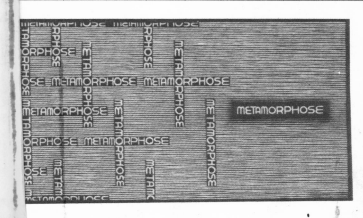

By the same authors
Fischer v. Spassky: Reykjavik 1972

Edited and designed by Derek Birdsall

Harper & Row

The thyrd chapitre of the first tractate treteth Wherfore
the playe Was founden and maad Capitulo iij

The causes Wherfore this playe Was founden ben iij
¶ The first Was for to correcte and repreue the kyng
for Whan this kyng enylmerodach saWe this playe / And
the barons knyghtes and gentilmen of his court playe
Wyth the phylosopher / he merueylled gretly of the beaulte
and nouelte of the playe. And asked to playe agaynst
the phylosopher / The phylosopher ansWerd and sayd to hym
that hit myght not be Won / but yf he first lernyd the play
The kyng sayd hit Was reson and that he Wold put hym
to the payn to lerne hit / Than the phylosopher began to

A Book of Chess by C.H.O'D. Alexander

Harper & Row Publishers
New York, Evanston, San Francisco, London

© C.H.O'D.Alexander and Derek Birdsall 1973

FIRST U.S. EDITION 1973

0-06-010048-6

LIBRARY OF CONGRESS CATALOG CARD NUMBER: 73–11894

Made and printed in Great Britain by
Westerham Press Ltd, Westerham, Kent
Set in Monotype Walbaum

The authors would like to thank F.D.Buck, G.H.Diggle,
Edna Ellis, John Ernest, Peter Jay & Clive Phillpot
for their help in the preparation of this book

Designed and produced by Omnific/London
Art Editor: Fiona MacGregor
Picture research: Zoë Henderson

Contents

Prologue

Section 1: The nature of Chess

Section 2: The history and development of Chess

Section 3: Chess for blood

Section 4: Chess for fun

Section 5: The Iconography of Chess

Prologue

'Chess . . . is a foolish expedient for making idle people believe they are doing something very clever, when they are only wasting their time.'   Bernard Shaw

' . . . master chess grips its exponent, shackling the mind and brain so that the inner freedom and independence of even the strongest character cannot remain unaffected.'   Einstein

'My entire life has been devoted to the game . . . I don't believe a day has gone by that I have not played at least one game of chess – and I still enjoy it as much as ever.'
                                        F.J.Marshall, former US champion

'Chess is a sea in which a gnat may drink and an elephant may bathe.'   Indian Proverb

The scene is the USSR *v.* Yugoslavia match at the 1972 Skopje Olympiad; on the right, the top board game, where Svetozar Gligorić, the leading Yugoslav Grandmaster since 1945, is playing the Soviet ex-World Champion Tigran Petrosian. Many of the older spectators – and certainly Gligorić and Petrosian – will remember their encounter at Belgrade eighteen years earlier when Gligorić won a famous victory and '. . . pandemonium broke out at the end of the game, and the playing hall, which was overflowing with spectators, was cleared by the police. While this expulsion was in progress the players' clocks were stopped and the lights turned out and after about half an hour some of the spectators were allowed to return to their seats and play (in the other games) was able to continue.'* But this game is only one of about 150 in progress; 63 countries from every continent in the world, ranging in strength from the World Champions, the USSR, to the Virgin Islands are contesting the 20th chess Olympiad, and 23 women's teams are playing for the Women's Team Championship. Each of the players is wholly absorbed in his game; whether you are good or bad, nothing else matters when you are playing. This obsession doesn't just affect the players – it spreads to anyone with an emotional stake in the games. As well as playing in these events, I have frequently been non-playing captain of the English team; then one is as completely involved as if playing – I always used to go away from the games for periods, not through lack of interest but in an attempt to avoid getting too tense and transmitting nervousness to the players.

The Olympiad, although the biggest of all the international events, is very far from being the only one. There are many other team events such as the European Team Championship, the six-country West European team tournament and individual matches between countries; there are student team tournaments and events at the school level such as the Glorney Cup in which England, Scotland, Ireland, Wales, France and Holland compete.

Important though these team events are, we still have not come to the heart of the chess scene – the individual tournaments and matches. First there is the cycle of events culminating in the gladiatorial displays of the World Championship matches, such as the 1972 Fischer-Spassky struggle – an Icelandic saga indeed. Then there are about 30 international tournaments a

*The Skopje game was less dramatic than this; after a hard struggle in which Petrosian was under some pressure, the game was drawn in 41 moves.

year, each with 10–20 players on an all-play-all basis, lasting 2 to 4 weeks. Finally there are much larger numbers of local congresses within countries, often with very large entries: the *Evening Standard* London week-end congress in December 1972 drew over 1,000 entries and several hundred is quite common. At the junior level, 1,500 children have played in one of the Merseyside tournaments – and over 800 schools play in the annual *Sunday Times* National Schools Tournament. This is in England; in the USSR the number of players runs into millions and the nationwide Trade Union Championship has drawn 700,000 competitors.

In addition to tournament and congress competitors there are social players; and correspondence chess players – another flourishing group; and problemists – a different breed altogether; and endgame composers – a bridging group between players and problemists; and rebels – who believe the game is played out and want new pieces, new rules, new boards, extra dimensions; not to mention a few million Japanese playing Japanese chess (SHOGI). And there is a long history of chess in literature: it is said that more books have been written on chess than on all other games combined – and the imagination of many writers has been caught by the psychology of the player and the fascination of the game. Nabokov's *The Defence* is the best modern example where a great writer who is also a chess addict has shown his insight into one kind of chess mind. It is not surprising that the second book to be printed in English was *The Game and Playe of the Chess*. Chess sets, too, are objects of considerable visual appeal – and sometimes controversy; chess got into trouble with the Muslims in its early days (about AD 600) because the Elephant (now the Bishop) was carved as an elephant, thus transgressing Muhammad's prohibition of images – and in modern times there have been propaganda sets such as those in the USSR with the pawns being slaves in chains on one side and free workers on the other (for a fuller discussion of these, see page 132). Chess figures, to a minor but not negligible extent, in painting as well as literature – and, in recent years, as a prestige symbol in advertising.

Why all this? What is it about chess – pushing bits of wood in an arbitrary manner about a small board – that makes a small number of intelligent people give their lives to it and makes it a lifelong source of pleasure to a large number of others? In this book, I try to give a personal answer to these and other questions, to give some idea of what chess is, of what goes to make a great chessmaster, what the life of a professional is like, and

of the various types of enjoyment that the amateur can get from the game.

Chess notation and methods of scoring
I assume that any reader of this book knows the moves; there may however be some who are unfamiliar with methods of recording positions and game scores.

There are two main systems in use in this country; the algebraic and the descriptive. The algebraic is concise, rational and international; the descriptive is, alas, still the notation most widely used in this country. I describe both and will – reluctantly – use the descriptive.

Diagram 1: Algebraic notation

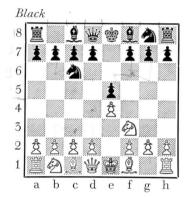

Each square has one name, a letter denoting the file, a number denoting the rank. White's first move is written e4, Black's reply e5; White's second move is Nf3.

Set up the pieces in their original positions and play through the following opening. 1. White moves his King's pawn two squares, Black does the same. 2. White brings out his King's Knight in front of his King's Bishop pawn, Black brings out his Queen's Knight similarly. These moves will be written (using the symbol N for Knight in algebraic)

(*a*) In algebraic. 1. e4, e5; 2. Nf3, Nc6.

(*b*) In descriptive. 1. P–K4, P–K4; 2. Kt–KB3, Kt–QB3.

Each system names the piece to be moved (in algebraic, when a pawn moves, no symbol is given for the pawn; in descriptive, P is used) and the square to which it goes. In algebraic, each square has one name allocated on the system shown in diagram 1.

Diagram 2: Descriptive notation

Black

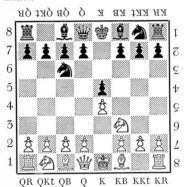

White

Diagram 3: The Forsyth* notation

Black

White

In descriptive, each square has two names, one used by White, one by Black, each player numbering the ranks from his own side of the board. Moreover the files, instead of being lettered *a* to *h*, are named after the piece which originally stands on the file (see diagram 2). Castling King's side is 0–0, castling Queen's side is 0–0–0 in both systems; captures are indicated by ':' in algebraic (sometimes omitted), by 'x' in descriptive; pawn captures are indicated by PxP (or – if necessary – KPxQP, specifying the files) in descriptive, simply by the files involved in algebraic (KPxQP would be 'ed'); 'en passant' is e.p. in descriptive, usually omitted in algebraic; check is + or ch in descriptive, + in algebraic; ! is a good move, ? a bad move in both systems. Here is an opening carried to seven moves using the two methods:

(*a*) Algebraic.   1. e4, e5; 2. Nf3, Nc6; 3. Bc4, Bc5; 4. d4, ed; 5. 0–0, Nf6; 6. e5, d5; 7. ed, Bd6.

(*b*) Descriptive.   1. P–K4, P–K4; 2. Kt–KB3, Kt–QB3; 3. B–B4, B–B4; 4. P–Q4, PxP; 5. 0–0, Kt–B3; 6. P–K5, P–Q4; 7. PxP e.p., BxP.

The descriptive is perhaps slightly more vivid but the greater brevity, international usage and simpler naming of squares gives the algebraic an undoubted all-round advantage.

This is very convenient for recording positions. In this the position is described rank by rank, starting at Black's QR1. Capital letters are used for White pieces, small letters for Black; numerals for unoccupied squares. The diagrammed position – the position reached after the seven opening moves given above – would be recorded: r1bqk2r/ppp2ppp/2nb1n2/8/2Bp4/5N2/PPP2PPP/RNBQ1RKI.

---

*Named after David Forsyth of Glasgow, who emigrated to New Zealand and died there in 1909.

Section 1: The nature of Chess

THE FAMOVS GAME
of Cheſſe-play.
Being a Princely exerciſe; wherin the
Learner may profit more by reading of
this ſmall Book, then by playing
of a thouſand Mates.
Now augmented of many materiall things
formerly wanting, and beautified with a three-
fold Methode, viz. of the Cheſſe-men.
of the Cheſſe-play, of the
Cheſſe-lawes.
By Jo. BARBIER. P.

If on your man you light,
The firſt draught ſhall you play:
If not, 'tis mine by right,
At firſt to leade the way.

Printed at London for *John Jackſon*, dwel-
ling without Temple-Barre. 1640.

Chapter 1 : The game and its players

'It is a game too troublesome for some men's braines, too full of anxiety, all out as bad as study; and besides it is a testy cholericke game and very offensive to him that looseth the mate.' Robert Burton, *The Anatomy of Melancholy*

'In the idea of chess and the development of the chess mind we have a *picture* of the intellectual struggle of mankind.' Richard Réti, *Modern Ideas in Chess*

'Now my question is this: How much of the fascination of chess comes from the excitement of carrying out a purpose under opposition; a suggestion or after-image of difficulties *in living*? And how much comes from the interest in *formal relations*, as in mathematics or stained glass or arabesques?' George Santayana, *Chess Review*

Game, Art or Science?

We can make unnecessary difficulties and confusion for ourselves by assuming that a question like 'What is chess?' has only one answer: it has many answers, depending on the skill and psychological make-up of the chess player. When a child draws, he isn't creating a work of art; he is playing – just as he is playing, not being a scientist, when he produces a nauseating stink from his No. 1 Chemistry Set. But in his play he is engaged in an activity, and developing a skill which may lead to his being an artist or a scientist; the subject matter of his play contains within itself the potentiality of something more than play in a way that the subject matter of Snakes and Ladders does not. The question to be asked about chess is not 'Is it a Game, Art or Science?' but rather 'It is a game; has it the potentiality of being anything more?' And, an allied but slightly different question: 'Whatever it is, is it worth taking seriously?' Remarks like those of Shaw, quoted in the Prologue, or Burton's (above) or Montaigne's 'I hate and avoid this idle, childish game . . . and I am ashamed to spend as much thought on that, as would serve to much better uses' all express the writer's opinion that chess is not worth taking seriously; on the other hand Einstein's comment (though hostile), Santayana's and Réti's all indicate that there can be more to chess than just the pleasure of a game.

Take the case for the prosecution first. If we compare it with an art or a science, its two great weaknesses are its artificiality and its small scale. Put it against mathematics for instance. Although as abstract as chess, mathematics is nevertheless embedded in the structure of nature. Euclidean geometry is – or can be made – purely abstract, i.e. one has a number of axioms which can be abstractly stated without any reference to physical reality and the propositions of geometry deduced from them by formal reasoning alone. Nevertheless, the origin of Euclidean geometry is the physical world we live in – and it is a remarkable illustration of the way mathematics is built into nature that after non-Euclidean geometry had been developed it was unexpectedly discovered that a form of it was necessary for the description of the post-Einstein universe. Chess on the other hand is entirely man-made; the size and shape of the board, the rules, the moves of the pieces, their positions are all arbitrary. Put it another way; if Sirius has some inhabited planets we can be confident that their mathematics will be the same as ours – but if they play a board game of the chess type, all the detail will be different. And the scale; not only is mathematics incomparably more varied and 'larger' than chess, it is also 'open-ended' in a way that chess is not. There are almost certainly new branches of mathematics to be discovered or developed from an embryo state; there are probably new techniques to be developed in chess, but they operate within a closed and defined area. An 18th-century mathematician would find much modern mathematics unintelligible; but Philidor could perfectly easily follow a modern game of chess – though there would be much that would surprise him and he would be struck by the much higher standard and greater subtlety of the play.

If we take a major art, say music, for comparison chess is again going to have a hard time, though not I think as hard as with mathematics; but perhaps I say this because I was once a mathematician and have never been a musician. The same weaknesses appear again in slightly different modes. Music, though less fundamental than mathematics, is more so than chess; our inhabitants of the planets of Sirius might not have any chess – but, given the equivalent of ears, there must be a good chance that they have something recognizable as music. Again, there is a range and depth in music greater than in chess; we can see this sometimes in the praise that a great game gets. When Najdorf said of one of Fischer's victories over Spassky that it was 'like a Mozart symphony' he paid a compliment that would not be given in reverse. Even the most ardent chess fan would not say after first hearing some Mozart 'Marvellous; it's like a Fischer/Spassky game'.

I have compared chess with mathematics and music because amongst the sciences and arts these are the closest to chess in that they are the most abstract and the most concerned with formal structure and pattern; and we are forced to admit that in some fundamental way they are superior to chess. What can be said on the other side?

First, we chessplayers should not be too overcome by the small scale and range of our activity compared with that of mathematics or music. For when we come to compare what the individual chessmaster does with what the individual mathematician or musician does we find that the gap is much smaller. Within the vastness of mathematics even the greatest intellects can only cover a small part of the field; and the average professional mathematician can only hope to work on a microscopic part of the whole. And in music it is possible to be a great artist and yet very limited – one can be a great singer and yet have little understanding of music as a whole and no ability as a composer or as an instrumental executant. In chess, a great player will master far more of the much smaller field. What is important is not so much the scale of the activity compared with other activities; though that is of some absolute significance, it will be reflected in – and to some extent balanced by – the number of people who take it up. No: what really matters as regards scale and depth is that there should be enough of both to ensure that if an intelligent man devotes his life to it he will find sufficient to satisfy and extend him – that he won't be able to exhaust it. Chess seems to pass this test; no one has yet been able to play it perfectly, nor to exhaust all the ideas in it.

What about its artificiality? Does this reflect a triviality in the game that, despite its difficulty, makes it not worth serious thought? It is easy to imagine jigsaw puzzles and crosswords so large and so difficult that it might take a lifetime to solve them; yet we should regard it as a waste of time to spend a life doing this – it would be too meaningless a task and it is meaningless because it is totally dissociated from anything else in life. Chess is not meaningless in this way; it is artificial in detail, but not in principle. The struggle involved in chess meets a deep-seated need in our natures: if we go back to our Sirius illustration, while it is most unlikely that we should find chess being played there it is probable that we would find some game of the same type being played, differing entirely in detail but meeting the same psychological need.

All competitive games, physical or mental, meet a need of this kind – in all of them there is (to re-quote Santayana) 'the excitement of carrying out a purpose under opposition'; but in meeting this need, the master chessplayer produces an end-product which differs in kind from the results of a physical game and in degree from a game of bridge or draughts. A great game of chess is capable of giving those who see it, or those who play through it afterwards, something that is not just pleasure; it is a feeling of wonder at such a product of the human mind and of being caught up, emotionally involved, in something more than just a game. In a great attacking game (such as the sixth in the Fischer/Spassky match) the rightness and inevitability with which the attack is developed excites the same kind of feeling as some works of art (or mathematics for that matter); the game has to be like that and no different – its logic and clarity give it a beauty which one feels as such. Other games (such as the thirteenth of the match*) which are intricate, fluctuating struggles full of crises and hairbreadth escapes give us an intense feeling of drama – we feel (as do the players) that their lives, not their Kings, are at stake. Bridge does not give this feeling; the 'unit' in bridge – a hand – is too small.

Now if we agree that this quality in chess – the emotions a great game is capable of arousing, not just in the players, but in those few who see it played and the many who play through it afterwards – coupled with its permanence, make it something worth taking seriously, the question still remains 'Is it just a superb game, or can it be more – and if so what?' I think that we must reject any claim for chess as a science. It uses many of the weapons that the scientist uses; there are principles to be mastered, techniques to be learnt, facts to be acquired and systematic, logical methods of thought to be used – but there is not the subject matter or aim of a science. Science sets out to discover the nature of the world by studying the data with which this world presents us; while it may be argued that this is only partially true of mathematics, this merely illustrates the dual nature of mathematics lying on the borderline between science and art. The case for chess being an art as well as a game is much stronger. On this the former World Champion Botvinnik says, 'There is a science which studies the world of sound – acoustics. But there is also an art operating within the ocean of sound – music. Clearly it is the same with thought. Logic studies the laws of thinking, but chess in the form of

---

*The sixth and thirteenth games are given at the end of this section

artistic images reflects, as an art, the logical side of thought . . .'
It is very striking how close this clear, careful dissection of the
problem – so typical of Botvinnik's mind – comes to the
bolder statement, quoted at the beginning of the chapter, by
the more intuitive, artistic Réti.

I myself believe that Réti and Botvinnik are right; that it is
because we see in a great game of chess a picture of the mind in
action, of the response to an intellectual challenge, that we react
as we do – and that because of this, a great game is a work of art as
well as a game. Whether you accept this conclusion or not is largely
a question of how one defines art; if you take the view that the
subject matter of art must be part of the general human
background you will reject it – though even then one must feel
that there is, at least, much common ground between chess and
art. But however we decide this, we must be careful not to
confuse the nature of the end product with the motive of the
producer. A great player does not sit down saying to himself
'Today I will produce a work of art'; he sits down determined to
win if he can and it is this desire for victory that is the driving
force. He plays chess for two reasons – because he is good at it
and because it meets a psychological need in his nature, i.e. he
can play and he enjoys it; and also he enjoys the by-products –
the admiration that success arouses and the prestige that he
acquires. But is this any different from the attitude of the
artist and scientist? The best work in any creative field is done
through an inner compulsion, not through objective consideration of the nature of the end product; the attitude of society will
affect the question negatively in that it may not be practicable
in some societies to earn a living as, say, a chessplayer or a poet –
but the positive drive is provided by inner needs and innate
abilities that have little to do with the classification of the
results. The mathematician Hardy says, with a good deal of
truth, that there are only two honest justifications for what one
does: (*a*) 'I do it because I can do it well', (*b*) 'There is nothing
that I can do particularly well. I do what I do because it came
my way'.

What about the distinction between the creator and the
executant? Is a chessplayer like a concert pianist or a composer?
Basically he is an executant; like an actor or a pianist he
exercises his skill to order – he sits down and plays at the
allotted time. However most great players will have some
element of the composer as well; Philidor, Morphy, Steinitz,
Nimzovich all introduced new ideas into the game and most of
the leading players have made some contribution of this kind.

One sees this purely creative element in chess undiluted in chess
problems and endgame studies. Here the competitive side has
vanished: the problem composer is struggling not with an
opponent but with the raw material of the chess pieces and their
moves out of which he tries to create an aesthetically satisfying
representation of a chess idea.

Finally, let us return to Santayana's question. For the
problemist the interest is purely in the formal relations and he is
consciously attempting to create a minor work of art. The
player's motive power on the other hand is 'the excitement of
carrying out a purpose under opposition'; and this meets a
psychological need either because (as Santayana suggests) it
echoes the problems of living or because it provides in the game
a success which the player is unable to achieve in life. Chess can
be for a player an echo, a substitute or – in the case of a successful
professional – a way of life; but in each case it is the struggle that
supplies the driving force. The interest in formal relations is the
reason for the individual choosing chess – rather than, say,
football, poker or the stock exchange – for meeting his needs;
his ability to handle formal relations makes him enjoy the
problems of play and enables him to solve them. This leads us
from the game to its players; what is the psychological and
mental make-up of a chessplayer?

The Players

Here we can distinguish three types – social, obsessive and professional. For the social player chess has many functions. It
releases his aggressive instincts; he may – like Napoleon (who,
typically, lost his temper when beaten) – have an excessive
supply, or (like a country clergyman) have insufficient natural
outlets for normal aggression. Or he may enjoy the planning;
Sherlock Holmes (and what a chessplayer he would have made),
explaining how he had detected yet another villain in 'The
Adventure of the Retired Colourman' says: 'Amberley
excelled at chess – one mark, Watson, of a scheming mind'. A
just observation, though he might have said a good planner
instead of a scheming mind. Another function of the social
game is pointed out by the psychologist Dr Peter Wason when
he says 'The distinguished British master, Stuart Milner-Barry,
told me that, when the Russian physicist, Peter Kapitza, was
working with Rutherford at the Cavendish laboratory, he
would often come to Milner-Barry's room in a distressed state,
and crave a game of chess because of frustration with a research
problem. I have had a similar experience in my research. It

would seem that an equally demanding, but totally different, intellectual task may allow a "block" to be overcome without dissipating the mental energy required to solve a problem'. In all these cases chess is play; the social player is exercising his powers in a field difficult and absorbing enough to engage his full attention, but free from the responsibilities and anxieties of real life.

For the obsessive player – weak or strong – chess is not play, but a substitute for life. He has the normal aggressive instincts and desire to succeed but for one reason or another shrinks from expressing these in real life. 'Willing to wound and yet afraid to strike', he escapes from the complications of human relationships into the tidy, restricted world of chess. Sometimes people say that chess has ruined a man's career – he spends so much time on the game that he fails in the rest of life. This puts the cart before the horse; it is not chess that causes his failure – it is his weaknesses that turn him obsessively to chess. This group overlaps with both social and professional players; amongst the latter I would put Rubinstein and Steinitz – the fictional Luzhin, in Nabokov's novel *The Defence*, if slightly larger than life, is still a marvellous picture of this type of player. However the chessmaster is not typical of this group; the successful master has a strong practical reason for putting chess first – it is the unsuccessful player, who still puts chess first, who is the prototype.

There is nothing particularly abnormal in this. Many people seek escape from life; some of them – those with fairly strong feelings of aggression and with analytic minds – find it in chess. The Freudian idea – put forward by Ernest Jones in his famous essay on Morphy (whose ambivalent love-hate relationship to chess is a happy hunting ground for the chess psychologist) – that chessplayers are engaged in killing their fathers will seem to most of us as more of a comment on Freudians than on chessplayers. In victory in chess a man may often be trying to build up or recover his self-confidence, which may be linked to breaking away from a father's dominance or neglect; but this is true of a very high proportion of all human activities – self expression is usually self assertion as well – and it seems to me a piece of Freudian fantasy to attach this exotic label to chess.

In considering professionals, it is worth looking separately at Communist and Western players. For a Soviet player, especially in Stalin's time, there were great advantages in being a professional. Prestige, opportunities for travel, state support and much less danger of disgrace through ideological deviation than for any other intellectuals, all made chess an attractive profession. An eccentric, offbeat occupation in the Western democracies, chess is respectable in the Communist world. To become a chess professional was a perfectly sensible choice for an able man in the USSR and the Soviet master strikes one as much like any other successful professional man. A small example: at Tel Aviv in 1964, one of our team – the well-known player and writer, Peter Clarke – wanted to see Botvinnik. I happened to be in Botvinnik's hotel and mentioned this to him; Botvinnik replied, 'If it is convenient for Mr Clarke to be here at 11.00 tomorrow I shall be glad to see him'. It was the head of the profession agreeing to see a more junior member. Alekhine would never have made an appointment – and if he had he wouldn't have kept it.

The Western professional is more of an individualist, a rebel, an artist in temperament; the intellect and will power needed to make a successful chessmaster would normally bring success in other careers carrying, in the West, more prestige and money. The Western professional is likely therefore either to have something of the obsessive love of the game of our second group or to want to avoid the network of professional and social obligations implied by a more orthodox career. Fischer shows both of these characteristics in an extreme form; equally, Spassky is not untypical of the Soviet professional.

Overall, chessplayers are much less odd than is generally supposed. It is unfortunate that Fischer is such an extreme type; his unbalanced behaviour has inevitably encouraged journalistic muck-raking for other eccentricities amongst chessmasters. I find the references to Steinitz and his statement that he could give God odds at chess particularly repugnant; Steinitz's mind broke down when he was old, ill, unhappy and within a year of his death. It is as misleading as it is heartless to represent his conduct then as if it were his normal behaviour. To quote Dr Wason again, 'There is no evidence to suggest that the incidence of mental illness amongst chessmasters is greater than among other comparable groups'. What is interesting, however, as Dr Wason says, is the nature of their breakdowns when they have them and the commonest form amongst chessplayers is paranoia. This is not surprising; chess is a suspicious game, with its mixture of positive planning and constant alertness for enemy counterstrokes.

What about the mental make-up of chessplayers? The strongest correlation is between chess and mathematics. If we take the greatest champions from Anderssen onwards, five of them – Anderssen, Steinitz, Lasker, Capablanca and Botvinnik – all had mathematical ability far above the average; of the other three, two – Morphy and Alekhine – trained as lawyers, and all that I know about Fischer's undeveloped abilities outside chess is that he is said to have an I.Q. of over 180. The connection with law – there are many examples besides those of Morphy and Alekhine – is interesting. One can see why; the resemblance between the cut-and-thrust of a legal argument and the interplay of ideas on the chess board, the opportunism of a cross-examining counsel, the common element of victory and defeat. Mathematics is intellectually like chess but psychologically very different; law picks up some of the sides of chess that are absent from mathematics.

A quality covered neither by law nor mathematics arises from the element of judgment. Chess operates in a field in which proof (the possibility of analysing the game out to a forced win or draw) is usually impossible, and at the end of analysis one has to make an act of judgment. Here there is something analogous to 'taste' in the arts. In giving simultaneous displays, I am constantly struck by how one's opponents, after careful thought, will play moves which I know instantly to be wrong, without any conscious analysis whatever. A good player in most positions can tell at a glance who stands better – and can tell whether the players are strong or weak; a strong positional player will have a very fine appreciation even of difficult positions. On the whole – though it is a generalization with many exceptions – the non-mathematicians tend to be positional players.

Finally, all attempts – I am happy to say – to show that chess players have some unique mental faculty (e.g. exceptional memory) have been unsuccessful: the only respects in which they are superior to non-chessplayers of the same general calibre seem to be those in which their experience of chess is directly relevant.

Summing up, can we form any kind of composite picture of a chessplayer? He is likely to be an individualist with a good deal of aggression in his make-up, better with things than with people, mathematically oriented and at home with abstractions, and an opportunist; in his feeling for positions he has something of the artist in him, he has some creative power but on a small scale – he is a miniaturist, better at detail than at large-scale ideas. He is no crazier than anyone else – but when he is crazy, he will probably be paranoiac. And – as is shown by the millions of players in the USSR – there are potentially many of him; given suitable soil, *caissa vulgaris* is a common enough growth.

The Psychological Struggle

In correspondence chess, the game is an intellectual struggle between the players; over the board it is also a struggle between their psyches. Nearly all the leading players have had dominating personalities which, consciously or unconsciously, they try to impress on their opponent and weaken his will to win: Fischer's brutal remark 'I like to feel the other fellow's ego crack' is true of most great masters. Players react to the strain of the struggle in very different ways. Some are confident and play with ease against weaker players but are overcome by a feeling of helplessness against stronger opposition. Others (of whom I was one) are nervous against weaker players – 'how awful if I cannot beat *him*' – and more relaxed against stronger opposition, where they feel there is nothing to lose. But whichever group you belong to, you cannot help feeling some strong psychological pressure when struggling against a great player.

I had a curious personal example of how helpful an insight into the opponent's psychology can be when I played Alekhine in the Margate 1938 tournament. In the early part of the game Alekhine (who won the tournament) played a move that looked wrong to me; thinking it was probably my own judgment that was wrong, I made what seemed the right reply. Alekhine sat down – and started twisting his hair; suddenly I remembered that I had been told 'Alekhine always twists his hair when he is worried'. This unexpected confirmation of my judgment both invigorated and relaxed me and I played with increased confidence. It was the last round and there was no adjournment; Alekhine sat from 10.00 a.m. until 2.30, never leaving the board, always twisting his hair. On the 44th move I made an error; Alekhine moved, took out a comb and ran it through his hair, got up and stalked majestically up and down the room. I was in no danger, but I knew my chance of victory had gone; a few moves later I offered a draw. I have never been less tired by a hard game.

It is no wonder that in preparation for a serious event, the Russians make a close study not only of the technical side of an opponent's play but of his psychology. The Soviet player Efim Geller in his book *Grandmaster Geller at the Chessboard* quotes the following as a typical dossier: 'Grandmaster Oscar Panno, 24 years old, former Junior World Champion, Argentine Champion in 1953 . . . Plays best in simple positions. Plays attacks quite well. Doesn't defend so well. In playing Soviet opponents he will be very careful in the opening, probably somewhat passive. Therefore it is recommended to play sharp opening lines against him and go in for complications.' One may be sure that no minor quirk like Alekhine's hair-twisting would escape the Russian eye. Indeed – a less happy recollection – I remember at Munich 1958 making a positional error against Botvinnik which ultimately led to the loss of the game. When I was wandering round the room (it was Botvinnik's move and I am a peripatetic player) and gossiping with Kotov, the Russian captain, Kotov said with some relish 'Botvinnik always fingers his tie when he likes his game'; I returned – alas, Botvinnik's tie was getting a real mangling.*

If you play through not just the best games but all the games in a match between two players or in a major tournament you are bound to be struck by how many really bad moves there are, especially near the time limit: I still think with shame of some of my more horrible blunders. These occur because of the nervous strain on the player. Chess, like cricket, is a game in which a single error can be fatal; it is in fact much worse than cricket – it is bad enough to be bowled when you have made 99, but at least you keep your 99. A blunder at chess after hours of good play is as if when bowled your score was recorded as 0 however many you had scored. The strain of simply avoiding serious errors throughout a five hour session, with one's clock steadily advancing is very great – especially when one is winning.

Different psychological types cope with this in different ways. The strain is greatest on the pessimist and few if any players who doubt themselves can reach the very front; this streak of self-doubt and pessimism is all that has prevented Jonathan Penrose, the most gifted British player born in this century, from becoming a Grandmaster. The optimists – like Bogolyubov ('when I am White I win because I am White; when I am Black I win because I am Bogolyubov') and Najdorf – always expect to win and the strain on them is least; but they pay for their optimism in lack of judgment – they tend to overrate their positions – and therefore are unlikely to become World Champions. The fighters – like Lasker – enjoy the struggle; they feel the strain but they do not mind it. Vain players – like Alekhine – feel and dislike the strain, but dislike defeat far more; they fight because they cannot bear to lose. The strong-willed, self-disciplined players like Botvinnik train themselves methodically to endure the strain; Botvinnik always prepared himself with the greatest thoroughness for every event (a small illustration – he dislikes smoking and, to reduce this feeling, in one of his

training matches he got his opponent to smoke throughout and puff the smoke in his face) and followed a rigid routine throughout. If you play Botvinnik, it is even alarming to see him write his move down. Slightly shortsighted, he stoops over his score sheet and devotes his entire attention to recording the move in the most beautifully clear script; one feels that an explosion would not distract him and that examined through a microscope not an irregularity would appear. When he wrote down 1. . . . c2–c4 against me, I felt like resigning. Then there are those few who know they are better than anyone else – the Capablancas ('as one by one I mowed them down, my superiority became evident') and the Fischers ('I am the best player in the world'). As long as this supreme self-confidence (something much more fundamental than the hopefulness of the optimist) is justified by results it is probably the best of all approaches; but it is also the most vulnerable.

Finally, how does the obsessive player of master strength react? In a curious way, by ignoring the opponent. In the course of a wonderful description of the great Polish master Akiba Rubinstein, Réti – the finest of all writers on chess – says: 'Rubinstein . . . lives only for his self-appointed task . . . It is not a matter of a fight for him, but the working out of a victory, and so his games create the impression of a great structure from which not one stone dare be shifted'. Rubinstein's struggle was with himself and the chessboard; his opponent was merely part of the raw material of the game. The antithesis of Lasker, for whom the psychology of the struggle lay at the heart of the game, Rubinstein had no doubts about the nature of chess – it was an art and his only struggle was that with his own imperfections as an artist.

The Prodigies

'Chess is his mother tongue'   Réti on Capablanca

One cannot have a child novelist because a child does not know enough of life; when the 9-year-old Daisy Ashford writes *The Young Visiters* it is the inadequacies of the book that are its charm. There are however some areas – elementary mathematics, music and chess – in which, because of their abstract nature, experience and knowledge are less essential; it is here that we get the infant prodigies – Gauss correcting the wages bill at the age of three, Mozart composing when six, Capablanca beating his father at the age of four.

The four most famous names amongst chess prodigies are

---

*But see page 89 for a different view of Russian thoroughness

Morphy, Capablanca, Reshevsky and Fischer but I would not put Morphy and Fischer in the same class as the other two. Morphy did not learn until he was ten and Fischer's exceptional talent did not show until he was about twelve; one does not have for their early performances the feelings almost of awe and disbelief that are aroused by Capablanca and Reshevsky. We know the story of Capablanca's first game so well that it is difficult to look at it with fresh eyes – but it is worth trying. Take Capablanca's own unemotional description in *My Chess Career*: 'I was not yet five years old when by accident I came into my father's private office and found him playing with another

gentleman. I had never seen a game of chess before; the pieces interested me, and I went the next day to see them play again. The third day, as I looked on, my father, a very poor beginner, moved a Knight from a white square to another white square. His opponent, apparently not a better player, did not notice it. My father won, and I proceeded to call him a cheat and to laugh. After a little wrangle, during which I was nearly put out of the room, I showed my father what he had done. He asked me how and what I knew about chess. I answered that I could beat him; he said that that was impossible, considering that I could not even set the pieces correctly. We tried conclusions and I won. That was my beginning.'

The third day! A four-year-old does quite well if he plays

Young Reshevsky during Washington, DC *match, 1922*

snakes and ladders and very well indeed if you can teach him the moves of all the different pieces in chess; and yet after three days watching, Capablanca picks up all the moves for himself, detects his father's error and can show him after the game what it was. This indeed is genius. At the end of this section I give a game (taken from Reinfeld's *Great Games by Prodigies*) in which a leading member of the Havana Chess Club attempts (with hopeless lack of success) to give the four-year-old Capablanca the odds of a Queen; the child's grasp of the game is quite extraordinary.

Reshevsky offers an equally remarkable case; he played quite well when four, was giving simultaneous displays when six and toured the capitals of Europe when he was eight. He too became a great master when an adult, though never quite reaching Capablanca's level. Not all prodigies last the course, however. 15 to 20 years ago I published an account of a Korean boy, Ernest Kim; this drew a letter in which the writer said that, travelling along the 'Golden Road to Samarkand' he had stopped overnight at Tashkent. He admitted to playing a little chess and was at once pressed by the locals to play 'our champion'; he reluctantly agreed – and a tiny four-year-old boy was brought in. It was Kim. But now he must be about 20 – and I have never seen his name as an adult player.

I cannot offer any explanation of this extraordinary facility. Believers in reincarnation will have no problems; they will point out that Morphy died in 1884 and Capablanca was born in 1888 – and, Capablanca dying in 1942, Fischer was born in 1943. For the rest of us, one can only say that if there are to be prodigies at all, it is natural to find them in a self-contained activity like chess; that their existence is a remarkable example of the power of a child to learn; and that it is an illustration of the innate differences in ability which the most convinced environmentalist will find it hard to explain away.

Women in Chess

'During the reign of David, King of Israel, it was said that the daughter of a Rabbi was a match for any man at chess.'
Koltanowski, *En Passant*, 1938

'Male Chauvinist Pig'   Women's Lib.

First, a fact: women are now, and always have been, much weaker players than men. Nona Gaprindashvili has been the Women's World Champion since 1962 and has successfully defended the title three times; but there are at least 200 men with a higher rating than she has. Before the war, Vera Menchik-Stevenson, the Czech-born, English-domiciled World Champion established complete dominance in the women's game; in the six tournaments in which she defended her title she scored 64 wins, 1 loss and 4 draws. Yet in the British Championship she was only able to score about 50% against the male competition. Why?

It may simply be unequal opportunity, but I don't think so; in the USSR when there is no obvious sign of unequal conditions, the gap is as great as anywhere else. I believe that there are two reasons, one intellectual, one psychological, which are independent of opportunity. Women do less well at all the more abstract forms of thought – philosophy, mathematics, composition in music, chess. Music offers the most interesting example; there are many good women executants, but few composers and none in the very front rank. Why should this be

Left: 1972 USSR *Women's Chess Champion, Marta Shul, a 23-year-old engineer-mathematician from Lvov*

Right: Nona Gaprindashvili, of the Soviet Union, in 1962, when she became Women's World Champion

if it is simply a question of opportunity? And why should one get many good women writers and not composers of music? If one looks at the question without prejudice – i.e. without any prior assumption as to whether the mental make-up of men and women is the same or different – the balance of the evidence is quite clearly that abstract thought is more suited to men. On the psychological side, aggression is very necessary if one is to be a strong player; and there is some evidence that men are inherently more aggressive than women. If you want to put these points in a slightly different way, you can say that women are too practical and too sensible to take chess seriously.

However, we must not exaggerate the difference. Men are, on average, taller than women and the tallest man is taller than the tallest woman; but tall women are taller than short men. When Gaprindashvili played at Hastings in 1964, she came, she was seen, she conquered; charming and lethal, she scored 4–0 against the four British men (and, I believe, beat most of them at table tennis for good measure). And in pre-war years I played in seven tournaments with Vera Menchik; while I don't think I ever finished below her in the final order I never won a game against her, losing 2 and drawing 5. These two losses made me a member twice over of the 'Menchik Club'; distinguished fellow members were Sir George Thomas (also twice qualified) and the former World Champion Professor Max Euwe. Nevertheless, in chess the female is not as deadly as the male and in my view never will be.

Chess and Nationality

'The Americans are the best poker players, the Russians are the best chess players, the French are the best domino players'   Stephen Graham, *Characteristics*, 1936

When non-chessplayers make polite conversation to me about chess and have exhausted remarks such as 'You must be very clever to play chess' and 'How many moves ahead do you think?' (alas, I have long passed the point when I can any longer draw 'You look very young for a chessplayer'), we almost always come to 'Why are the Russians so good at chess?'. It always interests me that no-one asks 'Why are the Jews so good at chess?' though taking total numbers into account the performance of Jews is more remarkable than that of Russians. At one time (it is much less true now) if one divided the world into four groups, Russian Jews, Russian non-Jews, non-Russian Jews and non-Russian non-Jews the first would have been the

strongest and the last the weakest in chessplaying strength.

It is easy to explain the Russian dominance on the lines indicated in 'The Players' above; I consider chess in the USSR in more detail in the next section – here it is enough to say that chess is strongly encouraged, and chessplayers supported, by the State. Similar support in any industrialized state would produce similar results. The case of the Jews is more interesting. Steinitz, Lasker, Botvinnik, Fischer – four of the greatest World Champions – all wholly or partly Jewish; the three great American players between Marshall and Fischer – Kashdan, Fine and Reshevsky – all Jewish; Tarrasch, Rubinstein, Tartakower, Flohr, Najdorf, Bronstein, Tal . . . there is a galaxy of great Jewish names. The reason for this, it seems to me, is psychological. Over the centuries, Jews in the Western world have to a greater or less degree been discriminated against and have felt the need to prove themselves; chess has offered a field in which discrimination does not operate and in which success is peculiarly clearcut and satisfying – and both the artistic and the aggressive sides of the Jewish nature, so strongly developed in and by Western culture, get full play in chess. This view – that the Jewish genius for the game is the result of psychological pressures produced by the social environment – is supported by what has happened in Israel. If the causes were not environmental but racial (whatever that means) one would expect Israel to excel; but, despite the flying start given by the many chessplayers amongst the immigrants, Israel – though good – is not an outstanding chessplaying country and there is no sign of an Israeli grandmaster appearing.

As we shall see in the chapter on the history of the game, chess dominance has passed from country to country with the passage of time; there is no good evidence for any one race being inherently better than any other. You may well ask why, if I am prepared to explain a dominance as striking as that of Russian or Jewish players on social grounds, I resort to inherent difference to explain the chess superiority of men over women. There are a number of reasons. The discrepancy to be explained is greater and longer lasting; *a priori*, inherent differences are more likely between men and women; and one can see more clearly how the environmental causes have operated in the case of national differences. But I accept that the fact that such great differences can be so rapidly created by a change in social environment must make one cautious about one's assessment of the reason for the difference in existing chessplaying strength between men and women.

Chapter 2: Chess and Computers

A perspective view of the Automaton, seen in front, with all the doors thrown open.

An elevation of the front of the chest, showing the concealed player in his first position when the door A is opened.

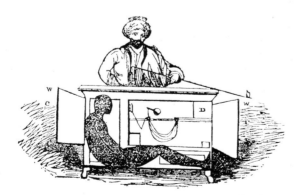

A front elevation, showing the concealed player in his second position, when the door B is closed and A C C open.

'The question is not merely whether a computer can be taught to play chess, but whether a computer can replace human perception to any great extent. If it is possible to arrive at an answer using chess as an example, a great contribution will have been made to the understanding of how the mind functions.'

Professor Max Euwe, 'Computers and Chess' in *The Encyclopedia of Chess*, 1970

'Such key concepts as "advantage", "sound sacrifice" and "simplification by exchange" . . . are far too indeterminate, far too subjective and historically fluid to be rigorously defined and formalized.'

Dr George Steiner, 'Fields of Force', *New Yorker*, 1972

'Hence if the knowledge of the chess-master were built into a computer program we should see not master chess but something very much stronger. . . . To capture in a formal, descriptive scheme the game's delicate structure – it is here that future progress lies.'

Professor Donald Michie, 'Programmers' Gambit', *New Scientist*, 1972

The idea of a chess-playing automaton has gripped the imagination in fiction and real life for at least 200 years. In fiction there are stories such as 'Moxon's Master' by Ambrose Bierce; in real life there was Baron Wolfgang von Kempelen's celebrated hoax 'The Automaton Chess Player'. In this device a man was hidden amongst the machinery with an ingenuity which successfully concealed the secret from 1770 – when it

A front elevation, showing the concealed player in his third position, or that in which he plays the game.

was first exhibited – until 1834. Even then, despite intense interest and speculation wherever it had been exhibited, it was not exposed by external analysis; one of its former 'Directors' (i.e. concealed players), Mouret, who had operated it from 1819 to 1824 fell on hard times and sold the secret to the French *Magazin Pittoresque* (a detailed account is given in an admirable article by Harkness and Battell, *American Chess Review* 1947, which is reprinted in Reinfeld's *Treasury of Chess Lore*).

It is only in the last twenty years, however, with the development of modern computers that a genuine 'automaton' has become possible; during this time, a considerable effort has gone and is going into attempts to produce a chess program that can match the human player. Why?

Chess is one of the simplest forms of creative thought. It is not easy, but it is simple in that it works on a very small amount of clearly defined data; thus it is easy to supply the computer with all the basic information needed to play the game. And creative thought is involved. One cannot – as one can in noughts and crosses or in solving simultaneous equations – lay down cut and dried rules which, if followed, will lead to success. We do not understand exactly how we decide what to play (except in the small fraction of positions where there is a clearcut winning line); we examine a range of possible continuations, we compare the resulting positions and weigh them up – we use our 'judgment'. And we get 'ideas'; we think of ways in which we might try to demolish the enemy position. Judgment, ideas – what do these abstractions mean? What are the mental processes that produce ideas and judge whether they are good? Can we break them down into definable components, feed these into a computer program and thus enable the program to play a 'human' game, to produce ideas and to exercise judgment? Suppose that this can be done and that the program can play games indistinguishable from those of a great master – games that give us the same feeling of originality and depth that we get from the games of Alekhine, Capablanca, Botvinnik, Fischer: then this has important, and not very comfortable, implications about the nature of thought. If we can make the computer program travel the journey from knowing the moves to playing grandmaster games, then why not the journey from doing mathematical calculations to solving problems and thence to original discoveries; and from composing random electronic music to producing a computer Beethoven. A real success – i.e. the production of great games and not just the avoidance of blunders – in the attempt to mechanize chess must

at the very least teach us a good deal about the nature of thought. I believe myself that it would go further than this; that it would have considerable philosophical importance – that it would strengthen mechanistic and behaviourist schools and weaken the more idealistic schools of thought.

There are two common misconceptions that are worth removing. The first is that the program can only do what the programmer tells it, so it can never do anything that he can't. This is wrong in several ways. By avoiding blunders it clearly might do better: and if the programmer is able to define 'good' and 'bad' positions then by being able to do more work than the programmer can (i.e. to examine more possible lines of play) it may discover good lines of play that he would never get round to examining. There is also the possibility that if the machine were programmed to take advantage of its previous experience it might improve its play and in this way too surpass its parent. The second fallacy is that with the speed of modern computers one should be able to rattle through all possible games and thus settle chess once and for all. It is worth doing a simple sum to dispose of this.

There are probably somewhere about 10^{120} (1 followed by 120 zeros) possible games, give or take a factor of 10^{20}: but we can afford to be much more modest than this. Suppose we restrict ourselves to 40-move games and suppose that for one White move and the Black reply there are 10 'reasonable' possibilities (i.e. we have fitted up our program with some mechanism for rejecting outlandish moves). Since 10 possibilities only means about 3 White moves with 3 replies to each, we have already endowed our program with considerable perception. How many possible games are there now? 40 moves, with 10 possibilities each is 10^{40}. Suppose now that our program can play through 10^9 games a second; a game in one ten thousand millionth of a second (a nano-second) is not bad going – light only travels about a foot in that time. And let us put a million (10^6) machines on the job night and day. Between them then they will plough through 10^{15} games a second; and I won't make a fuss about just how the final positions are examined – we will assume that after the 40 moves the result is obvious. The solar system has been in existence, so it is said, for about 10^{18} seconds and let us suppose that this examination has been going on since its creation. This brings us up to $10^{15} \times 10^{18} = 10^{33}$ games; we are still short by a factor of 10^7 of our modest figure of 10^{40} – we have only done one ten-millionth of the work. No, this method may exhaust time and space but not the game.

What can a program do? It can carry out any instructions, however complex, provided that they unambiguously define a course of action and that there is enough time available. There is therefore no problem in learning the moves, in avoiding gross blunders which lose material and in finding short combinations. When the Euratom Committee under Euwe's chairmanship set out 'to investigate the possibilities of programming chess for a computer' they gave the following numerical values: Pawn = 10, Bishop = 30, Knight = 30, Rook = 45, Queen = 85, King = 1,000.

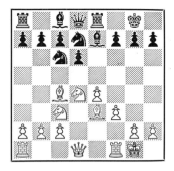

Now, look at the diagrammed position (given in Euwe's article); this illustrates how a winning combination can be found and the kind of problem one encounters even in such a simple position. Suppose the program is capable of examining all possibilities to a depth of four moves on each side and is solely interested in material gain, material being assessed on the scale above – so that mate will give the maximum gain possible. After a bit, it will look at 1. B x P ch; now it is + 10. It will consider three replies: K–R1, K–B1 and K x B. After 1. . . . K–B1 or R1; 2. Kt–K6, White will win the Queen and will emerge 35 up (10 − 30 − 30 + 85) against K–B1 and 65 up against K–R1, no further continuations (for the remaining two moves) changing this. However, after 1. . . . K x B Black is + 20; the program now tries all possible second White moves and finds that after 2. Kt–K6 Black must play 2. . . . K x Kt or else lose his Queen which would leave White + 10 − 30 + 85 − 30 = + 35. So 2. . . . K x Kt (leaving Black temporarily 50 up) and now 3. Q–Q5 ch, K–B3; 4. Q–B5 mate winning the jackpot with 1,000 for the King. Thereafter after 1. . . . K x B White is bound to be at least + 35; as 1. . . . K–R1 and 1. . . . K–B1 gave him + 65 and + 35, the program sees that 1. B x P ch nets White at least 35 whatever Black does, and will therefore play 1. B x P ch in the absence of any move showing a greater plus.

Note, however, that if the program had only been able to look three moves ahead it would have rejected 1. B x P ch, since 1. B x P ch, K x B; 2. Kt–K6, K x Kt; 3. Q–Q5 ch, K–B3 leaves White at −50. On the other hand four moves each is vastly in excess of what is needed for most of the variations and is very expensive; there are 47 possible first White moves and even if we take an average of 30 moves each in each variation we get almost a million million possibilities. How can we see that the machine only follows up 'promising' lines? We might say 'follow up all captures, all attacks on an enemy piece (this would get in 2. Kt–K6), all checks; abandon after two moves each all lines not involving a capture, an attack or a check'. In this kind of way we could equip the program with some tactical ability and enable it to pursue the more promising lines and abandon the others – but it is clearly going to be far from easy, even in situations where there are clearcut tactical chances, to raise its performance above that of crude bludgeoning.

Our problems here, however, are nothing to those that face us in positional play, i.e. in the selection of the best plan and the correct method of implementation when the advantages and disadvantages are small and hard to define. We can isolate components: it is good to develop, to control space, to occupy open files, to attack weak points, to have a sound pawn structure, to secure forward posts for one's Knights, to make pawn advances against the enemy King, to pin his pieces, to have protected passed pawns and so on. Can we construct a 'scoring system' which will combine all these elements, check that there are no tactical snags or opportunities by an exploratory analysis on the lines indicated and thus arrive at the right move? (It is curious, incidentally, that finding a winning combination is much less difficult for the program than playing positionally; what the average player most admires – the 'brilliancy' – is a type of chess that is easier to reproduce, and therefore less human, more mechanical, than the strategic struggle which has much less general appeal.)

It is clear that we can do something but the difficulty is how to supply the program with the experience of the master. There are two central problems here, involved in most forms of thought and allied to each other; they are the recognition of similar positions and the problem of learning. An experienced player rarely if ever faces a wholly new situation; consciously or subconsciously, he relates the positions that he sees to similar but not identical positions that he has met in the past. What is 'similar'? Can we define and enable the program to search its memory for 'similar' positions? If we could, then we would have gone a long way to solving the other problem – that of learning – since one of the major methods by which we learn is through using experience in this way. A very interesting example of machine learning is given by A.L.Samuels' system for draughts. His program evaluated positions in draughts by giving scores for various favourable and unfavourable features in a position. The program played through a number of master games and compared the result of its evaluation with the move actually played, making the assumption that the winner made the best move throughout. It noted all cases where its evaluation gave a different result from the actual move and compared the contributions made to the total score for its move and for the 'correct' move by the various elements in the evaluation function. By considering all its failures it was able to improve its evaluation function, i.e. to change the scores so as to produce fewer failures. To quote Euwe: 'After the computer had thus undergone self-instruction for a number of months, its program had been improved to such a degree that on one occasion it even outplayed a master'.

This is potentially a method of great power. The Euratom committee tried it for chess but 'soon came to the conclusion that it would have to deal not with 31 component numbers but with 31 million or even more, which means that the whole method is impossible'. They should know – but I can't help wondering whether in the end one will not return to this type of method.

So far, the strongest program is good enough to beat most social players but would have no chance against a master. The following table – based on one given by Professor Michie – illustrates this. Rating players on the ELO scale (a numerical system for assessing merit on the basis of results) we have:

Fischer	2800
Average Grandmaster	2600
International master	2450
National master	2200
'Expert'	2000
Strong Amateur	1700
Best Program	1500
Average Amateur	1250

Roughly speaking, a difference of 100 points means that in a match the stronger player would expect to score 65–35; 250 points would be 80–20; and 500 points 97–3. So 'Best Program'

is hardly ready to challenge Bobby Fischer – but it would score 4 to 1 against the average amateur. Moreover the programs are steadily improving and in 1974 or 1975 we may see a program of a different order. Botvinnik has been working with a programming team and expects his program to be ready by about then – he thinks that existing programs are designed on the wrong lines and that programs of master strength can be produced. The Scottish International Master, David Levy (rating 2380) has wagered £1,000 with Professor Michie and two others that no computer program will be able to beat him by 1978: Botvinnik's ominous comment is 'I feel very sorry for your money'.

I give the final game won by the current Fischer of the computer program world, CHESS 3.6, against its chief rival, TECH, in the 1972 computer championships. It is won in the style of the oldest club member; CHESS 3.6 does nothing, but does it reasonably sensibly. As a parlour game for those interested, I suggest the following. Make up your own scoring system and play the moves dictated by this; you can do this in a finite time by rejecting ridiculous moves without examination. You then have in effect a pencil and paper computer program; in this way you will begin to see the practical difficulties involved.

Finally, suppose Botvinnik is right – and we might note in passing that Euwe does not agree with him – and a Grandmaster program is produced, will this degrade chess and remove its interest? I don't think so. It will affect our view of how the human mind works and what it is – but that is another and wider issue, with implications outside chess. It will not alter the beauty and fascination of a great human game, nor reduce the creative effort involved, any more than good computer music would devalue Beethoven. That an aeroplane can fly over Everest does not alter the human triumph in climbing it.

Chapter 3: Illustrative Games by Men, Women, Children — and Computers

*Fischer/Spassky 1972 World Championship match: 6th game**

This beautiful and harmonious game falls into three parts. First, the opening; moves 1–13. This is a psychological and technical struggle which lays the foundation for Fischer's victory. Fischer before this match had almost invariably played 1. P–K4 and had never been known to play the Queen's Gambit, an opening of which he has always been scornful. Yet he plays it here and although Spassky adopts a defence which he has often played and in which he had never lost, Fischer gets the upper hand.

Why? Here is the explanation as I see it. Fischer knew the Queen's Gambit would be a complete surprise to Spassky and that he would be less prepared, psychologically and technically, to meet Fischer on this ground – certainly he would be unlikely to have a special line ready for the game. In these circumstances it was clearly quite likely that Spassky would fall back on his old favourite, the Tartakower Defence. Now although this is a popular line, it is a little suspect in that Black gets a not wholly satisfactory pawn structure. Fischer – peculiarly gifted in exploiting small weaknesses of this kind – must have analysed the whole variation deeply and decided that, despite its popularity, the line was not good. The first 13 moves take us, roughly, to the end of the opening. Moves 14–20 are the critical part of the early middle game; here Fischer, in a series of fine moves, demonstrates the inferiority of Spassky's pawn structure and – helped by some slightly inferior play by Black – establishes a positionally won game. 'Positionally won' in that Spassky's weaknesses in pawn structure are 'fixed'; he cannot remove them and as a result he cannot prevent Fischer getting the superior piece position. In the third stage, moves 20–41, Fischer transmutes this positional advantage into a winning attack on the King; this ability to build a winning attack on the basis of a positional advantage is one of the most attractive sides of a great master's virtuosity. The game ends with a pleasing sacrifice of the exchange leading to mate or overwhelming gain in material. The logic and unity of the game is such that it all seems inevitable; you feel that nothing after the opening could

---

*Notes on this and the next game are based on those in my book, *Fischer v. Spassky, Reykjavik 1972.*

have saved Spassky – that he was helplessly struggling against perfect and remorseless technique.

WHITE R.J. FISCHER   BLACK B. SPASSKY
Queen's Gambit (Tartakower Defence)

1.	P–QB4	P–K3
2.	Kt–KB3	P–Q4
3.	P–Q4	Kt–KB3
4.	Kt–B3	B–K2
5.	B–Kt5	0–0
6.	P–K3	P–KR3
7.	B–R4	P–QKt3

The Tartakower Defence. A more solid line is Lasker's Defence, 7. . . . Kt–K5; 8. BxB, QxB but this gives Black no chance of more than a draw. The modern masters prefer on the whole to take a slight positional risk in order to get more freedom.

8.	PxP	KtxP
9.	BxB	QxB
10.	KtxKt	PxKt
11.	R–B1	B–K3
12.	Q–R4	P–QB4

Now Black has got some space on the Queen's side and some long term counter-attacking chances; but, as we shall see, the same pawn moves that gave him space, also give him weaknesses.

13.	Q–R3	R–B1
14.	B–Kt5!	

With the idea that if 14. . . . Kt–Q2; 15. 0–0 White will threaten to double Rooks on the QB file with BxKt and PxP at appropriate moments when Black will have difficulty in protecting his centre pawns.

14.	...	P–QR3
15.	PxP	PxP

15. . . . RxP; 16. 0–0! also leaves Black with bad pawns.

16.	0–0	R–R2

Geller suggests 16. . . . Q–Kt2; 17. B–K2, Kt–Q2 but White's position remains superior. He has two blocks of pawns, with only the QKtP at all weak; Black has three blocks and QRP, QBP and QP are all shaky.

17.	B–K2	Kt–Q2

It would be a little better to forestall White's next move by Q–B1 or to play 17. . . . P–B5; when the pressure on White's QKtP would to some extent (but not wholly) offset Black's central weakness.

18.	Kt–Q4!	Q–B1

And here 18. . . . Kt–B3 is slightly better; the text is too passive.

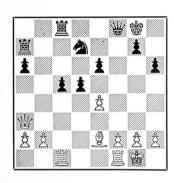

19.	KtxB	PxKt
20.	P–K4!	

20.	...	P–Q5?

After 20. . . . PxP; 21. R–B4 Black will lose at least one of the isolated pawns quickly and, at best, reach a very inferior endgame. However, after the text move, there is no strength left in the black centre and the White Bishop is extremely strong. 20. . . . Kt–B3 is relatively best though after 21. P–K5, Kt–Q2; 22. P–B4 White has a clear advantage. It is fascinating to see how a series of slightly inferior moves, coupled with very fine White play, have got Spassky into a lost position. The hardest part of White's work is now done.

21.	P–B4	Q–K2
22.	P–K5!	R–Kt1

The plausible 22. . . . Kt–Kt3 is met by 23. P–B5! (23. . . . PxP?; 24. Q–Kt3ch), Kt–Q4; 24. B–B4 and Black is under severe pressure.

23.	B–B4	K–R1

23. . . . Kt–Kt3; 24. Q–QKt3!

24.	Q–KR3!	Kt–B1

24. . . . RxP; 25. BxKP followed by P–B5–B6 with a winning attack.

25.	P–QKt3	P–QR4
26.	P–B5!	

From now on, as that great master of attack Mikhail Tal said, it is a textbook attack.

26.	...	PxP
27.	RxP	Kt–R2

So that he can answer R–B7 with Kt–Kt4.

28.	R(1)–KB1	Q–Q1
29.	Q–Kt3	R–K2
30.	P–KR4	

Depriving the Kt of KKt4; White gradually reduces Black to a position in which he can only move to and fro.

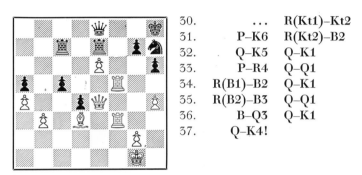

30.	...	R(Kt1)–Kt2
31.	P–K6	R(Kt2)–B2
32.	Q–K5	Q–K1
33.	P–R4	Q–Q1
34.	R(B1)–B2	Q–K1
35.	R(B2)–B3	Q–Q1
36.	B–Q3	Q–K1
37.	Q–K4!	

The threat is 38. R–B8ch, KtxR; 39. RxKtch, QxR; 40. Q–R7 mate. If 37. . . . P–Kt3; then 38. Q–K5ch, R–Kt2 (38. . . . K–Kt1; 39. R–B7); 39. R–B7, RxR; 40. RxR, Q–KKt1; 41. BxP followed by P–K7 winning.

37.	...	Kt–B3
38.	RxKt!	PxR
39.	RxP	K–Kt1
40.	B–B4	K–R1

40. . . . Q–R4; 41. R–Kt6ch, K–R1; 42. Q–R8ch and 40. . . . Q–Q1; 41. Q–Kt6ch are even worse. The threat was 41. R–B7, RxR; 42. PxRch.

41.	Q–B4	Resigns

41. . . . K–Kt1; 42. QxRP followed by 43. R–Kt6ch.

The 13th game of the match

This is a game of an entirely different type from the 6th; Fischer's play is far more flawed but in compensation it is a richer game, full of tension and drama. It occurred at a critical stage in the match. Spassky, after a terrible hammering in games 3 to 10 in which he lost 5 games and drew 3, had crushed Fischer in the 11th game and comfortably drawn the 12th; if he could win this he would only be a point behind. The result was (to quote myself!) 'a struggle of heroic proportions . . . without doubt one of the most interesting and remarkable encounters ever to take place in a World Championship'.

In the first phase of the game, moves 1–14, Fischer again wins the opening battle. This is much more surprising than in the sixth game, because the line he chose should have been no surprise to Spassky; I cannot understand Spassky's weak play. In moves 15–24, Spassky fights back; rather than accept a permanently inferior position, he sacrifices a pawn and with Fischer not finding quite the best line Spassky gets a dangerous attack. He misses his way however, is caught in a trap on move 29 and seems to be lost: however, on moves 32 and 33 Fischer – perhaps overconfident – again loses his way. Moves 34 to 54 see a tremendous cut-and-thrust struggle very well played by both sides and culminating in the sacrifice of a piece for three pawns by Fischer. Still, this should not be enough to win; Spassky counters strongly and by move 69 has a clear draw. But he is understandably tired and has – with four moves to make in four minutes – run himself short of time; on move 69 he blunders fatally and on move 75 is forced to resign.

Despite its errors this is a great game – a struggle of character as well as technical ability in which the stronger and more determined player justly won: it settled the match. For ordinary mortals, it is encouraging to see how even the greatest players are not able to play a game of this length and complexity without error. Chess has never looked less played out than here.

WHITE B.SPASSKY   BLACK R.J.FISCHER
Alekhine's Defence

1.	P–K4	Kt–KB3
2.	P–K5	Kt–Q4
3.	P–Q4	P–Q3
4.	Kt–KB3	P–KKt3
5.	B–QB4	Kt–Kt3
6.	B–Kt3	B–Kt2

7.	QKt–Q2	

Artificial and less good than the more natural move 7. 0–0; the line played by Keres, 7. 0–0, 0–0; 8. P–QR4, P–QR4; P–R3, Kt–B3; 10. Q–K2, P–Q4; 11. Kt–B3, preserves some initiative.

7.	...	0–0
8.	P–KR3?	

This is a good move when the White Knight is going to QB3 since it prevents B–Kt5 putting pressure on the KP; but one of the few merits of 7. QKt–Q2 is that it removes any menace from 8. ... B–Kt5 which would be met by 9. P–KR3, BxKt; 10. KtxB. The combination of White's 7th and 8th moves is as baffling as it is bad. Better 8. Q–K2 or 8. 0–0.

8.	...	P–QR4!
9.	P–QR4?	

Now White loses the QRP; P–QR3 was correct.

9.	...	PxP
10.	PxP	Kt–R3!
11.	0–0	Kt–B4
12.	Q–K2	Q–K1
13.	Kt–K4	Kt(3)xP
14.	BxKt	KtxB
15.	R–K1!?	

White could regain the pawn by 15. Q–B4, B–Q2; 16. QxP but after 16. ... Q–B1; 17. QxQ, KRxQ Black's two Bishops and better development would give him a superior endgame. Against Fischer – a superb endgame technician – I think Spassky is right to let the pawn go and try for the attack.

15.	...	Kt–Kt3
16.	B–Q2	P–R5
17.	B–Kt5	P–R3
18.	B–R4	B–B4?

Better 18. ... B–Q2! threatening B–Kt4 and Kt–B5. Now White begins to get some real chances of attack.

19.	P–KKt4	B–K3

After 19. ... BxKt; 20. QxB White has Queen's side pressure, e.g. 20. ... P–QB3; 21. Q–Kt4 or 20. ... R–Kt1; 21. Q–Kt4, P–Kt4; 22. B–Kt3 followed by P–KR4 renewing the King's side threat.

20.	Kt–Q4	B–B5
21.	Q–Q2	Q–Q2

21. . . . BxP; 22. P–B4!, BxKtch (22. . . . B–Kt2; 23. Kt–B6ch!); 23. QxB, Q–Q1; 24. Q–B5, R–K1; 25. QR–Q1, Q–B1; 26. BxP with a winning game.

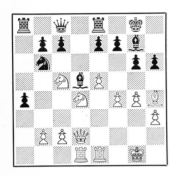

22.	QR–Q1	KR–K1
23.	P–B4	B–Q4
24.	Kt–QB5	Q–B1

25.	Q–B3	

I am not sure, but I think that he should have tried 25. P–K6, Kt–B5!; 26. Q–K2!, Kt–Q3! (26. . . . KtxP?; 27. Kt–B5! is good for White) and now 27. PxPch, 27. P–B5 and 27. Kt–B5 are all possible, though none conclusive. A fascinating position. After the text move, Black stands better.

25.	...	P–K3
26.	K–R2	Kt–Q2
27.	Kt–Q3?	

Overlooking Black's 29th move. 27. Kt–Kt5, KtxKt; 28. QxKt, B–QB3; 29. Kt–Q4, B–B1; 30. Q–B3 preserves some pressure for the pawn.

27.	...	P–QB4
28.	Kt–Kt5	Q–B3
29.	Kt–Q6	QxKt!
30.	PxQ	BxQ
31.	PxB	P–B3

Now Fischer must have thought it was all over – but he underestimates the trouble that the pawn on Q6 can cause.

32.	P–Kt5	RPxP

It is simpler to play 32. . . . P–B5!; 33. Kt–Kt4, RPxP; 34. PxP, P–B4; with no access to K5 for his Knight White has no counter attack and the passed QRP will win.

33.	PxP	P–B4?

After this Black's weakness on the dark squares plus the pressure of the QP makes it very hard – maybe impossible – to win. The right move was 33. . . . . PxP!; 34. BxP, R–KB1! and with threats on both wings Black should win, e.g. 35. Kt–K5, KtxKt; 36. RxKt, R–B7ch; 37. K–Kt1, R–Kt7ch; 38. K–B1, R–B1ch; 39. K–K1, B–B5.

34.	B–Kt3	K–B2
35.	Kt–K5ch	KtxKt
36.	BxKt	P–Kt4
37.	R–KB1!	

Threatening R–B4–R4–R7ch.

37.	. . .	R–R1!

He does not mind 38. BxR?, RxB since he will pick up the QP and then win with his own passed pawns.

38.	B–B6	P–R6
39.	R–B4	P–R7
40.	P–B4	

The last move before the time control; by this sacrifice White opens the diagonal to allow his Bishop to protect QR1 and gains time to advance the QP.

40.	. . .	BxP
41.	P–Q7	B–Q4
42.	K–Kt3!	

Threatening R–R4 followed by a Rook exchange after which the QP will cost Black a whole Rook.

42.	. . .	R–R6ch
43.	P–B3	

And not 43. K–B2?, R(6)xP!; 44. P–Q8 = Q, RxQ; 45. BxR, P–K4! regaining the Rook and winning easily!

43.	. . .	R(1)–QR1!

Another splendid conception; he must during the adjournment have analysed at least up to move 52 and reckoned that he would have good winning chances.

44.	R–KR4	P–K4!
45.	R–R7ch	K–K3
46.	R–K7ch	K–Q3
47.	RxP	RxPch

47. . . . P–R8 = Q?; 48. R(5)xBch, K–B3; 49. RxQ, RxR; 50. P–Q8 = Q, RxQ; 51. RxR and White is winning.

48.	K–B2	R–B7ch
49.	K–K1	KxP
50.	R(5)xBch	K–B3
51.	R–Q6ch	K–Kt2
52.	R–Q7ch	K–R3
53.	R(7)–Q2	RxR
54.	KxR	P–Kt5
55.	P–R4!	

He must force a passed pawn himself to tie down the Black Rook.

55.	. . .	K–Kt4
56.	P–R5	P–QB5!

Threatening P–B6ch, cutting off the Bishop, followed by P–R8 = Q.

57.	R–QR1	PxP
58.	P–Kt6	P–R5
59.	P–Kt7	P–R6
60.	B–K7	R–KKt1
61.	B–B8	

Now we have another extraordinary phase in an extraordinary game. With the White B and KtP neutralizing the Black Rook we have 5 Black pawns *v.* White Rook; it is slightly better for White than this as he can in an emergency use his Bishop (which also hampers Black's King) whereas Black cannot use the Rook except by White's permission.

61.	. . .	P–R7
62.	K–B2	K–B3

| 63. | R–Q1 | P–Kt6ch |
| 64. | K–B3 | P–KR8 = Q |

To have a chance of winning he must bring his King down the centre – and this is the only way to do it.

65.	R x Q	K–Q4
66.	K–Kt2	P–B5
67.	R–Q1ch	K–K5
68.	R–QB1	K–Q6

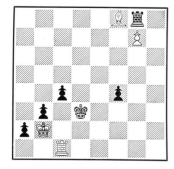

| 69. | R–Q1ch ? | |

Alas! Time and fatigue cost him the game. 69. R–B3ch draws: (*a*) 69. . . . K–K7; 70. R x BP, P–B6; 71. R–B1, P–B7; 72. K x P, P–B8 = Q; 73. R x Q, K x R; 74. K x P. (*b*) 69. . . . K–Q5; 70. R–KB3, P–B6ch; 71. K–R1, P–B7; 72. R x Pch, K–B6 (72. . . . K–K6?; 73. R–B1, K–Q7; 74. K–Kt2 and White wins); 73. R–B3ch, K–Q7; 74. B–R3!, R x P; 75. R x P and draws.

69.	...	K–K7
70.	R–QB1	P–KB6
71.	B–B5	

Now 71. R x P, P–B7; 72. R–B1, P–B8 = Q is a move too late.

71.	...	R x P
72.	R x P	R–Q2
73.	R–K4ch	K–B8
74.	B–Q4	P–B7
75.	Resigns	

75. R–B4 (nothing better), R x B!; 76. R x R, K–Kt7 and White must give up the Rook for the KBP.

And so no doubt it was when the great Achilles (who had a lot in common with Fischer) slew Hector.

The following is a game played by Capablanca when 4 years 10 months old – just after he had learnt the moves by watching his father play. The game is of no interest in itself – White had not the faintest chance of successfully conceding a Queen – but there are two interesting points that arise from it. The first is the truly amazing grasp of the game shown by the four-year-old – what intuition told him to develop, to centralize, to increase his advantage by exchange, to use his King in the endgame? The second is the comparison between this game and the next – the game won by CHESS 3.6 against TECH; my impression is that the prodigy would have held his own with the program. If so it is remarkable to think that years of thought and the most powerful of modern machines cannot yet better the performance of an untaught four-year-old genius.

WHITE IGLESIAS   BLACK J.CAPABLANCA
Petroff's Defence (Havana, 1893)
(*Remove White's Queen*)

1.	P–K4	P–K4
2.	Kt–KB3	Kt–KB3
3.	Kt x P	Kt x P
4.	P–Q4	P–Q3
5.	Kt–KB3	B–K2
6.	B–Q3	Kt–KB3
7.	P–B4	0–0
8.	Kt–B3	Kt–B3
9.	P–QR3	P–QR3
10.	B–Q2	P–QKt3
11.	0–0–0	B–Q2
12.	K–Kt1	Kt–QR4
13.	R–QB1	Kt–Kt6
14.	R–B2	P–B4

One's impression is that Iglesias would not have had it all his own way if they had been playing level.

15.	P–Q5	R–K1
16.	P–KR4	P–QKt4
17.	P–Kt4	Kt–Q5
18.	Kt x Kt	P x Kt
19.	Kt–K4	P x P
20.	Kt x Ktch	B x Kt
21.	B x BP	B x KtP
22.	B–Q3	B–B6
23.	R–R3	B x QP

Take Black's Queen off and he would still have the better of it.

24.	P–R5	B–K3
25.	R–Kt3	P–Kt3
26.	P–B4	B–R5
27.	R–Kt1	K–R1
28.	P–B5	BxP
29.	BxB	PxB
30.	B–R6	

At last a threat – disposed of by the infant with contemptuous ease.

30.	...	R–KKt1
31.	R(B2)–Kt2	RxR
32.	RxR	Q–B3
33.	B–Kt7ch	QxB
34.	RxQ	KxR
35.	K–B2	K–B3
36.	K–Q3	K–K4
37.	P–R6	P–B5
38.	K–K2	K–K5
39.	Resigns	

No one could accuse White of giving up prematurely.

Now, for comparison, the struggle of the automata.

WHITE CHESS 3.6   BLACK TECH
Ruy Lopez (Boston, 1972)

1.	P–K4	P–K4
2.	Kt–KB3	Kt–QB3
3.	B–Kt5	Kt–B3

The Berlin Defence, discovered by TECH – which doesn't know any opening theory – for itself.

4.	0–0	B–B4
5.	Kt–B3	P–Q3
6.	BxKtch	

According to David Levy, who acted as tournament controller for this event – he does not say how he disciplined recalcitrant machines – CHESS 3.6 is very fond of doubling its opponent's pawns. It strikes me altogether as a pawky sort of player; never does anything much, but plugs steadily along. We all know players like this in the club; members for many years, slightly despised by the younger players, they sit stolidly at the board outlasting their opponents and bringing home one dismal win after another. I'm sure 3.6 is a pipe smoker.

6.	...	PxB
7.	P–Q4	PxP
8.	KtxP	0–0
9.	B–Kt5	

9. KtxP is met by 9. . . . Q–K1; now however the win of a pawn is threatened.

9.	...	B–KKt5
10.	Q–Q3	BxKt
11.	QxB	R–Kt1
12.	BxKt	QxB
13.	QxQ	PxQ

Having isolated or doubled all pawns within reach, White settles down to the ending. Computers have the great advantage of being – I assume – immune to boredom.

14.	P–QKt3	R–Kt5
15.	P–KR3	B–K3
16.	P–Kt4	R–Q5
17.	QR–Q1	RxR
18.	KtxR	

I am interested by this recapture, preparing to get the Kt to K3; I wonder why the program rejected the more obvious RxR.

18.	...	K–Kt2?

It should play either R–Q1 followed by K–B1–K2 or else P–Q4.

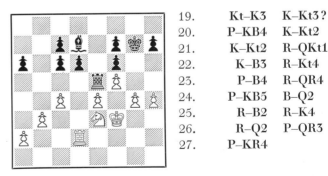

19.	Kt–K3	K–Kt3?
20.	P–KB4	K–Kt2
21.	K–Kt2	R–QKt1
22.	K–B3	R–Kt4
23.	P–B4	R–QR4
24.	P–KB5	B–Q2
25.	R–B2	R–K4
26.	R–Q2	P–QR3
27.	P–KR4	

27.	...	P–B4?

It should sit tight with P–R3. Nobody can have told it about weak squares.

28.	Kt–Q5	B–B3
29.	KtxQBP	BxPch
30.	K–B4	P–KR4!

A good try, but Black now has too many weaknesses.

31.	P x P	P–R4
32.	R x P	B x P
33.	P–R6ch!	K–Kt3
34.	P–R5ch!	K x P(R4)
35.	R x P	R–K7
36.	K x B	R–B7ch
37.	K–K5	R–R7
38.	Kt–Q5	K–Kt4
39.	Kt–B3	R–R5
40.	R x P	K x P
41.	Kt–K4	R–R4ch

A less determined machine would resign.

42.	K–Q6	K–Kt3
43.	R–QR7	P–R5
44.	R x P	K–B2
45.	R–R7ch	K–Kt3
46.	P–R4	R–B4

Now almost any being, animate or inanimate, would give up, but TECH fights to the last watt.

47.	P–R5	R–B6
48.	R–QKt7	K–B4
49.	Kt x P	R–B6
50.	P–R6	R–R6
51.	P–R7	Black exceeded the time limit

This, however, is carrying things too far. TECH should learn that that is not the way that a properly programmed computer should lose.

What I find impressive about this game is that I could not have told that it was not by human players: many club games are like this. In tactical situations, CHESS 3.6 is quite competent and it sets about winning the endgame in a sensible, straightforward way; in position play, it has the fairly crude ideas of weakening Black's pawn structure, of centralizing and of gaining space by advancing its own pawns, but there is little sign of strategy of any depth. (It might reply perhaps that against TECH there was no need for any.) Although no masterpiece this is a lot better than computer games of even two years ago, and Botvinnik may yet prove to be right in thinking that we shall see Grandmaster programs.

The Women's Game

The two strongest women players in the world are the World Champion Nona Gaprindashvili and her contemporary and great rival Alla Kushnir. Both Soviet players, they were both born in 1941; Gaprindashvili won the championship in 1962 and has three times successfully defended it against Kushnir. She beat her $8\frac{1}{2}$–$4\frac{1}{2}$ in 1965, $8\frac{1}{2}$–$4\frac{1}{2}$ again in 1969, but only $8\frac{1}{2}$–$7\frac{1}{2}$ in 1972. In the latter half of the 1972 match Kushnir played very strongly and if they meet yet again in 1975 she might well win.

The players differ completely in style; Gaprindashvili is essentially an attacking combinative player and Kushnir a strategist. In the 1972 match each player stuck firmly to her favourite opening – a marked contrast to the Fischer/Spassky match where a wide range of openings were played. When Gaprindashvili was White, Kushnir played the Sicilian Defence every time – score 4–4. When Gaprindashvili was Black, she played the Grünfeld the first six times; with its numerous tactical points this was a good choice and she won the match with this defence by scoring 4–2. In games 14 and 16 she changed, perhaps unwisely, to the Nimzo-Indian when she scored a loss and a draw. Here is one of her Grünfeld wins. Like Petrosian, Gaprindashvili was born in Georgia, so from 1963 to 1969 it had the proud distinction of being the birthplace of both the World Champions.

WHITE A.KUSHNIR   BLACK N.GAPRINDASHVILI
Grünfeld Defence (4th game of match, Riga, 1972)

1.	P–Q4	Kt–KB3
2.	P–QB4	P–KKt3
3.	Kt–QB3	P–Q4
4.	P x P	Kt x P
5.	P–K4	

This is the most critical and complex of the various ways of playing against the Grünfeld. It might have been wiser for Kushnir to adopt one of the quieter lines.

5.	...	Kt x Kt
6.	P x Kt	B–Kt2
7.	B–QB4	P–QB4
8.	Kt–K2	Kt–B3
9.	B–K3	0–0
10.	0–0	Q–B2

11.	R–B1	R–Q1

The critical position in the opening. White has a massive pawn centre and prospects of a King's side attack based on the advance P–KB4. On the other hand her centre is under pressure and if it comes to an endgame Black's pawn majority on the Queen's wing will be valuable. It is not clear who has the better position, though in practice Black's game seems to be rather harder to play correctly than White's and White tends to have the edge. Kushnir now tries a new idea.

12.	B–B4	Q–Q2
13.	PxP	

This surprising move is a lot stronger than it looks at first sight. White's better development fully compensates for the broken pawns – and after all she has an extra pawn, however bad it is. In trying to assess the players' strength, one must always remember that each had a strong master as her second and this striking variation was undoubtedly fully prepared in advance.

13.	...	Q–K1
14.	B–Q5!	Kt–K4

Not 14. ... P–K3?; 15. BxKt!, PxB; 16. B–Q6 with the better game. However 14. ... B–Q2 looks better than the text; if then 15. Q–Kt3, P–K3; 16. BxKt, BxB with equality.

15.	Q–Kt3	P–K3
16.	BxKtP?	

She should play 16. BxKt!, BxB; 17. BxKtP, R–Kt1; 18. P–B6 with some advantage.

16.	...	BxB
17.	QxB	Kt–Q6!
18.	B–Q6!	

This gives better winning chances than 18. QR–Q1, KtxQBP. It also gives better losing chances, but neither player lacks courage and this is a justified sacrifice.

18.	...	KtxR
19.	KtxKt	P–K4
20.	Kt–Q3	

Better 20. P–KB4, PxP; 21. Kt–K2 and 22. KtxP with plenty for the exchange.

20.	...	B–B1

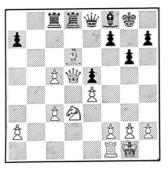

21.	Q–Q5	QR–B1!

22.	R–Q1?	

She must play P–KB4! after which the game is still in the balance. Black's play is altogether more incisive than White's. After the text move, White is quite lost. Black wins the ending in vigorous and efficient style.

22.	...	BxB
23.	PxB	R–B3!
24.	P–Q7	QxP
25.	KtxP	QxQ
26.	PxQ	RxBP
27.	P–Kt3	K–Kt2
28.	Kt–Kt4	R–B7
29.	R–R1	R(1)–QB1
30.	K–Kt2	R–B8

With the exchange of Rooks White's position is completely hopeless; as long as it was 2 Rs *v.* R and Kt there was a faint chance perhaps, but with the scattered pawns the Knight on its own has no chance – it cannot cover the ground.

31.	RxR	RxR
32.	K–B3	P–B4
33.	Kt–K3	K–B3
34.	P–Kt4	K–K4
35.	PxP	PxP
36.	P–KR4	R–B6
37.	K–K2	P–B5
38.	Kt–Kt4ch	KxP
39.	Kt–B6ch	K–Q5
40.	KtxP	P–B6ch
41.	K–Q2	R–R6
42.	Resigns	

The position is hopeless, e.g. 42. Kt–Kt5, RxPch; 43. K–K1, K–Q6 and 44. ... R–R8mate. Not a Grandmaster game but I shouldn't like to run up against either lady on a dark chess night.

Section 2: The history and development of Chess

Chapter 4: Fourteen Centuries of Chess

In the beginning

'Before the seventh century of our era the existence of chess, in any land, is not demonstrable by a single shred of contemporary or trustworthy documentary evidence. . . . Down to that date it is all impenetrable darkness.'

Professor D.W.Fiske quoted by H.J.R.Murray in
A History of Chess.

Until quite recently it seemed fairly certain that chess was invented in North-West India in the sixth century AD. Earlier ideas that it was a much older game arise from the habit of referring to any pieces used in an unknown boardgame as chessmen; so-called 'chessmen' found in Tutankhamun's and other Egyptian tombs have in fact nothing to do with chess. However, in 1973, Russian archaeologists working near the Afghanistan border of the Uzbek Republic found a china jar filled with gold, rubies, emeralds and two ivory figures which look very like chessmen. If they are, then this moves the origins of the game back to the 2nd century. Even so, on present evidence, the Chinese game of WEI-CHI (or 'GO' in Japan) is over twice as old as chess, having been traced back at least as far as the emperor Kieh Kwei (1818–1767 BC). So although chess is of respectable antiquity, we chess players should not give ourselves too many airs on this account.

Once invented, however, it fairly quickly showed its universal appeal. From India it spread out in all directions. It reached

Satirical papyrus XIXth/XXth *Dynasties*

Right: Excavations on the site of the ancient town of Dalverzin-tepe in southern Uzbekistan, Central Asia

Below: 'Chess' pieces from the second century AD *unearthed during the excavations in 1973*

Europe by three routes: direct to Russia through Persia, via the Moors to Spain and then to France and England and – again through Persia – via the Saracens to Italy, Germany, Bohemia and Hungary, and Northern Europe. It was probably about the tenth century when it reached Western Europe. Travelling East, the game went to China and Japan where, although popular, it took second place to the older (and equally good) game of WEI-CHI; it also went direct to South-East Asia and has always been very popular in Malay countries, especially Sumatra where the Bataks rival Russians, Jews and Icelanders in their passion for the game.

In its travels, the game was gradually modified, in different ways by different people. One can see how great the effect of these cumulative changes is by comparing the modern game as we know it with Japanese Chess or *Shogi* (see Section 4); while the common origin is evident, a western player will have to learn *Shogi* as an almost completely new game. Nevertheless it is surprising how well the original concept has stood the test of time, as we can see if we look at the primitive game.

'The Original Game'

'According to Moslem Law it is an Abomination to play at Chess . . . the prophet has declared all the Entertainments of a Moslem to be vain, except three, viz: the breaking-in of his horse; the drawing of his bow; and the playing or amusing himself with his wives.

Several of the learned, however, deem the game of Chess to be allowed, as having a tendency to quicken the understanding'

The Hectaya or *Persian Guide*, 1791

'Your rose-water has turned to urine'

The Caliph al-Muktafi, to his dependant al-Mawardi on the latter's losing the World Championship to the Turk as-Sūlī, *c.*905.

Chess is undoubtedly a war game and the complications of the various pieces with their different moves arise from its inventor's attempt to reproduce on the chessboard the structure of the Indian army of those days. There were equivalents – though not all with identical moves – to all the modern pieces, and the initial set-up was the same as in the modern game. The King, the Horse (Knight), the Chariot (Rook) and the Foot-soldier (pawn) all had their present-day moves except that there

was no castling, no initial double move for the pawn and the pawn could only promote to a Queen (Minister) – a very important point as we shall see. The Elephant (Bishop) was much weaker than his modern counterpart; he could only move two squares (not one) diagonally, jumping an intervening piece if there was one there – thus he never had more than four squares available. Most important of all, the Minister (Queen) was not the strongest but one of the weakest pieces, being confined to moving one square diagonally. This not only greatly limited the initial force available but meant that the long-term importance of a pawn was much less; to promote to a Minister was a comparatively trivial advantage. Finally, victory could be of one of three kinds: (*a*) checkmate, (*b*) by the 'bared King', i.e. capturing all the other enemy pieces, or (*c*) by stalemate.

In addition to this, the basic game, there was also a four-handed game played with dice. Here each player had a 'half-set' – King, Bishop, Knight, Rook and four pawns – placed in the four corners at right angles to each other, i.e. one set from QR1 to Q1, one from KR1 to KR4 and so on. At each turn the player threw the dice to decide which piece to move and could then exercise some skill in deciding where to move it. One might have expected people to prefer this to the more rarified atmosphere of the game of pure skill but, although it survived for some time in Europe, it never achieved the popularity or status of the main game; the reason may be the strong disapproval of gambling by both Muhammadan and Christian religions. They also intermittently anathematized the main game for various reasons, ranging from Muhammad's denouncement of 'images' (as shown in the carving of the pieces) to the more practical Catholic disapproval of chess as a waste of time. But these objections were less fundamental and were either satisfied (e.g. by symbolic rather than representational carving) or died away naturally – and chess survived.

Returning to the main game, how did the original chess, as played by the Arabs when they brought it to Europe, compare with our own? It was inferior in various ways. First of all, if played at modern master level, almost all games would certainly be drawn. Without the power of the modern Queen, successful direct attacks on the King would be very rare; and small material gains, such as that of a pawn, which can be decisive in the modern game – because in the end it leads to queening a pawn – would be of little importance in the old game. And while the total force would be too weak for the checkmate victory, it would be too strong for the 'baring' victory. In draughts, where the moves of the individual men are very weak, an advantage of a man will lead without too much difficulty to the final capture of all the enemy men; but with the much greater mobility of the chess pieces, this is unlikely to be possible without a great material advantage.

The other drawback of the old game was its slowness. The absence of the initial double move of the pawn (what genius first thought of this? – I suppose boredom was the spur) makes the openings tedious to a degree: no contact with the enemy was normally made for a dozen moves or more. This is brought out clearly in the nature of Arab opening theory; an opening was something carried out behind your own lines without interaction with the enemy – it didn't matter what order you played the moves in, you just played to reach your own basic position. The Mujannah, The Sayyāl, the Mashā'ikhī, the Saif – these exotic creatures were one-player openings.

One must not however underrate the skill of the great Arab players. As late as the thirteenth century they were clearly much superior to any Europeans, as is shown by the fact that in 1266 the Saracen Buchecha played the three best players in Florence simultaneously, two of them blindfold, and scored two wins and a draw – and Italy, with Spain, was the leading European country. Blindfold play was highly developed; five games at once had certainly been played and probably ten. As late as 1783, when Philidor played two games blindfold at once, *The World* described this feat with journalistic inaccuracy as a 'phenomenon in the history of man'; when we look forward and compare this with the fifty games at once played by modern blindfold masters, we should also look back to the ten games of the Arabs.

Further, the Arabs appear – for better or for worse – to have invented not only the World Championship but also Grandmasters. In 820 there were four 'aliyāt' or 'players of the highest class'; and in 847 the Persian ar-Rāzī defeated al-'Adli (then the only aliyāt) in the presence of the Caliph al-Mutawakkil' – an international contest that seems over the centuries to carry a faint flavour of Fischer/Spassky. Finally, they wrote on the game; according to Murray in his *History of Chess*, my title *A Book of Chess* was first pre-empted by al-'Adli while ar-Rāzī, as-Sūlī (the Turkish historian and World Champion) and his disciple al-Lajlāj ('the Stammerer') also all wrote on chess.

As a farewell to the Arabs, here is a game given by al-Lajlāj and quoted by Murray: it is said to have been won by as-Sūlī, the greatest of all the early players.

Opening: Sayyāl ('The Torrent')

	WHITE	BLACK
1.	P–KKt3	P–KKt3
2.	P–KKt4	P–KB3
3.	P–K3	P–K3
4.	Kt–K2	P–Q3
5.	R–Kt1	P–B3
6.	P–KB3	P–Kt3
7.	P–B4	P–QR3
8.	P–B5	

The KBP is 'The Torrent', hence the name of the opening. As-Sūlī was the first player to think of interfering with his opponent's opening plans, and to make contact with the enemy on move 8 was indeed a torrential advance in those days.

8.	...	KPxP
9.	PxP	PxP

It would be better to play 9. ... P–KKt4 and avoid breaking up his pawns.

10.	B–KR3	

Threatening BxBP – this is not protected, of course, by Black's QB.

10.	...	Kt–K2
11.	R–B1	R–Kt1
12.	Kt–Kt3	R–Kt4
13.	BxP	P–R3
14.	B–KR3	Kt–Q2

Better to protect the pawn by K–B2, followed by Kt–Kt3 and R–R2–K2 and only then bring out the QKt.

15.	P–Q3	P–Q4
16.	P–B3	Q–B2
17.	P–Kt3	R–R2
18.	P–B4	B–Q3

He should play 18. ... PxP; 19. KtPxP, P–Kt4 followed by Q–Q3; as played the Bishop is in the way on Q3, and his pawn formation is further weakened.

19.	Kt–B3	B–K3
20.	P x P	P x P
21.	P–Q4	B–KB1
22.	R–B2	Q–Q3
23.	P–Kt4	R–B2
24.	K–Q2	P–Kt4
25.	B–R3	Kt–QKt3
26.	B–QB5	Kt–B3?

After this he is lost. He should play Kt–Kt1. Note incidentally that White was threatening B x Kt, a major gain in material.

27.	P–R3	K–B2
28.	Q–B2	B–B5
29.	R(R1)–KB1	R–Kt3

29. . . . Kt–Q2 is met by 30. R–B5 and White will win either KBP or QP (which is not protected by either Q or B!).

30.	Kt–R5	K–K1

30. . . . Kt–Q2; 31. Kt x QP and wins.

31.	Kt x P ch	K–Q1
32.	Kt(B6) x P	R–QKt2
33.	R x B ch	K–Q2
34.	B–B5 ch	K–K3
35.	Kt–B4 mate	

A good game by White, but much of Black's play was very weak.

Early European chess

'The association of nobility with chess was so characteristic that for one of lower rank to admit a knowledge of chess was sufficient to raise suspicions as to his identity. Huon of Bordeaux, travelling disguised as a minstrel's varlet, is suspected when he boasts of his skill at chess, and the Devil is discovered in the guise of a servant (Miracles de la Sainte Vierge) through his unusual accomplishments of which chess is one.'

H.J.R.Murray, Shorter History of Chess

Despite periodic troubles with the church – chess players were at one time threatened with excommunication – the game's popularity in Europe gradually increased. However two factors kept the standard of play low. One was that it was largely a court game and so the total number of players was small. In a game like chess where defeat is peculiarly irritating owing to the difficulty of explaining it away by extraneous circumstances such as bad light and bad cards (though we do our best), playing with royalty clearly taxed one's diplomacy as much as one's skill. On the one hand there were monarchs like the Caliph Al-Ma'mum who, observing that his opponent was being unduly co-operative, overturned the board saying to the assembled spectators, 'Bear witness to the vow which I now make that I will never play chess with this person again' – and yet one wonders whether you really gained the Caliph's favour by consistently defeating him. At the other extreme was King Canute; less philosophical at chess than when sitting on the sea shore, he meant to win by fair means or foul. To quote from Snorri Sturluson's saga, 'As King Canute and Earl Ulf were playing at chess, the king made a false move, in consequence of which the earl took one of his Knights. But the king would not allow this, and replacing the pieces played differently. Whereat the earl waxed wroth, overturned the chessboard and made to depart. "Ulf, thou coward" called the king, "Dost thou flee?" "A longer flight", retorted the earl, "would have been thine in the River Helga, had I not run to thy assistance when the Swedes beat thee like a dog. Thou didst not then call me coward". So the earl retired, and next morning the king ordered his life to be taken.' In fairness to Canute, I should add that he and the earl were on very bad terms anyway.

The other limiting factor was the lack of communication between players. To quote Murray, 'There was no organized chess life comparable with the club and tournament of the present day, and the real representatives of the medieval players are not the club players . . . but the home players who have never opened a chess book or troubled their heads over the theory of the game'. Travel was difficult and there was very little literature on the game that gave any worthwhile technical information. The isolation of the European chessplayers from each other emerges vividly from the fact that minor changes in the rules and moves took place in different countries and by the fifteenth century Spain, Italy, France, England and Germany all played slightly different versions of the game.

So progress up to the fifteenth century was negligible; I doubt whether the best of the medieval players could have beaten the old Arab masters. But about 1500 a revolution took place.

The New Game

'Paoli Boi embarked at Barcelona, was taken by corsair, and sold at Algiers for a slave. His patron, having discovered his ability in Chess, won considerable sums by this means, and gave him his liberty, and a thousand sequins.'

Richard Twiss, *Chess*, 1787

(Paoli Boi (1528–98) and Leonardo were the two leading sixteenth-century players, both Italians. Boi, one of the earliest European professionals, is said to have made 30,000 crowns at chess during his life.)

'Whoever is to play an important game must avoid filling his belly with superfluous food, because fulness is contrary to speculation and obfuscates the sight.'

Pietro Carrera, *Il Giogo degli Scacchi*, 1617

(Bad advice for a five hour session; you will suffer for it in the fifth hour)

'Eschés de la Dame Enragée' appeared first in Italy and rapidly spread to France and Spain; it killed the old game in Europe as quickly and completely as contract bridge killed auction. It was not just that with the introduction of the modern moves of Queen and Bishop the effective force available to the players was greatly increased; the spirit of the game was changed. The old subsidiary wins by baring or stalemate gradually disappeared – but more important, the whole tempo of the game altered. Take a very simple example – Scholar's mate: 1. P–K4, P–K4; 2. B–B4, B–B4; 3. Q–R5, Kt–QB3??; 4. QxBP (incidentally, many people call this Fool's mate – but Fool's mate is 1. P–KKt4?, P–K4; 2. P–KB3??, Q–R5 mate; Maniac's mate would be a better name for it). Imagine the impact of this on players used to the Double Mujannah where no contact with the enemy is made for 15 moves; it would have taken the old Queen six moves to limp from Q1 to KB7 and the King's Bishop could never have got to KB4 at all – in the new game, the *dame enragée* and the revitalized Bishop could combine to give mate on the fourth move. It was no longer possible to conduct the openings on a sort of 'holidays abroad' basis – think of a nice place and then go there; from the first move you were liable to interference from the opponent. This in turn gave rise to detailed opening analysis of a quite new kind; a sharp, tactical study of the possibilities.

From now on there was a gradual advance, slow at first and accelerating from the middle of the nineteenth century, when international matches and then tournaments were introduced.

I deal with the technical side of this in the next chapter, so here I will merely sketch general and organizational changes. First, however, I give a game played shortly after the introduction of the new chess into Spain. It was played between two Catalan players and a poem 'Scachs d'Amor', with Mars as White and Venus as Black, was based on it; so it must have been regarded as a passable game at the time – to our eyes it is a game from the third class afternoon reserves at the Little Ditchley congress.

WHITE FRANCISCO DE CASTELLIZ   BLACK NARCISO VIÑOLES
Centre Counter

1.	P–K4	P–Q4
2.	PxP	QxP
3.	Kt–QB3	Q–Q1
4.	B–B4	Kt–KB3
5.	Kt–B3	B–Kt5?
6.	P–KR3?	

White can get a winning advantage by 6. BxPch, KxB; 7. Kt–K5ch and 8. KtxB. It is interesting to see how the most familiar tactical devices were still waiting to be discovered.

6.	...	BxKt
7.	QxB	P–K3??

Presumably a complete oversight.

8.	QxP	QKt–Q2
9.	Kt–Kt5	R–B1?

9. ... B–Q3 is necessary.

10.	KtxRP	Kt–Kt3?
11.	KtxR	KtxKt
12.	P–Q4	Kt–Q3
13.	B–Kt5ch	KtxB
14.	QxKtch	Kt–Q2
15.	P–Q5	PxP
16.	B–K3	B–Q3
17.	R–Q1	

Castling was not introduced in Spain for another 100 years.

17.	...	Q–B3
18.	RxP	Q–Kt3
19.	B–B4	BxB??
20.	QxKtch	K–B1
21.	Q–Q8 mate	

This is said to be the first recorded game in the modern style. White seems to be far the stronger player but, judging by his error on move 6, even he is at the level of a very ordinary club player of today.

In the sixteenth and seventeenth centuries, Italy and Spain remained the leading chessplaying countries with Italy on the whole the better; in 1574 Leonardo da Cutri visited Madrid and beat the leading Spanish player, the priest Ruy Lopez, in a match played before Philip II. Leonardo, it is said, lost the first two games intentionally and then won the next three as an 'I am the greatest' demonstration; no wonder his rivals poisoned him when he was 44. In the late seventeenth century supremacy passed to France, helped there (and in England) by the opening of coffee houses, and France remained the leading country until well into the nineteenth century. Gradually however its position was challenged by England and in the famous series of games in 1834 between de la Bourdonnais and McDonnell, the latter, although defeated (W28, L44, D13) was far from disgraced; the best games of this match can still arouse our admiration. In 1843 the French ascendancy was finally destroyed when the English historian Howard Staunton beat the leading French player, the wine merchant Pierre Charles Fournié de Saint-Amant, in Paris by 11–6, with 4 drawn. Then eight years later, in 1851, an event took place which brought in competitive chess as we know it today.

The era of tournament chess

'Every game of chess in a way is a contest of the nerves. Tournament play . . . is a relentless intellectual struggle before a numerous public, at a prescribed hour and with a prescribed time limit . . . most chess masters suffer a sort of nervous collapse after a mistake, especially after a game has been lost.'

R.Réti, *Masters of the Chess Board*

Tournaments are to us so much the natural form of competitive chess that it is difficult to visualize how great an innovation the 1851 'Great Exhibition' tournament was. For the first time in chess history there was a meeting of the leading players from a number of countries – England, France, Germany and Hungary were all represented. Anderssen's victory inaugurated a period of central European dominance. Anderssen was German, Steinitz – the first recognized World Champion – an Austrian, Lasker – World Champion from 1894, when he beat Steinitz,

Howard Staunton, 1810–74

until 1921 – was German; the main challenge to this supremacy was from Americans – Morphy who for a dazzling year in 1858 overwhelmed all opposition, Pillsbury who also had a brilliant but tragically brief career, dying in 1906 at the age of 33, and Capablanca. The introduction of tournament chess had a number of important effects. It led, through increased exchange of ideas and more books on chess, to a general rise in standards; top class chess became more and more a professional game – the time required for tournaments and to acquire the knowledge and technique needed to succeed made it increasingly difficult for the amateur to hold his own, and success in tournaments began to give the money and international prestige to make life as a professional feasible; and, through bringing all the leading players into fairly frequent contact with each other, tournaments led naturally to the emergence of a World Champion.

The World Championship

'(The World Championship) is a gladiatorial contest compared with which Joe Frazier *v.* Muhammad Ali is just a friendly little chat.'

Myself, *Fischer v. Spassky, Reykjavik 1972*

'Emergence' is, I think, the correct word; no formal organization created the World Championship – embodied in the indomitable, eccentric figure of Wilhelm Steinitz, it emerged. He himself thought that he was World Champion from the time of his victory over Anderssen in 1866; from then on he described his matches as 'matches for the World Championship'. However, like a high proportion of chess players, Steinitz was quarrelsome – and had no problem in finding people to quarrel with; further, he was less successful in tournaments than in matches. So it was not until he defeated his chief rival Zukertort in 1886 that he was finally accepted by the whole of the chess world as champion; since then there has never been any doubt as to who was champion (except for the brief interregnum after Alekhine's death, from 1946–1948).

From 1886 to 1946, however, the World Championship was the property of the holder; he played whom he liked, when he liked. On the whole the system – or lack of it – worked better than one might have expected; in the end pressure of public opinion meant that an outstanding opponent had to be faced. However some matches that should have been played – Lasker/Rubinstein and a return Alekhine/Capablanca match for example – never took place; some, notably Lasker/Capablanca,

took place years too late; and some were played – such as the second Alekhine/Bogolyubov match – that were not worth playing.

During this period an international chess body had come into existence; the *Féderation Internationale des Échecs* – FIDE – was born in 1924. Too weak a body to wrest control of the World Championship from a dominating champion such as Capablanca or Alekhine, it began, as its first major contribution, the Chess Olympiads – the biennial World Team Championship, first held in London, 1927 with 16 teams; the 20th Olympiad was in 1962 with 63 competing countries.

Over the years FIDE gradually increased its standing and in the immediate pre-war years had succeeded in nominating a challenger; the war prevented a match from taking place and in 1946, just when a match between Alekhine and Botvinnik had been arranged, Alekhine died. This gave FIDE the chance it needed; in 1948 it sponsored a pentangular tournament for the vacant title – easily won by Botvinnik; and since then the title has been firmly under FIDE control. A detailed description of the present system is given in Section 3; meanwhile there are two more developments to be described in this historical review – the rise of the Soviet School and the revival of the West.

The Soviet School of Chess

'. . . The USSR is becoming the classical land of chess. The famous masters of Western Europe and America watch the growth of our chess culture with astonishment and envy. There is nothing like it in their countries.'

Pravda, 29th August, 1936 following Botvinnik's victory in the Nottingham 1936 Grandmaster Tournament

There has always been a tradition of chess in Russia. Tchigorin was one of the great rivals of Steinitz and twice played a match against him for the title, losing $10\frac{1}{2}$–$6\frac{1}{2}$ in 1889 and $12\frac{1}{2}$–$10\frac{1}{2}$ in 1892; at the great International Tournament at St Petersburg in 1914, the Czar awarded the title of 'Grandmaster of Chess' to the five finalists – Lasker, Capablanca, Alekhine, Tarrasch and Marshall; and from that time until his death in 1945 Alekhine was of course one of the greatest of all the Grandmasters. But imperialist Russia, although it had many good players, was not outstanding. What then is the reason for the dominance of Soviet Chess from 1945 on – a dominance that was unchallenged until the 1960s and is only now being seriously shaken?

I can best summarize the reasons by quoting what I have

already written in my book on the Fischer/Spassky match.

'Very soon after the revolution, certainly no later than 1920, the USSR decided to develop and encourage chess in every way. There were a number of reasons, internal and external. It was regarded as a gateway for leading people into an interest in general culture; at the lowest level, many who could not read or write were led to do so by their wish to be able to read chess books – at a higher level, the elements of art and science in chess helped to bring people into contact with these ways of thinking. A stranger reason to Western minds was that chess was a dialectical game illustrating, in its resolution of conflicts, the Marxist mode of thought.

Unexpressed, but I believe important, were two other reasons; chess is a very cheap game and it is as safe from 'dangerous thoughts' as any intellectual activity can be.

More compelling than any of these reasons, however, was the propaganda value – internal and external – of success in chess. Here was the only intellectual field in which a decisive objective comparison between the communist and capitalist ways of life was possible; if the USSR could surpass the West this would be strong evidence for their own people and for sympathizers abroad of the superiority of communist culture. I have no doubt at all that the USSR got very good value in this way for their investment of effort.

These are the advantages for the state; what about the players? Their motives overlapped but were not identical and the differences in outlook between state and individual are a source of intermittent, and probably increasing, friction. From the player's viewpoint, to be a chessmaster is a secure, distinguished career; when, in the course of his match in 1933 with the Czech Grandmaster Salo Flohr, Botvinnik attended the Bolshoi ballet the whole audience rose and applauded him – I have seen the same thing happen with the Yugoslav champion Gligorić. Further, chess offered opportunities for travel to the West when these were hard to come by; and liquidation for unorthodox views was a minimal risk. So, both by the state and by chess players the new programme was embarked on with enthusiasm.

... We can get an idea of the staggering increase in popularity of chess over the period as a whole by looking at the figures of registered chess players in the USSR: 1923 – 1,000, 1929 – 150,000, 1934 – 500,000, 1951 – 1,000,000, 1963 – 3,000,000.'

In view of this there is nothing in the least surprising in the Soviet supremacy in postwar chess. On the contrary, what is really surprising is not the success of Soviet chess but its comparative failure in the last decade. Why is it that only one world-class player – Karpov – has appeared since 1957 (the year in which Tal became a Grandmaster)? Look at the 1972 Skopje team – completely representative if one were to replace Savon by the ex-World Champion Spassky. Board 1, Petrosian – age 43; 2, Korchnoi – 41; 3, Smyslov – 51; 4, Tal – 35; 5, Karpov – 21; 6, Savon 43. The top four boards all played in the 1960 team and Smyslov played in the 1952 side. Of course many strong Soviet masters appeared in the 1960s but the standard has clearly declined since the great period of 1945–59. Why?

Keres put one reason to me succinctly a few years ago: 'There is more to do nowadays'. In the oppressive days of Stalin the attractions of chess as a career were very great; in the less restricted atmosphere of the present, its advantages – the opportunities for travel, the elements of safety and escape – are much fewer. Next, the original missionary zeal has departed. When after his victory at Nottingham in 1936 Botvinnik cabled[*] Stalin: 'Dearly beloved teacher and leader . . . I am infinitely happy to be able to report that a representative of Soviet chess has shared first place in the tournament with ex-champion of the world Capablanca. . . . Inspired by your great slogan "catch up and surpass" I am glad that I have been able to realize it', I don't think it was just sycophancy; to a considerable extent he meant it. There was an ambivalence in the Soviet attitude to the West – on the one hand, a keen curiosity tinged with envy as to what the wicked capitalists were up to in their native haunts; on the other, an equally keen desire to demonstrate that, however uncomfortable it might be at the moment, communism was best. Both these strands favoured chess; the first increased the attraction of the professional game to potential masters, the second strengthened their will to win. Now all this has gone; the Soviet professional is a chess professional first, a communist very much second.

A factor of a different kind is that of age. In the thirties and in the immediate postwar years the Soviet school was young and so were its players; in 1945, for example, Botvinnik – its unquestioned leader and senior citizen – had reached the advanced age of 34. In the main it was a group of players in their twenties who were making the running. This produced vigorous, original, self-confident play; the contrast often drawn by communist

---

[*] This cable is said to have been concocted in Moscow – but Botvinnik knew and agreed the contents.

propagandists between positive creative socialist play and the negative decadent bourgeois attitude, in so far as it was valid at all, was largely the difference between young and middle-aged players. As this young group of players got older their attitude gradually changed, until we see Petrosian saying 'Obviously many people forget that nowadays in chess the struggle for points prevails over creative considerations'. Yes – and nowadays Petrosian is 43 not 23. In the last decade the young players have been following not leading.

Age has had an even more marked effect on the Soviet chess establishment and organization. It is difficult to judge this from outside but my impression is that increasingly the value of the State support for chess is masked and weakened by the clumsiness and vested interests of a vast bureaucratic machine. Anyone who has ever had the experience of getting the Soviet Chess Federation to nominate two players for a tournament abroad – the nightmare feeling of an endless struggle with an infinite mass of jelly – will know exactly what I mean. As Larsen said when I interviewed him (see Section 3), the Soviet players often have considerable practical difficulty (there is no problem in theory) in getting hold of foreign tournament bulletins and complain of finding Western players better prepared than they are – an amazing change from the forties and fifties. There seems, too, to be more friction between players and establishment. When Spassky had to meet the challenge of Fischer did he feel that he had the support of the Soviet chess organization? I suspect that he was more oppressed by their probable reaction to failure than buoyed up by their support.

Summing up, much of the early motivation, enthusiasm and drive has gone; in its place one has a large but creaky machine in urgent need of oiling. Still, it is very large and should not be underrated; with the loss of the world title to Fischer and the timely appearance of a potential challenger in Anatoly Karpov we may see a new vigour in Soviet chess in the seventies.

The Revival of the West

'I am the best player in the world'

R.J.Fischer (numerous occasions)

During the period of Soviet dominance, the Western players accepted a subordinate role. It was assumed that whenever a Soviet master played in a tournament he would win it – unless there was another Soviet player there to match him; it was a familiar sight to see two Soviet players jog side by side past the winning post followed at a respectful distance by a sweating mass of lesser breeds. Apart from the decline within the USSR, already discussed, two Western players were responsible for breaking through this mastery – first Larsen, then Fischer. Larsen caused a major sensation when at the age of 21 he made the best score of any top board player (including Botvinnik) in the Moscow 1956 Olympiad; for some years in the 1960s he was the most successful of all tournament players except Fischer. When Fischer or Larsen plays in a tournament, then he – not the Soviet representative – is favourite to win. More recently the young German Grandmaster, Robert Hübner, repeated Larsen's feat by making the best top board score at the Skopje 1972 Olympiad.

The climax of the Western revival was of course Fischer's $12\frac{1}{2}$–$8\frac{1}{2}$ victory over Spassky at Reykjavik in July/August 1972. I do not intend to retell this story again but will end this chapter with a brief look at its implications. The unprecedented excitement aroused by the match has led to a great world-wide increase in chess; some of this is purely temporary but a good deal will remain. When one combines this special cause with the more general one of increased leisure and increased need for creative activities like chess, there will certainly be an expansion and maybe an explosive one in chess in the Western world. We may be in a period when chess history is not just being written, but made.

Chapter 5: The dialectic of chess: the development of style

'What we are disposed at first to take as immediate and self-complete presently, by reason of the fact that it is not such a complete whole but only a portion of reality, shows it incompleteness by passing into its opposite: and then follows the process of reconciliation through which both sides get their rights. Every partial truth is thus preserved and enters into the final synthesis of reason.'

Professor A.K.Rogers on Hegel in
A Student's History of Philosophy

'First Boy! "Nohow." Next Boy. "Contrariwise."'

Tweedledum and Tweedledee in
Alice through the Looking Glass

If Marx is the Messiah of communist hagiography and Lenin its first Pope, then Hegel is its John the Baptist; he is the forerunner of Marx, whose doctrine of economic determinism was developed from Hegel's philosophy. That in turn rested on Hegel's idea of *development*. In this one has the sequence thesis–antithesis–synthesis; first there is an idea (thesis) which, while appearing to be the whole truth is in fact only part of it – the incompleteness of the idea leads to the generation of its opposite (antithesis) and then there is a reconciliation (synthesis) of the conflict at a higher level, which will last until this synthesis itself is seen to be incomplete and the process starts again. In this way intellectual and economic progress take place. The communists thought that chess was a Hegelian game and thus ideologically respectable; that in it, one could see in miniature the universal process of thesis–antithesis–synthesis taking place. With reservations, I think that this is right; and it is worth looking at it not just in the context of the struggle in an individual game, but rather in the development of chess style over the years.

One must, however, preserve a sense of proportion. In any analysis of this kind, it is only too easy to over-simplify and by picking the most extreme cases to make trends seem much more clearcut than they are. At any time in chess there are players of many different temperaments and styles playing – and the same player plays in different styles at different times; when one talks of a change of style, the change is neither sudden nor uniform – in certain games new ideas begin to appear and over a period there is a change in the balance of games of different types. Also, it is wrong to think altogether in terms of 'better' or 'worse'; perhaps a more important effect of new ideas is that they make

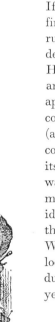

the game richer – it contains more possibilities than one had thought. It also becomes more difficult – so there is more scope for the stronger player to show his superiority.

We can (oversimplifying) isolate four types of player.* First, the tacticians – e.g. Greco, Anderssen, Marshall, Keres, Tal; players for whom the heart of the game is in its combinative possibilities. Second, the strategists – e.g. Philidor, Steinitz, Réti, Nimzovich, Bronstein, perhaps Larsen and Petrosian; for them the interest lies in the positional ideas, the underlying logic of the game. Third, the technicians – e.g. Staunton (I think), Tarrasch, Maroczy, Flohr, Fine; they master current ideas and learn how to apply them safely and effectively – they learn all that can be learnt. Fourth, the greatest world class players – Morphy, Lasker, Capablanca, Alekhine, Botvinnik, Fischer; they overlap all the other groups, combining technical mastery with great tactical power and strategic insight. Now no great player – especially amongst the moderns – belongs wholly to one group. Of course a great tactician like Tal has also a deep understanding of positional ideas and a first class technique, and a strategist must be a good combinative player to reap the fruits of his strategy: and you can't be a successful technician unless you have the strategic and tactical ability to produce an advantage on which to employ your technical skill. This division is not so much based on what a player can do as on what he wants to do – it is temperamental rather than technical: and many players do not fall clearly into one group or another.

Nevertheless, there are these types of players – and even more clearly there are the corresponding types of play. When we try to do our Hegelian analysis, the two main conflicting elements – the thesis and the antithesis – are represented by the tactics and the strategy, the special situation and the general principle, the detailed analysis and the positional judgment.

In the primitive game – watch any beginners – tactics dominate. Take for example Greco's seventeenth-century *Traité du Jeu des Échecs*, the outstanding chess book of the day, and look at what Greco has to say on the *Giuoco Piano*. Comments in inverted commas are his own. *1. P–K4, P–K4; 2. Kt–KB3, Kt–QB3; 3. B–B4, B–B4; 4. 0–0* (he later considers 4. P–Q4 and 4. P–B3), *Kt–B3; 5. R–K1, 0–0; 6. P–QB3, Q–K2?* ('P–Q3 would be better'); *7. P–Q4* (' it would be better to play P–Q3'),

Paul Morphy, 1837–84

---

*I am painfully aware how crude these labels are – especially 'tacticians' and 'strategists'. I hope that the kind of distinctions I am trying to make will become clear in the subsequent discussion and that even if (as I do!) readers dislike the labels they will be interested in the ideas.

P x P; 8. P–K5 ('this move is less good than the capture of the QP'), *Kt–KKt5; 9. P x P, Kt x QP* (see diagram); *10. Kt x Kt, Q–R5; 11. Kt–KB3, Q x BPch; 12. K–R1, Q–Kt8ch; 13. R x Q, Kt–B7 mate.* And his second variation is *6. . . . R–K1?* (Greco's '?'); *7. P–Q4, P x P?; 8. P–K5, Kt–KKt5; 9. B–KKt5, Kt x BP; 10. B x Q, Kt x Q; 11. R x Kt, P x P dis ch; 12. K–B1, P x P; 13. QKt–Q2, P x R = Q; 14. R x Q, Kt x B* and Black wins. Now these are not opening variations in the modern sense – they are purely tactical traps. If in the first variation (where Greco wrongly criticizes 7. P–Q4) White had played 8. P x P he would have had a greatly superior game – but the other line is given because (who knows?) White might play P–K5 and then you might be able to give up the Queen and mate. Further, no clear distinction is made between an opening and a game he (Greco) has won. Here, in Greco, we have our first statement of the tactical 'thesis'.

André Danican Philidor (1726–95) states the first antithesis, in his *Analyse du Jeu des Échecs.* 'My chief aim is to earn praise (*me rendre recommendable*) through a novelty which no one has observed or perhaps been able to put into effect; it is to play the pawns properly. They are the soul of chess; it is they alone who create the attack and the defence and victory or defeat depends solely on their good or bad arrangement.' This was a generalization, a positional idea of the greatest importance. If we look at a variation, given in his book, of Philidor's Defence we can see the strength and weakness of his approach. *1. P–K4, P–K4; 2. Kt–KB3* (Philidor thought this inferior because it blocked the KBP), *P–Q3; 3. B–B4, P–KB4; 4. P–Q3, P–B3; 5. P x P.* Here Philidor comments that if White does not take, you leave your pawn on B4 and do not advance to B5 unless he plays 0–0 – because if you advance at once, he may castle Queen's side. Right or wrong, this is a piece of general advice different in kind from Greco's purely tactical comments. *5. . . . B x P; 6. B–KKt5, Kt–B3; 7. QKt–Q2* ('If he plays B x Kt, you must retake with the pawn, to increase your central pawn strength'), *7. . . . P–Q4; 8. B–Kt3, B–Q3; 9. Q–K2, Q–K2; 10. 0–0, QKt–Q2; 11. Kt–R4* ('To follow with P–KB4, trying to break the line of your pawns'), *11. . . . Q–K3; 12. Kt x B, Q x Kt; 13. B x Kt, P x B* (see diagram); *14. P–KB4, Q–Kt3; 15. P x P, P x P; 16. R–B3, P–KR4; 17. QR–KB1, 0–0–0; 18. P–B4, P–K5!* (Here Philidor gives a long note to show why this pawn sacrifice – opening lines for Black and giving him a passed QP – is good), *19. P x KP, P–Q5!; 20. B–B2, Kt–K4; 21. R–B6, Q–Kt2; 22. Q–B2, Kt–Kt5; 23. Q–B5ch, K–Kt1; 24. R x B* (fearing B x Pch), *R x R; 25. Q–B4, Q–K4; 26. Q x Q, Kt x Q; 27. R–B5, Kt–Kt5; 28.*

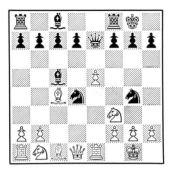

Greco on the Giuoco Piano: a tactical trap

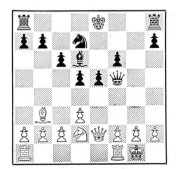

Philidor's Defence: Black conquers the centre

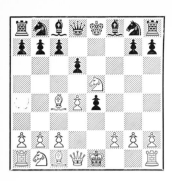

Philidor's Defence:
a tactical rebuttal

P–B5, R–Kt3; 29. *Kt–B4, Kt–K6*; 30. *KtxKt, PxKt*; 31. *R–B3, R–Q1*; 32. *RxP, R–Q7* and wins. This is analysis of a different order from Greco's; Philidor has a positional idea – to create a strong pawn centre. And he shows how to carry it through. However the idea had comparatively little immediate impact for two reasons: (*a*) it was too far in advance of his time to be readily assimilated, (*b*) his detailed analysis was not sufficiently accurate, so that the tacticians were later able to demolish substantial parts of it and thus cast doubt on the principles. We can see this if we look again at the position after 1. *P–K4, P–K4*; 2. *Kt–KB3, P–Q3*; 3. *B–B4, P–KB4*. Here Philidor makes White play peacefully 4. *P–Q3* and allow Black to set up his centre undisturbed; but White is ahead in development and Black has weakened his King's defensive position by *P–KB4* so White can instead attack vigorously as follows: *4. P–Q4!, PxKP* (other moves are no better); *5. KtxP!* (see diagram) *P–Q4* (5. . . . *PxKt*; 6. *Q–R5ch*); *6. Q–R5ch, P–Kt3*; 7. *KtxP, Kt–KB3*; *8. Q–K5ch, B–K2*; 9. *B–Kt5ch, P–B3*; 10. *KtxB, QxKt*; *11. QxQch, KxQ*; *12. B–K2* and White is a pawn ahead and should win. This tactical refutation of a positional plan illustrates the weaknesses in Philidor's implementation of a fundamentally sound idea.

Despite Philidor's ideas, the pendulum swung back to the tacticians and the combinative school reached its peak under the leadership of Adolf Anderssen (1818–1879) – influenced to some extent by Philidor, play was less purely tactical than in Greco's day, nevertheless combinative play was dominant. The first real synthesis now took place – by Paul Morphy for the open game. Morphy realized that the purely combinative school attached too much importance to immediate threats, too little to development. Réti quotes as an example the position in the Evans Gambit after *1. P–K4, P–K4; 2. Kt–KB3, Kt–QB3; 3. B–B4, B–B4; 4. P–QKt4, BxP; 5. P–B3, B–R4; 6. P–Q4, PxP; 7. 0–0, P–Q3; 8. PxP, B–Kt3* (see diagram). Here the fashionable moves were the directly attacking *P–Q5* or *Q–Kt3*; Morphy saw that in the end the developing move 9. *Kt–B3* was stronger. Most of Morphy's opposition was relatively weak and he could win with brilliance just as Anderssen did; but when he played Anderssen himself, he won by superior positional play – the fourth game of this match (see games), which is also taken from Réti's *Modern Ideas in Chess*, illustrates this very clearly.

Now a major step forward was taken with the positional game by perhaps the greatest of all chess thinkers, Wilhelm Steinitz. Realizing the fundamental correctness of Philidor's ideas about

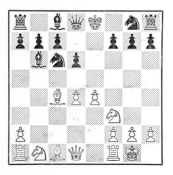

Evans Gambit:
development is best

pawn structure, he had a deeper and more far reaching understanding of how to apply these to the area in which they were most important – the close game. Philidor does not seem clearly to have distinguished between open positions – where rapid development is all important – and closed positions (those, basically, which lack open lines for the pieces), where permanent features such as pawn structures dominate. His error in the Philidor Defence variation that we examined lay in adopting a closed game technique (i.e. striving for a superior pawn structure at the expense of development) in a position in which White could open up the game. Steinitz laid down a comprehensive set of principles which should guide one; for a brilliant account of these, read the chapter on Steinitz in Euwe's *Development of Chess Style* on which the summary here is based. Steinitz distinguished between transient advantages (e.g. a lead in development) which had to be quickly exploited, and permanent advantages (largely arising from superior pawn structure, such as more room to manoeuvre or basic weaknesses – like isolated pawns – in the opponent's position); he preached the accumulation of small advantages until the moment was right to strike. Whereas the older school of purely tactical players thought that – especially with White – one should go for an attack at once, Steinitz realized that there was a critical moment when it was right to launch it; attack too soon and you were repulsed, leave it too long and your chance was lost. He also had a deeper understanding of the importance of the pawn centre; for the older players the object of central control was purely for immediate attack – Steinitz saw that it could also be used to cramp the opposition. The game Steinitz *v.* Blackburne (see page 58) shows a typical Steinitz victory.

Woodcut of Wilhelm Steinitz, in 1886

Like many of the great strategic innovators, Steinitz had the fault of his virtues; like Philidor and Nimzovich he was too much in love with his own theories. So now, just as Morphy had produced a synthesis of tactical and strategic ideas for the open game, the Steinitz school, led by the great systematizer Dr Siegbert Tarrasch (1862–1934) produced a synthesis for closed positions. They refined Steinitz's methods, got rid of his extravagances and saw that tactical considerations were given their proper place. Naturally there was great variety amongst the players of the day. At one extreme the brilliant American master, F.J.Marshall, a throwback to Anderssen who could never reach the very top because he was too weak positionally; then there was the World Champion, Emanuel Lasker, who fully understood Steinitz's theories but, basically a superb practical player and psychologist, was always looking for ways of getting into uncharted waters where a player was thrown on his own resources; and at the other end of the scale there was the man of method, Tarrasch, who believed that the correct application of Steinitz's principles would solve all problems – and could never quite understand why he lost to Lasker. By and large, however – to quote Euwe again – this period, from about 1900 to the first world war was the age of the virtuosi, the perfecters of Steinitz; as an example of their play I give the game Tarrasch *v*. Lasker in which we see Tarrasch defeated by the better practical player.

During the period 1900–1920, chess gradually stagnated; there were many fine games played but no new ideas produced and it began to seem that there was nothing more to discover. The victory of Capablanca in the 1921 World Championship match, though thoroughly deserved, was not good for chess; a conservative opening player (he was too lazy and too self-confident to bother to study the openings) and fundamentally uninterested in chess theory (he was altogether much less interested in chess than most great masters) Capablanca won by a combination of a very fine natural feeling for positions and tremendous tactical skill. He made the game look easy and himself invincible; indeed he said that he thought that the game was played out.

Happily he was wrong; the Steinitz synthesis now came under fire in two different ways. It was positionally attacked in the 1920s and early 1930s by the 'hypermoderns'; and it came under a mixed tactical and positional fire from the rising Soviet school from the middle thirties onwards, the full force of the Soviet school not being felt until after the 1939–45 war.

The 'hypermoderns', for whom Réti was the leading propagandist and one of the leading players, attacked one of Steinitz's central doctrines – that one must establish, slowly perhaps, as massive a centre as possible. Players as a matter of course therefore occupied as much of the centre as possible, as soon as they could safely do so. The hyper-moderns saw that this was not essential; that if you controlled the centre, i.e. prevented the opponent from establishing himself firmly in it, you could delay occupying it. This gave increased popularity, and new meaning, to fianchetto defences (P–Kt3 and B–Kt2) and moves like 1. P–QB4 or 1. Kt–KB3 which put pressure on the key central squares without occupying them. At the same time they saw that if White could be persuaded to over-extend himself in the centre, Black might be able to get the upper hand by counter-attack. It is this idea that underlies Alekhine's

Alexander Alekhine, World Chess Champion, 1927–35, 37–45

Defence *1. P–K4, Kt–KB3.* After *2. P–K5, Kt–Q4; 3. P–QB4, Kt–Kt3; 4. P–Q4, P–Q3; 5. P–B4* (see diagram) by all the classic canons Black should be hopelessly lost; his Knight is displaced on QKt3 and White has completely occupied the centre. However, White's problem is that he may have occupied it too completely; his advanced pawns are potentially targets for attack and it is still an open question who in fact has the better of this position. The hypermoderns also realized that whereas Steinitz's rules were applicable in most situations, there were exceptional situations where they were not. A famous example of this is in the opening of the game Alekhine/ Rubinstein (The Hague, 1921) where the opening went *1. P–Q4, P–Q4; 2. Kt–KB3, P–K3; 3. P–B4, P–QR3.* A loss of time and the source of his subsequent troubles. *4. P–B5, Kt–QB3.* The struggle now centres round Black's efforts to force P–K4 which would equalize. *5. B–B4, KKt–K2; 6. Kt–B3, Kt–Kt3; 7. B–K3* (see diagram). A move that the older players would never have considered – but if White plays 7. B–Kt3, then 7. . . . P–K4!; 8. PxP, P–Q5! and Black gets a good game. *7. . . . P–Kt3.* Realizing that he cannot force P–K4 he hopes to free his game by getting rid of the cramping pawn on B5 and exploiting the awkward position of the B on K3. *8. PxP, PxP; 9. P–KR4!* A remarkably imaginative idea; he will force a weakness in Black's pawn structure which will allow him to post his QB effectively. *9. . . . B–Q3.* Here Alekhine comments (*My Best Games of Chess 1908–23*) 'if 9. . . . P–KR4; 10. B–KKt5, P–B3; 11. Q–B2 followed by B–Q2, P–K3, P–QR3, and B–Q3 with the better game for White'. *10. P–R5, KKt–K2; 11. P–R6!, P–Kt3; 12. B–Kt5, 0–0; 13. B–B6!* (see diagram) and White has a clear advantage – more space, a grip on the dark squares and attacking prospects – which ultimately led to his winning the game.

One must not exaggerate the effect of the hypermoderns; Alekhine's own comment on this opening are a useful corrective. 'Black has given himself over to several eccentricities in the opening (3. . . . P–QR3; 5. . . . KKt–K2; 6. . . . Kt–Kt3) which without the reaction of his opponent (for example 7. P–K3 instead of 7. B–K3, or 9. P–KKt3 instead of 9. P–KR4) would in the end have given him a good game. It is therefore, as a necessity, and not with a preconceived idea, that I decided upon the advance of the KRP, preventing Black from securing an advantage in the centre. But, as a rule, in the opening stages of a game such eccentricities are in accordance neither with my temperament nor my style'. As with Steinitz, so now the new

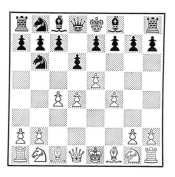

Alekhine's Defence: the problem of the extended centre

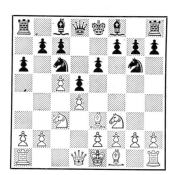

Alekhine v. Rubinstein: the start of a 'hypermodern' manoeuvre

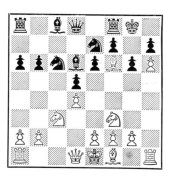

Alekhine v. Rubinstein: a positional plus for White

theorists – Réti and still more Nimzovich – were too interested in their ideas for the good of their play; Alekhine absorbed the new ideas and used them when and only when they were appropriate. I give two games from this period; Johner-Nimzovich (Dresden, 1926), illustrating Nimzovich's idea of 'The Blockade' (Larsen mentions this as the game which most influenced his own development as a player) and Réti-Alekhine (Baden-Baden, 1925), rated by Alekhine one of the two best games he ever played, his win against Bogolyubov (Hastings, 1922) being the other.

Finally, the modern Soviet school. While the hypermoderns attacked some of Steinitz's ideas positionally – making general statements such as 'no, it is not necessary to occupy the centre' the young Soviet players of the late 30s and the period 1945–60 distrusted all generalizations. They adopted the tactical battle cry 'analyse!'; don't generalize, work out exact variations, find the exceptions in which some peculiar feature of the position means that an unlikely move is right. We can see this fore-shadowed in the Alekhine/Rubinstein opening given above, but the process was carried much further by the Soviet players and later on by Fischer, Larsen and other Western players. Of course in doing this the Russians were not rejecting positional con-siderations; they were rejecting the attitude which led to too superficial a consideration and the use of positional clichés to reach premature conclusions. The positional idea which under-lay their new attack was that the Steinitz theories – even as modified by his followers – gave too much weight to static and too little to dynamic considerations; one could have a position with long-term weaknesses but with such tactical potential that the game will be won before the weakness has time to matter. I give the game Denker/Botvinnik (USA *v.* USSR radio match, 1945) to illustrate this. A remarkable example of this in the opening is shown in the third game of the Fischer/Spassky match; with

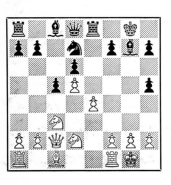

Spassky v. Fischer (3rd game); open lines make up for shattered pawns

Spassky as White the opening went *1. P–Q4, Kt–KB3; 2. P–QB4, P–K3; 3. Kt–KB3, P–B4.* The 'Modern Benoni', a double-edged defence typical of modern play; Black concedes a central pawn majority in return for Queen's side chances. *4. P–Q5, PxP; 5. PxP, P–Q3; 6. Kt–B3, P–KKt3; 7. Kt–Q2, QKt–Q2; 8. P–K4, B–Kt2; 9. B–K2.* 9. Kt–B4, Kt–Kt3; 10. Kt–K3 may be better. *9. . . . 0–0; 10. 0–0, R–K1; 11. Q–B2.* 11. P–KB4 is better. *11. . . . Kt–R4!* This is a move which no-one but a modern player (and very few of them!) would have dared to play. After *12. BxKt, PxB* (see diagram) – which was played – Black's pawn position is shattered and Tarrasch would certainly have given Kt–R4 a '?'; but Fischer correctly judged that his two Bishops and open lines would fully compensate for his pawn weaknesses and he justified this view by winning a fine game. I am not saying that Kt–R4 won or even that Black had the advantage after it; merely that it is a move which would have been rejected immediately by players of an earlier school but nevertheless one that gives Black great practical chances.

This leads to another feature of the Soviet school; making life difficult for the opponent. Technique nowadays is so good that if one plays simple openings there is a high chance of a draw. First the Soviet masters, and in the last 10–15 years the Western players also, have sought new lines which are not necessarily better than the old ones but which are difficult – for both sides – to play well, thus giving the stronger player more chance to show his superiority. One way of doing this is by the Flank Openings – where, for example, White plays 1. Kt–KB3, 2. P–KKt3 and 3. B–Kt2; or by Larsen's opening 1. P–QKt3, 2. B–Kt2, 3. P–QB4. In these openings White makes no direct threat and both players have so much choice that it is very easy to go wrong; at his best Petrosian was the great exponent of this style and I give his win against Korchnoi (Moscow, 1971) as an example.

In the present World Champion, Robert James Fischer (born 1943) we see a synthesis at the highest level of all the develop-ments so far described. The sixth game with Spassky (see page 25) shows his ability to exploit small advantages in classic style and his attacking power; the thirteenth game shows his Lasker-like fighting spirit; the opening of the third game (see above) shows his mastery of modern ideas; the sixth game of his match with Petrosian, which broke his opponent's spirit, showed his ability to beat Petrosian at his own game – and the seventh game of the same match was typical of Capablanca's perfect technique at its best.

How far, then, can we say that the Hegelian hypothesis holds water? Fairly well, I think: we see the two elements of tactics (the thesis) and strategy (the antithesis), opposing and inter-locking with each other and constantly synthesized by the greatest players, the whole process gradually spiralling upwards to produce a deeper and more varied game. We have Greco – fairly primitive tactics; Philidor – a deeper, but limited, positional idea; Anderssen – brilliant combinative play, defeated by the synthesis of tactics and strategy in Morphy. Next Steinitz – position play in close positions; and a further synthesis by his followers with Lasker and Capablanca in their different styles as the peaks. Then the positional inroads by the hyper-moderns and the tactical/positional developments of the Soviet school with Petrosian's 'elastic' play as a further devel-opment; and finally Fischer.

In this examination I have only considered the Hegelian idea in the context of the development of chess as a whole. We can also see it both in the move-by-move struggle in the individual game and in the development of the theory of an opening. If one looks at any heavily analysed opening such as the Sicilian, one sees the same process going on all the time. A line is produced in which White gets the advantage and the opening pundits (especially those who are not quite in the front rank as players) all say that the line must be abandoned by Black. Then the new line is subjected to deeper analysis by the top-level players and hidden weaknesses appear; so after all Black has a good game? Then there is another study of the new play for Black and so on; within the opening the process of thesis-antithesis-synthesis is constantly going on. Perhaps in a way all this is self-evident; it may be that it is a fundamental property of all non-trivial games, mental or physical, that they are Hegelian – certainly one can see similar processes taking place in football or cricket. The individual game in chess (as Soviet writers have pointed out) is clearly Hegelian.

Returning to chess, what further developments can we expect? If I knew, I would be a much better player than I am; it is in the nature of new developments that you can't imagine them until they arrive and when they do, they seem obvious. Maybe there will be a revival on a new level of Petrosian's methods; both Fischer and Spassky are basically classical players – Fischer strikes me as a mixture of the best of Capablanca and Alekhine – perhaps the next champion will be an improved version of Petrosian.

One thing is sure; we have not reached the end.

Capablanca in play at Margate, 1935

Chapter 6: Games illustrating the development of style

The development of the Lopez

The following three games, all Ruy Lopez openings, should be compared with each other; they show a steady deepening of positional understanding and an increase in complexity.

WHITE A. ANDERSSEN   BLACK P. MORPHY
Ruy Lopez (fourth game of match, 1858)

1.	P–K4	P–K4
2.	Kt–KB3	Kt–QB3
3.	B–Kt5	P–QR3
4.	B–R4	Kt–B3
5.	P–Q3	B–B4

Morphy, like Anderssen, was an open game player and therefore he brings out the Bishop onto the most aggressive square. However, this should react against him – it is too ambitious a move. White cannot of course win a pawn at once by 6. B x Kt, QP x B; 7. Kt x P? because of 7. . . . Q–Q5!

6.	P–B3	P–QKt4
7.	B–B2?	

An antipositional move. Unless Black can play P–Q4 himself, White will gain central control by P–Q4; therefore 7. B–Kt3! is correct, e.g. 7.B–Kt3, P–Q4; 8. P x P, Kt x P; 9. 0–0, B–KKt5; 10. R–K1, 0–0; 11. P–KR3, B x Kt (otherwise the KP is lost); 12. Q x B, Kt(4)–K2; 13. Kt–Q2 followed by Kt–K4 with strong pressure. White however has the tactical idea of an attack on KR7 and ignores the positional needs.

7.	...	P–Q4
8.	P x P	

Here 8. Q–K2 is better, maintaining the centre, but he wants to be able to open the Bishop's diagonal.

8.	...	Kt x P
9.	P–KR3	0–0
10.	0–0	P–KR3

Not wanting to be bothered by Kt–Kt5 after he plays B–K3.

| 11. | P–Q4 | P x P |

12.	PxP	B–Kt3

White has now some attacking chances but Black is well developed and centralized and should be able to defend himself, after which White's weak QP will be a serious liability.

13.	Kt–B3	Kt(4)–Kt5!

Forcing White to give up his attacking chances or shut in his QR.

14.	B–Kt1	B–K3!

Not 14. . . . KtxP?; 15. KtxKt, BxKt; 16. Q–B3, B–K3; 17. B–K4, R–Kt1; 18. P–R3! and wins. Black goes steadily on with his development – the pawn will always be weak.

15.	P–R3	Kt–Q4
16.	B–K3	Kt–B3
17.	Q–Q2	R–K1
18.	R–Q1	

Réti has criticized this move without however suggesting anything better; if for example 18. R–K1 then 18. . . . Kt–QR4 is unpleasant. The text at least threatens P–Q5 and is the best chance.

18.	...	B–Q4?

But here 18. . . . B–Kt6; 19. R–K1, Kt–QR4 followed by Kt–B5 is better, taking full advantage of the light square weaknesses.

19.	Kt–K5!	Q–Q3

And not 19. . . . KtxKt; 20. PxKt, RxP; 21. BxB, PxB; 22. B–R2 and wins a piece.

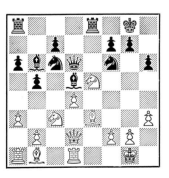

20.	Q–B2?	

A fascinating position. 20. KtxB, KtxKt (20. . . . QxKt?; 21. B–R2); 21. Q–B2, KtxB; 22. Q–R7ch, K–B1; 23. KtxKt!, QxKt; 24. PxKt, RxP; 25. Q–R8ch, K–K2; 26. QxKtP, Q–B3; 27. QxQch, KxQ would still save the day for White. Or here 21. . . . KtxKt; 22. Q–R7ch, K–B1; 23. PxKt, QxP; 24. BxB, KtxB; 25. B–B5, P–Kt3 (what else?); 26. QxRPch, Q–Kt2 with a probable draw. Finally 21. . . . KtxQP?; 22. BxKt, BxB; 23. Kt–B6! threatening both to take the Bishop and also 24. Q–R7ch, K–B1; 25. Q–R8 mate.

20.	...	KtxP!
21.	BxKt	BxB
22.	KtxB	QxKt(K4)!

And not 22. . . . QxKt(Q4)?; 23. Kt–B6, R–K5; 24. RxB, RxR; 25. Kt–K7ch.

23.	KtxKtch	QxKt
24.	Q–R7ch	K–B1
25.	B–K4	QR–Q1
26.	K–R1	BxKtP
27.	QR–Kt1	RxRch
28.	RxR	QxP
29.	Q–R8ch	

29. R–Q7?, Q–K8ch; 30. K–R2, B–K4ch and wins.

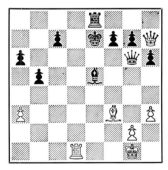

29.	...	K–K2
30.	Q–R7	B–K4
31.	B–B3	Q–Kt6
32.	K–Kt1	Q–Kt3

And with the Queens off the three extra pawns win easily.

Whilst this is by no means as clearcut an example as Réti makes out in *Modern Ideas in Chess* it is broadly true that Morphy wins through having a better idea of the positional requirements of the opening; the picture is muddied by some tactical inaccuracies by both players.

WHITE W.STEINITZ   BLACK J.H.BLACKBURNE
Ruy Lopez

1.	P–K4	P–K4
2.	Kt–KB3	Kt–QB3
3.	B–Kt5	P–QR3
4.	B–R4	Kt–B3
5.	P–Q3	

Nowadays 5. P–B3 and 6. P–Q4 is more usual, but Steinitz liked this very slow build-up. Its success depends on passive play by Black.

5.	...	P–Q3
6.	P–B3	B–K2

Another good method is 6. . . . P–KKt3, e.g. 7. P–Q4, P–QKt4; 8. B–Kt3, Q–K2; 9. 0–0, B–Kt2 and Black has a solid position.

7.	P–KR3

Preparing a King's side advance; the proper way to meet this is by a counterattack in the centre and Black loses largely because he never attempts this.

7.	...	0–0
8.	Q–K2	Kt–K1

A good alternative would be 8. . . . P–QKt4; 9. B–B2, P–Q4.

9.	P–KKt4	P–QKt4
10.	B–B2	B–Kt2
11.	QKt–Q2	Q–Q2

Now 11. . . . P–Q4; 12. PxP, QxP; 13. B–Kt3, Q–Q2 or 13. Kt–K4, Kt–B3 would still give Black good play.

12.	Kt–B1	Kt–Q1
13.	Kt–K3	Kt–K3
14.	Kt–B5	P–Kt3
15.	KtxBch	QxKt

Black – a fine combinative, but poor positional, player – has been outplayed. He is now weak on the dark squares and is cramped as well.

16.	B–K3	Kt(1)–Kt2
17.	0–0–0	P–QB4

Black's trouble is that now his only way of gaining space is by P–KB4, but this would open him to a direct attack on the King which would probably be fatal, e.g. 17. . . . P–KB4; 18. KtPxP, PxP; 19. B–R6.

18.	P–Q4	KPxP?

Not Blackburne's day; he should play 18. . . . BPxP; 19. PxP, QR–B1; 20. K–Kt1, PxP; 21. KtxP, KtxKt; 22. BxKt, Kt–K3 with some counterchances.

19.	PxP	P–B5?

Another positional misjudgment; there is no time for an advance by the Queen's side pawns before he succumbs to a combined central and King's side attack.

20.	P–Q5	Kt–B2

After 20. . . . Kt–B4; 21. BxKt, PxB White's centre pawns should win – but it would be a better chance than the text.

21.	Q–Q2!	P–QR4
22.	B–Q4	P–B3
23.	Q–R6	P–Kt5
24.	P–Kt5!	P–B4

Or 24. . . . PxP; 25. KtxP, Kt–R4; 26. P–K5!, PxP; 27. BxKP and the threat of BxKtP is decisive.

25.	B–B6

The positional grip is complete.

25.	...	Q–B2
26.	PxP	PxP
27.	P–Kt6!	QxP

Or 27. . . . PxP; 28. Kt–Kt5 followed by mate on R7 or R8.

Or 28. . . . QxB; 29. KR–Kt1.

| 28. | BxKt | QxQch |

He should resign.

29.	BxQ	R–B3
30.	KR–Kt1ch	R–Kt3
31.	BxP	

and wins easily.

Blackburne, who lost matches to Steinitz 7–1 and 7–0, plays like a beaten man throughout. The game, though much more sophisticated, has a strong family resemblance to the Philidor 'game' given in the text; unimpeded by Black, Steinitz obliterates his opponent with slightly elephantine skill. No modern master would have allowed White such free rein.

WHITE E. LASKER   BLACK S. TARRASCH
Ruy Lopez (5th match game, 1908)

This is a much more complex struggle than the Steinitz/Blackburne game; while the fundamental principles are Steinitz's they are seen here in the framework of a keen tactical struggle. This is an altogether more modern game than the Steinitz victory.

1.	P–K4	P–K4
2.	Kt–KB3	Kt–QB3
3.	B–Kt5	P–QR3
4.	B–R4	Kt–B3
5.	0–0	B–K2
6.	R–K1	P–QKt4
7.	B–Kt3	P–Q3
8.	P–B3	

Aiming at a quicker occupation of Q4 than that of Steinitz.

8.	...	Kt–QR4
9.	B–B2	P–B4
10.	P–Q4	Q–B2
11.	QKt–Q2	Kt–B3
12.	P–KR3	

If 12. Kt–B1 at once, then 12. . . . BPxP; 13. PxP, B–Kt5 gives Black pressure against the White centre.

| 12. | ... | 0–0 |
| 13. | Kt–B1?! | |

This pawn sacrifice is typical Lasker; it produces an unclear position in which he has excellent practical chances. In such a game he was better than Tarrasch, who preferred more stable positions.

13.	...	BPxP
14.	PxP	QKtxP
15.	KtxKt	PxKt
16.	B–Kt5	

In the third match game Lasker had played 16. Kt–Kt3 and after 16. . . . Kt–Q2; 17, B–Kt3, Q–Kt3 got the worst of the game and lost. However, modern theory says that 16. Kt–Kt3 is correct and that after 16. . . . Kt–Q2; 17. Kt–B5, B–B3; 18. B–Kt3!, Q–Kt3; 19. B–Q5 Black has nothing better than 19. . . . B–Kt2; 20. BxB, QxB; 21. KtxP(Q4) with equal chances. This is a good example of a position whose merits cannot be decided on general principles but only by detailed analysis.

| 16. | ... | P–R3? |

The correct line is 16. . . . Q–B4!; 17. B–KR4, B–K3; 18. R–QB1, Q–Kt5; 19, P–QKt3, QR–B1; 20. Kt–Kt3, P–Q4! and Black is better. Vigorous counter play by Black is essential.

| 17. | B–KR4 | Q–Kt3 |
| 18. | Q–Q3 | P–Kt4 |

He feared 19. P–K5 followed by BxKt and Q–R7 mate (Anderssen–Morphy!) but the text is very weakening. 18. . . . R–K1 has been suggested instead and in a better chance for Black.

19.	B–KKt3	B–K3
20.	QR–Q1	KR–B1
21.	B–Kt1	Kt–Q2

Otherwise 22. P–K5, PxP; 23. BxP threatening (amongst other things) Kt–Kt3–R5.

22.	P–K5	Kt–B1
23.	Q–KB3	P–Q4
24.	Q–R5	K–Kt2
25.	P–B4!	P–B4
26.	PxPep.ch	BxP
27.	PxP	PxP

28.   **B–K5!**

Winning the KKtP and completely denuding the Black King.

28.	...	P–Q6 dis ch
29.	K–R1	Kt–Kt3
30.	Q x P	B–B2
31.	Kt–Kt3	B x B
32.	R x B	R–R1
33.	B x P	R–QR2
34.	QR–K1	K–B1
35.	B x Kt	Q x B
36.	Q–K3	R–B2
37.	Kt–B5	Q–QB3
38.	Q–Kt5	Resigns

Not only 39. Q–Kt7 mate but also 39. Q–Q8 is threatened. Tarrasch after this game believed that this defence (the Tchigorin) to the Ruy Lopez was unsound. This was an over-dogmatic judgment based too much on his positional principles and too little on detailed analysis.

Dr Emanuel Lasker in March, 1921

Blockade and restraint

Aron Nimzovich (1886–1935) was one of the great original thinkers of the game and his book *My System* is a major contribution to chess literature; cranky and conceited (he had cards printed which read 'A.Nimzovich: candidate for the World Championship of Chess') he was not exactly popular with other masters and – as with Steinitz – too dogmatic an adherence to his own principles affected his success as a player. Nevertheless he was one of the finest players in the world in the 1920s and played some superb games which had a considerable influence on those who followed him. Bent Larsen, for example, told me that if he had to pick one game which more than any other had influenced his own development as a player, he would choose the following. Notes in quotation marks are by Nimzovich in *My System*.

WHITE P.JOHNER   BLACK A.NIMZOVICH
Nimzo-Indian Defence (Dresden, 1926)

1.	P–Q4	Kt–KB3
2.	P–QB4	P–K3
3.	Kt–QB3	B–Kt5
4.	P–K3	0–0
5.	B–Q3	P–B4
6.	Kt–B3	

Here 6. Kt–K2 to avoid the doubled pawns is stronger. White can later advance by P–B3 and P–K4.

6.	...	Kt–B3
7.	0–0	BxKt
8.	PxB	P–Q3

Black's plan is to 'fix' the White pawns on the QB file, leaving him with a permanent weakness.

9.	Kt–Q2!	P–QKt3
10.	Kt–Kt3?	

He should play 10. P–KB4. 'If then 10. ... P–K4, there would follow 11. BPxP, QPxP; 12. P–Q5, Kt–QR4; 13. Kt–Kt3, Kt–Kt2; 14. P–K4, Kt–K1 and [White's] weak point QB4. ... will be protected by Q–K2, while White ... can use the KB file together with P–QR4–R5 as a base for operations. The game would then stand about even.'

10.	...	P–K4
11.	P–KB4	

'11. P–Q5, P–K5!; 12. B–K2, Kt–K4! or 12. PxKt, PxB; with advantage to Black.'

11.	...	P–K5
12.	B–K2	Q–Q2

Beginning a remarkable manoeuvre, the object of which is to restrain White's King side pawns.

13.	P–KR3	Kt–K2
14.	Q–K1?	

14. P–Kt4 would be met by 14. ... P–KR4! but B–Q2–K1–R4 is preferable to the text.

14.	...	P–KR4!
15.	B–Q2	Q–B4!
16.	K–R2	Q–R2!

'It must be conceded that the restraint manoeuvre Q–Q2–B4–R2 represents a remarkable conception.' Yes, indeed; now White can make no headway on the K side and Black gradually takes over the attack.

17.	P–QR4	Kt–B4

'Threatening 18. ... Kt–Kt5ch; 19. PxKt, PxPch; 20. K–Kt1, P–Kt6 etc.'

18.	P–Kt3	P–QR4
19.	R–KKt1	Kt–R3
20.	B–KB1	B–Q2
21.	B–B1	QR–B1
22.	P–Q5	

If he does not play it now Black will force it by B–K3. With the centre blocked, Black can now continue undisturbed with his King's side attack.

22.	...	K–R1
23.	Kt–Q2	R–KKt1
24.	B–KKt2	P–KKt4
25.	Kt–B1	R–Kt2
26.	R–R2	Kt–B4
27.	B–R1	QR–KKt1
28.	Q–Q1	PxP

'Opens the KKt file for himself, but the K file for his opponent. This move, therefore, demanded deep deliberation.'

29.	KP×P	B–B1!
30.	Q–Kt3	B–R3

A very subtle idea. 'If (White) had limited himself to purely defensive measures such as say 31. B–Q2, a pretty combination would have resulted: namely 31. B–Q2, R–Kt3!; 32. B–K1, Kt–Kt5ch; 33. P×Kt, P×Pch; 34. K–Kt2, B×P!; 35. Q×B and now follows the quiet move 35. . . . P–K6; and Q–R6 can only be parried by Kt×P, which move, however, would cost White his Queen.' Not only the strategy, but the combinations, in this extraordinary game are unique.

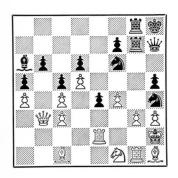

31.	R–K2	Kt–R5

32.	R–K3

'32. Kt–Q2, B–B1; 33. Kt×P, Q–B4; 34. Kt–B2, Q×Pch; 35. Kt×Q, Kt–Kt5 mate.'

32.	. . .	B–B1
33.	Q–B2	B×P!
34.	B×P	

34. K×B, Q–B4ch; 35. K–R2, Kt–Kt5ch and mate in 2 more moves.

34.	. . .	B–B4
35.	B×B	Kt×B
36.	R–K2	P–R5
37.	R(1)–Kt2	P×P dble ch
38.	K–Kt1	Q–R6
39.	Kt–K3	Kt–R5
40.	K–B1	R–K1
41.	Resigns	

There is no defence against the threat of 41. . . . Kt×R; 42. R×Kt, Q–R8ch; 43. R–Kt1 (43. K–K2, Q×Rch), Q–B6ch winning a piece and maintaining the attack. 41. K–K1, Kt–B6ch; 42. K–Q1, Q–R8ch would be a cure worse than the disease. One can see the influence of games like this in the fifth game of the Fischer/Spassky match.

An Alekhine brilliancy

In the other games in this section the primary object has been to show the changing chess styles. Here, however, is an example to show that the greatest moderns – in this context we can regard Alekhine as a modern – are capable of at least as much combinative brilliance as the old-style players such as Anderssen. In this game we see an outstandingly brilliant piece of play arising from a 'hypermodern' type of opening.

WHITE R. RÉTI   BLACK A. ALEKHINE
King's Fianchetto (Baden-Baden, 1925)

1.	P–KKt3	P–K4
2.	Kt–KB3	

One of Réti's less successful experiments. He intends to play Alekhine's Defence with a move in hand but this extra move – P–KKt3 – is worth very little.

2.	. . .	P–K5
3.	Kt–Q4	P–Q4

It would be better to play 3. . . . P–QB4!; 4. Kt–Kt3, P–B5; 5. Kt–Q4, B–B4; 6. P–QB3, Kt–B3 and now White would rather not have played P–KKt3.

4.	P–Q3	P×P
5.	Q×P	Kt–KB3
6.	B–Kt2	B–Kt5ch

6. . . . B–K2 is better; the text helps White's development.

7.	B–Q2	B×Bch
8.	Kt×B	0–0
9.	P–QB4!	Kt–R3

After all (thanks to Black's 3rd and 6th moves) White has come quite well out of the opening and has some pressure against the Queen's side.

10.	P×P	Kt–QKt5
11.	Q–B4	QKt×QP
12.	Kt(Q2)–Kt3	P–B3
13.	0–0	R–K1
14.	KR–Q1	

The prophylactic 14. P–KR3 depriving Black's QB of a good square would be better.

14.	...	B–Kt5
15.	R–Q2	Q–B1!
16.	Kt–QB5	B–R6!
17.	B–B3	

And not 17. B×B, Q×B; 18. Kt×KtP, Kt–KKt5; 19. Kt–B3, Kt(4)–K6!; 20. P×Kt, Kt×P; 21. Q×Pch!, K–R1! (21. . . . K×Q?; 22. Kt–Kt5ch); 22. Kt–R4, R–KB1 and wins the Queen since 23. Q moves is met by 23. . . . R–B8ch. It is extraordinary that Black can conjure up such a threat.

17.	...	B–Kt5
18.	B–Kt2	B–R6
19.	B–B3	B–Kt5
20.	B–R1!?	

White decides that, with the superior development, he should try to win, so he accepts an inferior square for his Bishop. While we can only feel grateful for his decision, it would have been prudent if ignoble to accept the draw. Fortunately for chess, most great players have the courage of their convictions.

20.	...	P–KR4!
21.	P–Kt4	P–R3
22.	R–QB1	P–R5
23.	P–R4	P×P
24.	RP×P	Q–B2
25.	P–Kt5?	

Réti is unaware of the coming storm. It would be better to play 25. P–K4, Kt–Kt3; 26. Q–Kt3 when he would retain a slight advantage, but he does not want to shut out his Bishop. Like all the hypermoderns, Réti had a peculiar affection for a fianchettoed KB and this several times (moves 20, 25, 27 – perhaps even

move 1) betrays him in this game. The danger signs are (*a*) that Black's pieces can rapidly be brought to bear on White's King, (*b*) that the defensive pawn structure has been weakened by the exchange of King's Rook's pawns, (*c*) that although for attack the White Bishop is as good on R1 as Kt2, it is not as effective on R1 in defence.

25.	...	RP×P
26.	P×P	

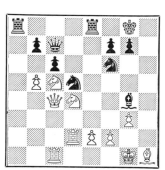

26.	...	R–K6!

One of the most spectacular and unexpected moves in tournament chess. The Rook dare not be taken – 27. P×R?, Q×Pch; 28. B–Kt2, B–R6 and Black threatens 27. . . . R×Pch!

27.	Kt–B3?

Alekhine gives as the only chance 27. B–B3!, B×B; 28. P×B!, P×P; 29. Kt(Q4)×P, Q–R4 with a slight advantage to Black (30. R×Kt?, R–K8ch; 31. R×R, Q×Rch; 32. K–Kt2, R–R8).

27.	...	P×P
28.	Q×P	Kt–B6!
29.	Q×P	

29. Q–B4, P–QKt4!

29.	...	Q×Q
30.	Kt×Q	Kt×Pch
31.	K–R2	

31. K–B1, Kt×Pch; 32. P×Kt, B×Kt; 33. B×B, R×Bch; 34. K–Kt2, R(R1)–R6; 35. R–Q8ch, K–R2; 36. R–R1ch, K–Kt3; 37. R–R3, R(B6)–Kt6! and wins (Alekhine).

31.	...	Kt–K5!
32.	R–B4!	

And not 32. P×R, Kt×R(7) winning the exchange. The long

new combination introduced by Kt–K5 finally wins the Kt on QKt7. The vitality of the position is extraordinary. If now 32. . . . Kt x R? then 33. Kt x Kt, R–Q6; 34. Kt–B5! threatening both Rooks.

32.	...	Kt x BP
33.	B–Kt2	B–K3
34.	R(4)–B2	Kt–Kt5ch
35.	K–R3	

35. K–Kt1?, R–R8ch.

35.	...	Kt–K4dis ch
36.	K–R2	R x Kt
37.	R x Kt	Kt–Kt5ch
38.	K–R3	Kt–K6dis ch
39.	K–R2	Kt x R
40.	B x R	Kt–Q5
41.	Resigns	

With the capture of the favourite Bishop, White must finally succumb. 41. R–K3, Kt x Bch; 42. R x Kt, B–Q4 and the Kt on Kt7 is lost. Alekhine says in *My Best Games of Chess, 1924–1927*, from which my notes are largely drawn, 'I consider this and the game against Bogolyubov at Hastings 1922 the most brilliant tournament games of my chess career'.

The new school

The following game was played in the famous 1945 radio match between the USSR and the USA in which the young Soviet players crushed the US team 15½–4½. This particular game, perhaps more than any other, illustrated both in its result and its style the strength and originality of the new school of play.

WHITE A.DENKER   BLACK M.M.BOTVINNIK
Queen's Gambit Declined (Radio Match, USA v. USSR, 1945)

1.	P–Q4	P–Q4
2.	P–QB4	P–K3
3.	Kt–QB3	P–QB3
4.	Kt–B3	Kt–B3
5.	B–Kt5	PxP
6.	P–K4	P–Kt4

Already we are in complications; assessment of such a position depends not just on positional judgment, but on detailed analysis of many variations with the positional judgment at the end.

7.	P–K5	P–KR3
8.	B–R4	P–Kt4
9.	Kt x KKtP	P x Kt
10.	B x KtP	QKt–Q2
11.	P x Kt?	

This releases the tension too soon. Botvinnik gives 11. P–KKt3 as best.

11.	...	B–QKt2
12.	B–K2	

Now it is too late for P–KKt3, because of the reply P–B4.

12.	...	Q–Kt3
13.	0–0	

To quote Botvinnik, '. . . almost all Black's K-side is destroyed, he has no pawn centre, he is a pawn down, and his King arouses serious anxiety. Yet in reality the Black King finds a secure haven on the Q-side, while White's central pawn at Q4 is a convenient object to attack and, with the continuation P–QB4 at the right moment, Black opens the diagonal for his Bishop, after which it is the White King's position that is hopeless. . . When this position arose in the game many masters considered Black's position very difficult; yet within five moves it was obvious that White's position was hopeless.'

13.	...	0–0–0
14.	P–QR4	P–Kt5!

And not 14. . . . . Kt–K4; 15. P x Kt!, R x Q; 16. QR x R followed by Kt–K4–Q6 and White has a good game.

15.	Kt–K4	P–B4

16.	**Q–Kt1**

Better than the obvious 16. Q–B2, P–B6!; 17. KtPxP, Q–B2!; 18. Kt–Kt3, PxQP; 19. P–QB4, Kt–B4 with a won game for Black.

16.	...	Q–B2
17.	**Kt–Kt3**	

After 17. P–KKt3 or P–R4, B–KR3 Black will get a winning attack on the KR file.

17.	...	PxP
18.	**BxP**	Q–B3!
19.	**P–B3**	P–Q6!

Threatening (*a*) 20. ... B–B4ch; 21. K–R1, RxPch; 22. KxR, R–R1ch (*b*) 20. ... Q–B4ch; 21. K–R1, QxQB. If 20. QxP then 20. ... Kt–K4; 21. Q–K2, B–B4ch; 22. B–K3, KtxB and wins.

20.	**Q–B1**	B–B4ch
21.	**K–R1**	Q–Q3!

Not at once 21. ... RxPch?; 22. KxR, R–R1ch; 23. B–R6!

22.	**Q–B4**

Or 22. B–B4, RxPch; 23. KxR, R–R1ch; 24. B–R6, P–Q7 or 24. Kt–R5, RxKtch; 25. K–Kt3, P–K4; 26. B–K3, P–K5 dis ch; 27. P–B4 (27. B–B4, QxP; 28. R–R1, Q–Kt3ch), R–Kt4ch; 28. K–B2, QxPch and wins.

22.	...	RxPch
23.	**KxR**	R–R1ch
24.	**Q–R4**	RxQch
25.	**BxR**	Q–B5
26.	Resigns	

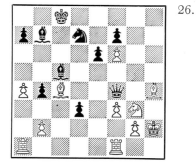

Mikhail Botvinnik, in March, 1963

*Below: Petrosian (to move) v. Spassky, 12th game of the World
Championship match in Moscow, May 1966*

The waiting game

In one of the semi-finals of the 1971 Candidates Tournament, Petrosian met Korchnoi. While Fischer was beating Larsen 6–0 at Denver, Petrosian and Korchnoi had played eight uninspiring draws in Moscow. In the ninth game, Petrosian as White adopted his most obscure style; appearing to do nothing in the most mysterious possible manner he reduced himself against one of the most dangerous attacking players in the world to a position of apparently complete passivity. Having reached this state he proceeded to show that Korchnoi's position was over-extended and in half a dozen moves it was shattered.

By a curious irony, this game which won him the match with Korchnoi lost the match against Fischer. In the sixth game, with the score 2½ all, Fischer's brilliant run of successes stopped and his confidence shaken, Petrosian chose this opening again; in a gruelling 66 move game, he was outplayed, outlasted and beaten. He never recovered and lost the next three games and the match.

The game with Korchnoi is not a great game; its interest lies in its type. It shows one of the directions in which there is scope for further development – whether we like the prospect or not. Play through it fairly quickly – but do play through it.

WHITE T.PETROSIAN   BLACK V.KORCHNOI
Double Fianchetto (*Moscow, 1971*)

1.	P–QB4	P–K4
2.	P–KKt3	P–QB3
3.	P–Kt3	

Why does Petrosian play such an opening? My guess is as follows. Korchnoi is a superb tactician and analyst, but his judgment is suspect; I think that Petrosian wanted to give him maximum rope to hang himself. He wanted to lure Korchnoi into positionally over-reaching himself; he therefore sets up a completely sound but rather backward position – and waits.

3.	...	P–Q4
4.	B–QKt2	P–Q5
5.	Kt–KB3	B–Q3
6.	P–Q3	P–QB4
7.	B–Kt2	Kt–K2
8.	0–0	KKt–B3

9.	P–K3	0–0
10.	QKt–Q2	B–K3
11.	P–K4	Kt–Q2
12.	Kt–R4	P–KKt3
13.	B–KB3	B–B2

Both sides prepare to deploy the Bishops on new diagonals; objectively, Korchnoi must have a good position but he understands this type of game much less well than Petrosian.

14.	P–QR3	B–R4

Not wrong, but the quieter R–K1 or Q–K2 reinforcing the centre is safer.

15.	B–B1	Q–K2
16.	B–Kt4	P–B4?!

Too loosening; he overrates his position.

17.	PxP	PxP
18.	B–B3	Kt–B3
19.	B–KKt2	

Magisterial calm. We call it 'fiddling while Rome burns' when White loses after such a manoeuvre.

19.	...	QR–Q1?

QR–K1 would be better; it is the KP that will need support – but Korchnoi does not suspect any danger.

20.	R–R2	B–B1
21.	R–K1!	K–R1

21. . . . KR–K1 is a little better, but Black's position is shaky anyway. After the text move he is – astonishingly – lost.

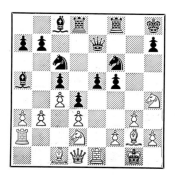

22.	P–QKt4!	P x P
23.	Kt–Kt3	B–Kt3

23. . . . P x P; 24. Kt x B, Kt x Kt; 25. B x RP and wins.

24.	B x Kt!	P x B
25.	P x P	P–QR3

Or 25. . . . R–KKt1; 26. KKt–B3 and KP or QP will fall (26. . . .
Q x P; 27. B–R3, Q–B6; 28. B–K7 and wins).

26.	Kt–B3	P–K5
27.	P–B5	B–B2
28.	Kt(B3) x P	Q–B2
29.	R–Q2	B–Q2
30.	B–Kt2	K- Kt1
31.	Kt–R5	B x Kt
32.	P x B	R–Kt1
33.	B–R1	R(B1)–K1
34.	R(2)–K2	Q–R4
35.	Q–Q2	K–B2
36.	P–R4	P x P
37.	Q x P	P–B5
38.	Kt–B3!	R x R
39.	Q x R	Q x BP
40.	Kt–K5ch	K–B1
41.	Kt x Bch	Kt x Kt

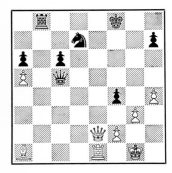

Here, with the time scramble over (the time control is after 40
moves) Black resigned without waiting for White's next move;
42. Q–Kt4 threatening both Q–Kt7 mate and Q x Kt is one simple
way of winning. A special prize to White's Bishops; one played
B1–KKt2–B3–Kt4–B3–Kt2 and was then exchanged – the other
B1–QKt2–B1–Kt2–R1 from which obscure spot it played a
major part in victory.

Section 3: Chess for blood

'First let me finish my move . . . and then hang me'

Chapter 7: A day in the life of an Olympiad

In this section of the book, I try to give an impression of what it's like to be a serious player – either a wholetime professional or a part-time player strong enough to compete from time to time in tournaments with professionals. With this in mind, it is worth looking at one particular event in detail – warts and all.

For this purpose I have chosen an Olympiad. It brings in almost all the factors that affect an individual tournament and several others of its own; it is the biggest event in the chess calendar and equal in importance to the world individual championship; and it is the only event which brings together serious players of all strengths.

Running the event

The first point to make is that organizing an Olympiad is a major task and a major expense. Each team will have 6 players and a non-playing captain, the women's teams 3 players and a captain; for 63 teams in the main event and 23 women's teams plus miscellaneous officials this makes about 550 people to be housed – at the expense of the host country – for $3\frac{1}{2}$ weeks (the Skopje Olympiad of 1972 lasted from September 19th to October 12th). There must be a hall which will permit 150 games at a time to be played in comfort and quiet, with room for about a thousand spectators, facilities for the press, demonstration boards to allow the most important games to be displayed outside the main hall, stewards – at Skopje there was an arbiter and two scorers for each match – controllers for the tournament as a whole and so on. The cost of the Skopje Olympiad was about £250,000 and 500 people (including, for example, 100 translators and team guides, 70 officials for the matches, 70 demonstrators and 100 writers for the games) were involved fulltime in managing it and seeing that all went smoothly. (The Yugoslav organizing committee listed in the book of the tournament had 54 members.) All this is a far cry from the first Olympiad in London in 1927 with its 16 teams, 70 players and 12 days; and then Argentina was the only non-European team – whereas in 1972 there were 34 European, 13 Asian, 12 American, 2 African, 2 Australasian teams.

Seeding the teams

After the teams have arrived there is a meeting, chaired by the President of the International Chess Federation (FIDE), which all the team captains attend. The central item of the agenda is the ranking of the teams in estimated order of strength; this task is impossible, but very important, because of the system on which the Olympiad is played. There are too many teams for them all to play each other, so the event is divided up into preliminary rounds and the finals. For the preliminaries at Skopje there were 8 groups – seven of 8 teams each, one of 7 teams: within each group, the teams all play each other and the first two teams go into the (16 country) A finals, the 3rd and 4th into the B finals, 5th and 6th into C finals and 7th and 8th into D finals. The policy in constructing the groups is to make them, as nearly as possible, of equal strength. With 63 teams this is done as follows. Write down the numbers 1 to 63 like this:

1	2	3	4	5	6	7	8
16	15	14	13	12	11	10	9
17	18	19	20	21	22	23	24
32	31	30	29	28	27	26	25
33	34	35	36	37	38	39	40
48	47	46	45	44	43	42	41
49	50	51	52	53	54	55	56
	63	62	61	60	59	58	57

Number the teams in order of strength and make up the eight preliminary groups by putting those corresponding to a column in this table into a group, i.e. the first group will be teams 1, 16, 17, 32, 33, 48, 49 and so on. If the preliminary seeding is correctly done, and if the gaps between the teams are equal, this will produce an equitable result. But in fact the seeding is very hit-and-miss; the results at the previous Olympiads are – except perhaps for the very best and very worst teams which maintain more uniform standards than most – extremely unreliable guides. Strong players who come to one Olympiad may not come to the next; and good new young players can make a team far stronger than it appears on paper. At Siegen 1970 when I was on the seeding subcommittee to decide the final order I thought the whole procedure extraordinarily subjective, not to say slapdash: I well remember being angrily accused by other captains, who disliked the results of the draw, of cheating to get a favourable draw for England (as a matter of fact, I hadn't cheated). At Skopje the seeding system was better, being based on the international ELO ratings (see page 77) of the players with a standard figure given for unrated players; but even this is an imperfect measure. The importance of the draw for 'marginal' teams is obvious. Suppose you are seeded 18; then you will be grouped with teams 2, 15, 31, 34 etc. Team 2 is clearly going to

make the A finals; you are going to have to struggle with team 15 for the second place. On the other hand if you can achieve a seeding of 14th, then you only have team 19 to contend with – a very big difference. Many people (of whom I am one) think that this whole system of preliminaries and finals is wrong and that the right course is to play a 15 or 20 round 'Swiss' tournament. The principle here is that after each round the teams are arranged in order of the scores they have made; in the next round a team plays the team whose score is nearest to its own – subject to the claims of other teams and to the same pair of teams not meeting twice. This system results in the strong teams rising to the top and playing each other and the weak teams sinking to the bottom and also playing each other; it has so many practical, as well as theoretical, advantages – for example, the number of rounds is largely independent of the number of teams and could be reduced well below the present number of 22 – that it is interesting to look at why it has not been adopted. The objectors are primarily the weak teams; they don't want just to play each other – they want their hour of glory playing strong teams, even if they do lose 4–0, and this they get under the present system. But I think that in the end the change must come.

Selecting the side

Now the draw is made and your team knows its section, the opposing teams and the order in which they are to be played. Of the six players, four will play in each match, 1 point is scored for a win and $\frac{1}{2}$ point for a draw and the final order is determined not by the number of matches won or lost but by the number of points scored; thus a win 3–1 against a weak team may be a disaster if your main rivals have won 4–0. England failed to qualify for the A finals at Skopje chiefly because they only beat Japan $2\frac{1}{2}$–$1\frac{1}{2}$, the other leading teams all scoring 4–0 or $3\frac{1}{2}$–$\frac{1}{2}$. The captain will select and hand in his team before each match, doing his best to weigh the various considerations; who is playing best, who needs a rest, whether he can afford to rest his strongest players against a weak team, whether A who was badly beaten yesterday should be dropped or whether it is better for him to play again and get the defeat out of his system and so on.

This selection of the team – justice being done and being seen to be done – is one, but not the only one, of the captain's functions. He also has the right to instruct his players to offer, or not to offer, a draw in a game or to tell them to accept or refuse a draw proposed by the opponent; in making these decisions he will be influenced by the score, the strength of the opposition and his own player's psychology. Some players won't want to offer a draw if there is any chance of winning, whereas others will want to offer it out of nervousness and if told they have to play on will do so with more confidence having had the responsibility for continuing taken off them and put on the captain. An unsatisfactory function of the captain – and a direct consequence of the sectional system – is that of arranging 'package deals' with the opposing captain. Suppose Ruritania is certain of qualifying for Group B and Mesopotamia needs a 2–2 draw with them to reach Group A (which cannot anyway be reached by Ruritania); then the captains may agree that all four games shall be drawn before play begins and an hour after the start all Ruritanian and Mesopotamian games have finished. Much worse things than this can happen; I quote without comment the facts of the Poland *v.* Greece match in the final round of the Group 1 Preliminaries at Siegen in 1970. Poland with $22\frac{1}{2}$ points out of 32 were sure to be in Group B finals; Greece, a much weaker side, had 15 points and needed to win $2\frac{1}{2}$–$1\frac{1}{2}$ to reach Group C. The result was a win for Greece by exactly $2\frac{1}{2}$–$1\frac{1}{2}$; and the two games that they won were both through the Polish players exceeding their time allocation – in one case, with the Pole in a winning position, the other, in an equal position. So far as I know, no Polish player exceeded the time limit throughout the rest of the Olympiad.

The time limit

To return from this digression, the teams are chosen; the round is due to start, play will be from 4.00–9.00 p.m. and unfinished games will be played from 9.00 a.m.–1.00 p.m. the next day. This brings us to one of the key elements in tournament and match play – the chess clock. This is a device composed of two clocks in a case with a button over each clock. When a player has moved he depresses the button over his clock which stops it, starts the opponent's clock and causes the button over the opponent's clock to rise: when the opponent has made his move, he does the same. Thus a player's clock is only going when it is his turn to move and one can measure the cumulative time taken by a player for a series of moves. $2\frac{1}{2}$ hours each for 40 moves (i.e. 5 hours for the two players) is the standard tournament time limit, so in the 5 hour session at least 40 moves must be played. Clocks are fitted with a small flag (as illustrated) which the minute hand pushes up as it reaches the hour; when

the minute hand passes the hour, the flag falls and the player's time has gone. Suppose the clocks are started at 3.30; then if a player has not made 40 moves before his flag falls at 6.00, he has lost. The introduction of the chess clock in the 1890s was a very important development in the game; a fixed time limit for each move is very unsatisfactory, since to allow enough time for the difficult moves you would have to leave far too much time for the average move – and no time limit at all leads to appalling stretches of boredom and frustration. On the famous 1834 match between Labourdonnais and McDonnell, Walker – an ardent fan of McDonnell – says '[McDonnell] sometimes dwelt on his moves till the sense of sight in the looker-on ached with the sickening of hope and expectation . . . I have known McDonnell [to take] an hour and a half, and even more, over a single move'; the only light relief offered to Labourdonnais and the spectators was to hear McDonnell muttering to himself 'I don't like it muchy'. Nowadays at least you know that if your opponent takes an hour and a half over one move he has to make the other 39 in an hour. The psychological pressure of the clock is severe; most players use nearly all their time and so there are many cases of errors in time pressure and some of exceeding the time limit – time trouble also leads to a fair number of disputes for the unfortunate tournament controller to settle. At Skopje, for example, Petrosian exceeded the time limit with three moves to play against the German grandmaster Hübner and at once claimed that the clock was defective; this claim was disallowed and Petrosian could be seen displaying the guilty clock in an aggrieved fashion to all his friends. In 1968 at Lugano, a time scramble in one of the Philippines *v.* West Germany games led to the Filipino banging his clock so hard that it fell on its face – and when picked up, showed both players as having passed the time control!

An immediate implication of the time control system is that players must keep an accurate, current score of their games. At Skopje to ensure that this was done each 4-board match had two official scorers attached to it each of whom kept a record of two of the games. This is desirable for many reasons. For example, a player may inadvertently miss out a move in his score and suddenly claim that the opponent has exceeded the time limit – thinking 39 moves have been played when in fact there have been 40; an independent score can settle this at once. Or if both players are very short of time and playing instantly – say they have 10 moves each still to make with a minute to go on each clock (this happens!) – they may not have time to write down the moves and just make ticks on their sheets, and an argument breaks out on the number of moves played. Curiously enough, replaying the game may not settle the matter. In the top board game between Israel and Mongolia (Czerniak *v.* Ujtumen), Lugano 1968, I remember seeing the following incident; Czerniak – who appeared to have exceeded the time limit – claimed that in the scramble the players (to gain time) had played two moves which led back to an unaltered position, i.e. that (say) moves 37 and 38 led back to the position after move 36. Ujtumen denied this, there had not been a neutral scorer present and it was just one word against another. A further complication was that immediately after the time scramble the players – who had no common language for communication with each other – had shaken hands. Czerniak claimed that in doing this Ujtumen was agreeing a draw – Ujtumen said that he had assumed that Czerniak was resigning! For anyone interested, a harassed committee – correctly, but to the disgust of the Israeli team – awarded the game to Ujtumen.

The sealed move

Well, suppose a game is unfinished when the 5-hour session is over; what then? Taking the Skopje schedule, the afternoon session has lasted from 4 to 9; unfinished games will be played from 9.00 am to 1 pm (occasionally from 8.00 to 12.00) the next day. In the intervening period there will be intensive analysis of adjourned positions – and now we come up against another problem. It is an obvious advantage in analysing to start from a position in which it is your move, not the opponent's; how can one put the two players on an equal footing? This is cunningly achieved by the device of the 'sealed move'. When a gong signals the end of a session, the player whose turn it is to move continues thinking until he has decided what to do; then, instead of playing this move over the board, he writes it down, puts it in an envelope, seals this and hands it to the controller. He is now committed to the move but his opponent doesn't know what it is – so each must start analysing from a position in which it is the other man to play. This ingenious and equitable system gives rise to further complications for the controller however; what happens if the player seals an ambiguous or impossible move? For example, he might seal Q×P when there are two pawns that can be taken; or he might seal P–Q5 (in error for P–Q6) when the pawn is already on Q5. Now the rule might be framed (and perhaps this would be best) in Draconian style to extract the death penalty for any offence; but this has not been done. It has left a kind-hearted loophole (deliberately) by the wording 'A game is lost by a player. . . 3. Who has sealed a move the real significance of which it is impossible to establish'. What exactly does this mean? No one knows. I sat on an appeals committee at the 1964 Tel Aviv Olympiad when Q x P had been sealed, with two pawns to be taken; one capture was sensible, the other lost the Queen. After almost an hour's discussion, involving the committee and both team captains, we ruled that it was possible to determine, beyond reasonable doubt, the real significance of the move. But were we right? It is a slippery slope when you bring your skill as a chessplayer into the decision – and this is what we were doing; where do you draw the line? A curious incident of a different kind occurred at Skopje in the USSR v. Bulgaria match. In a probably drawn position Tringov (Bulgaria) sealed against Korchnoi (USSR); when the envelope was opened there was no sealed move inside. Wild rumours at once flew round; the Russians had steamed the envelope open and extracted the move and so on. After various alarms and excursions the move was found – in Tringov's pocket. No one doubted that he had decided on his move at the time of adjournment and that this was the move on the score sheet in his pocket, but – inevitably – the game was scored to Korchnoi, an important half-point to the USSR which had made a bad start in the finals.

The adjourned games

Now the adjournment analysis. Originally a player was not supposed to get any help with an unfinished game – indeed, the ideal situation would be that he should not even look at it himself, since being able to move the pieces about introduces a new element not present in the rest of the play. However it is worse than useless to have unenforceable laws which only penalize the honest, so the rule is that players may analyse as a team if they wish. The captain must now sort out what is to be done; he will rapidly discover that if more than two players at a time look at a position, the result is chaos. He will therefore distribute the analysis as best he can amongst the six team members (plus himself, if he is a sufficiently strong player) and work continues. One more task remains for the captain – to get his players up the next morning and down to the playing hall in time; most chess players – particularly young ones – like to sleep on in the morning (especially if they have stayed analysing until 3 a.m.). That this is no sinecure is shown by the England v.

Philippines match in the penultimate round at Skopje. Only England or Israel – who had to meet in the last round – could win Group B; Israel had 35 points, England – with two games to finish against the Philippines – had 33½. But both these games were lost positions. However, play was due this day to begin at 8 a.m. and at 8 no Philippine players were present – and none appeared. Finally in desperation the Israelis sent a car to the Philippine hotel and brought the missing players down. Now, in adjourned sessions the time limit is 16 moves an hour; when the Filipinos arrived they each had 10 minutes of their hour left. One had such an overwhelming position that he won anyway – the other panicked and lost. So England went into the last round ½ point, instead of 1½ points, behind Israel, beat them 2½–1½ and won the group with 37 points against the Israeli 36½. An even more striking example was at Siegen, 1970 when Korchnoi overslept for the main session (at 3 pm!) against Spain and lost by default – inevitably headlined as Korchnoi's Complaint.

The end of the round

While these mopping-up actions are in progress, the players will be getting ready for the next round. The 4 players taking part (provided they are not involved in an adjourned game) will be working out who their opponent in the next round is likely to be – they know the country, but until the teams are posted (probably about 2 hours before play begins) they will not be sure who they will be playing since they do not know which 4 of the 6 enemy players will be chosen (their relative order cannot be changed, e.g. if No.2 and No.3 play, No.2 must play on the higher board). So they will examine their possible opponents' previous games in this and other tournaments and do some last minute opening homework – and perhaps take a gentle walk. On the whole violent exercise is best avoided and it is better to behave like a convalescent invalid; a state of pleasant fatigue – especially if fortified by alcohol – does not lead to good play.

This completes the account of a round; at Skopje there were 22 rounds in all and the event lasted from September 19th to October 12th, 1972. Like all major tournaments, a gruelling event in which chess skill is the main, but far from the only, factor. Physical and nervous stamina, resilience, the ability to rise to the occasion, good or bad team spirit all play a vital part. And it's work, not play; fascinating, absorbing work – but work, and the satisfactions, the successes and the failures are those one gets in work. You don't need to be there to realize this; look at the players' score sheets (below) in the famous Spassky–Fischer game, the top-board encounter in the USSR *v.* USA match at Siegen. Both were desperately anxious to win; Spassky to confirm his then position of champion of the world – Fischer to show that though he was not the champion, he was the best.

In addition, there was the national rivalry, at its most intense in this match. Spassky won – a misleading omen for the 1972 match – in a tense and brilliant game. Now look at Fischer's score-sheet – I don't need to say which it is. It is not easy being a chessmaster.

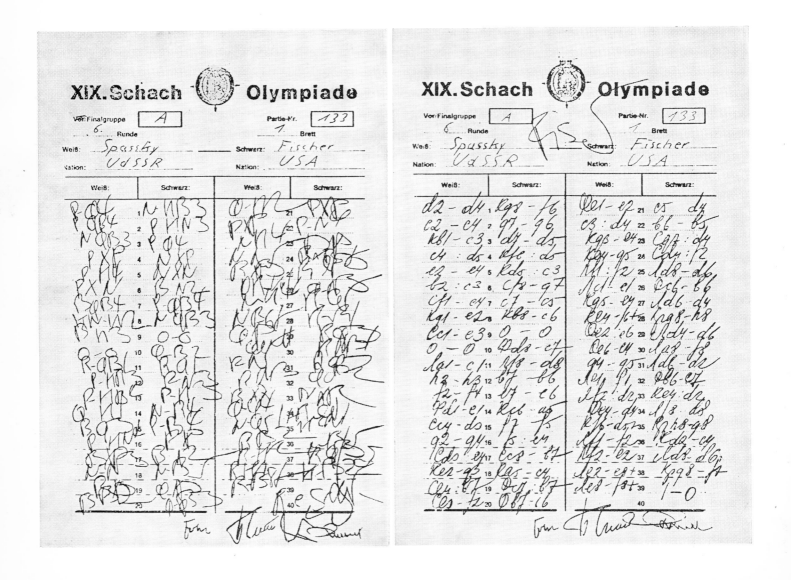

Chapter 8: The tournament circuit

In addition to team and individual matches, there are about 40 major international tournaments a year of a calibre to draw a selection of the leading players. There are about 100 Grandmasters (GMs), 200 International Masters (IMs) and about 1,000 internationally rated players all told; the typical make-up of a strong 16 player tournament would be 8 GMs, 4 IMs and 4 untitled players, all or most of these being players of the country holding the event. In this chapter I look at questions such as 'How are these titles awarded?', 'In what ways is a master stronger than other players?' and 'Where does the money come from?'

The title game

Until 1950, there were no official titles, except that of World Champion. In the bad old days, whose passing (in this matter at least) I greatly regret, the term of Grandmaster was employed, if at all, very loosely. Its first formal use was in 1914 when Czar Nicholas conferred the title of 'Grandmaster of Chess' on the five finalists of the great 1914 St Petersburg tournament – Lasker, Capablanca, Alekhine, Tarrasch and Marshall. Between then and 1950 the title was used (rightly) to describe a player of something near World Championship calibre – someone who might reasonably play a match against the champion.

In 1950, the title was formalized. It was awarded by FIDE on the basis of outstanding performance; and at the same time the title of International Master was introduced and awarded in the same way. The trouble with this system was nationalism; individual Federations lobbied for their own players and the usual wheeling and dealing went on in the hope – often justified – of getting marginal and sub-marginal candidates accepted.

In 1957 a change was made which removed this defect and introduced a worse one. It was decided that if in one major tournament, or two or three smaller ones of good enough quality (not necessarily consecutive), a player made a score equal to that got by scoring 55% against the Grandmasters, 75% against the International Masters and 85% against the non-masters he should get the GM title – with correspondingly lower percentages for an IM. Thus, if his opponents in a 16 player event were 8 GMs, 4 IMs and 3 untitled, the minimum score would be $0.55 \times 8 + 0.75 \times 4 + 0.85 \times 3 = 9.95$; so 10 points out of 15 would be needed.

This plausible scheme had two fatal defects. One was a theoretical weakness – the system was unstable; the more GMs and IMs it produced, the easier it became for the next contender to qualify – if the standard once began to fall the system would accelerate the process. But the practical defect was far more serious. Since all countries wanted to get titles for their own players, the most desirable competitors from abroad were bad GMs and bad IMs – the worse the better; and the last player to get an invitation would be a young, improving, untitled player. I well remember when I went to the Tel Aviv Olympiad as non-playing captain of the English team in 1964, having given up serious competitive play – but having the IM title. One of the Israelis approached me very politely and said what an honour for them it would be if I would play in an international tournament they were planning. Equally courteously (I hope) I expressed my extreme regret at being unable to accept but hoped that they would instead invite one of our young (untitled) players (by then, better than I was). They replied that they would certainly give this careful consideration – and nothing more was heard. Anyone can translate this little exchange, 'Come and play here and have a holiday; you aren't too hot now, but you've got a name and it will help our young players to get a title.' 'Sorry; but why not give one of our young players a break?' 'Not on your life; it's our young players, not yours, we're helping.' And some countries (I am not thinking of Israel here) were not above bribery. The scheme was a disaster.

In 1971 a major improvement was introduced, based on the ELO system, a rating system devised by Professor Arpad Elo, Professor of Physics at Marquette University, Milwaukee. All rating systems work on the following general principle. Suppose that we have somehow or other allocated figures which represent a player's strength at the beginning of the year; he then plays a number of games (say 30) and we want to find a new figure to estimate his strength in the light of these results – we can do this by giving him a score for each of the 30 games he has played and averaging these. Let us take the British system – this is simpler than ELO (though less accurate mathematically) which makes it better for explanation. A's grading is, say, 195 and he plays B, a stronger player with a grading of 210. If they draw, A receives a score for this game of 210 – this is clearly reasonable, as in this game he has shown himself equal to a 210-rated player; if A wins, he gets a bonus of 50 and scores 260 – if he loses, he gets a minus of 50 and scores 160. Average out the season's scores and you get the rating for that season. All rating systems work more or less in this way; there are many problems – such as how you introduce new players into the system, how long a period ratings should cover, how far you should give greater weight to more recent results, how in practice you keep ratings sufficiently up-to-date and so on – but, though important, they are matters of detail. By a system of this kind you can produce a fairly good numerical assessment of a player's strength and the ELO system has now been adopted by FIDE as the means of doing this.

This provides a much better method of assessing the strength of a tournament than the crude one of how many GMs and how many IMs are playing; the ratings of the players in a tournament are averaged (there is, for this purpose, a fixed figure for unrated players) and the average of these ratings determines the strength of the tournament – and according to its strength, there is a required percentage for a GM or IM title. A numerical example may help to show how this works.

In Section 1, page 24, we gave a table of the ELO ratings of various levels of player, showing that the average GM rated about 2600, the average IM about 2450. At Hastings, 1972/3, the average rating of the 16 competitors was about 2470. The official FIDE tables classify an event with an average rating in the range 2451–2475, as Category 9 (the range of classified tournaments is from Category 1, 2251–2275 to Category 15, 2601–2625) and in this category the requirement for a GM qualification is 64% and for an IM 50%. Hastings was a 15-round event, so this set a minimum of $15 \times 0.64 = 9.6$ (i.e. 10 points) for GM and $15 \times .5 = 7.5$ (7.5 points) for IM. The British IM, W.R.Hartston, scored 9½, thus missing a GM qualification by the narrowest possible margin.

If one must have a system, this is very nearly as good a one as can be managed. But it does make players count the points and half-points; what really matters is the quality of one's best games and one's best tournaments, but systems of this type emphasize average performance. In the pre-title days, everyone whose opinion was worth anything knew who were the great and who were the good players – and so they do now. All these systems do is to lead to the wrong sort of ambition, to jealousy and to various forms of sharp practice in the scramble for the extra half-point needed for a title.

The strengths of the masters

However, for better or worse, we have the titles and – titles or not – we have the great professional masters. They form a tightly knit group; they meet each other constantly in tournaments, study each others' play and know each others' psychological and technical strong and weak points. When a gifted new young player appears he may score some brilliant successes at first; that is one thing. To maintain and repeat these when his style is known and has been studied is quite another matter; only a player of true master strength can achieve this.

In 'The Nature of Chess' I have looked at the psychological and mental make-up of the chess player; here I add something on the various ways in which the superiority of the great master over the ordinary player shows in practice.

First there is his greater natural ability, which can be seen in many ways. There is the extraordinary precocity of the prodigy like Capablanca, the ease with which the mind moves in the medium of chess. Then there are the master's advantages in the three ingredients that make up a player – imagination, judgment and analytic power. Imagination: he has ideas which would never enter the head of a weaker player. A move like 26. . . . R–K6 in the Réti/Alekhine game (page 63) or an idea like that of Q–Q2–B4–R2 in Johner/Nimzovich (page 61) would not even occur to anyone except a great player; and similar differences at different levels distinguish players from each other all the way down the hierarchy. Judgment; given the ideas, a strong player can judge whether they are really good or merely plausible. In Anderssen/Morphy (page 56), for example, Anderssen's judgment of the correct strategy was worse than Morphy's; in Petrosian/Korchnoi, Korchnoi over-extended his position through misjudging its strength. Analytic power is the tool necessary to implement imagination and judgment. We can see this in any master game – Réti/Alekhine is again an excellent example; look at the power of calculation Alekhine shows in working out the exact consequences of his ideas – at move 31, he foresaw the final fork of Rook and Knight twelve moves later! I used to give 'depth' as a fourth category but I now think it is something that describes the quality of one's imagination and judgment rather than an independent element. One feels that Botvinnik's opening strategy against Denker had depth; in judging that the position was favourable to him, he saw and analysed far below the surface. Also Nimzovich's idea of Q–Q2–B4–KR2, though less immediately striking, is a deeper idea than 26. . . . R–K6 in the Réti/Alekhine game, brilliant though this was.

But if you want to see the innate superiority of the strong player in a very simple way, try the following experiment. Put

Black pawns on the board on QB3, KB3, QB6, KB6. Now put the White Knight on QR1, get from there to QKt1 (R1–B2–R3–Kt1) to QB1 . . . to KR1 from there to QR2 (KR1–B2–Q3–Kt4–R2 for example) and so on line by line to KR8; but you must never go to a square occupied or attacked by a Black pawn. How long does it take you? Get a friend to time you – and fine you 10 seconds for each time you break the rules. Some people get stuck and give up; 10–15 minutes is respectable; 7 minutes is good; a young Grandmaster will take under 2 minutes. All right – since you ask, I took 3 minutes 10 seconds first time, 2 minutes, 50 seconds second time. It gives an idea just how quick a sight of the board the master has.

Then there is technique. This serves exactly the same function in chess as in any other activity; through knowledge and experience you learn to do automatically what other people have to think about. This frees you to think about more difficult things. For example, one of the most frequent types of endgame is that in which each side has a Rook and pawns. First, a strong player knows various general principles; that the Rook is a better attacker than defender, that you should place it behind and not in front of its own or enemy pawns (so that as the pawn moves the Rook's range expands rather than contracts), that it is very strong on the seventh rank. He knows that the King too must be used aggressively, that it is desirable to force a passed pawn and so on. In addition to these general guides to play he has great detailed knowledge; a number of books have been written solely on these endings – a recent example is *Rook Endings* by Levenfish and Smyslov with over 200 pages and 300 diagrams. To take a very simple case, look at these three diagrams.

In all of them White wins with the move: but with Black to move, despite the fact that the positions are so similar, it is a draw in 1 and 3, a loss in 2 (solutions, for those who are interested, at the end of the chapter). More complicated – can you win with R, KP, KBP, KKtP, KRP *v.* R, KBP, KKtP, KRP? Sometimes you can, sometimes you can't. The expert knows that it is important for the defender to get his RP to KR4; if he can, he will probably draw – if he can't, he will probably lose. In endings like this, there are a large range of positions, some known to be won, some drawn. The expert has two advantages. He knows far more of these positions than his opponent, so he knows what to aim at; that is an advantage in technique. Secondly he is better at getting where he wants to get than his opponent; that is partly better technique (he knows the kind of move that is right), partly greater inherent skill.

Position 2
Black to play: White wins

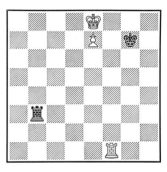

Position 1
Black to play: drawn

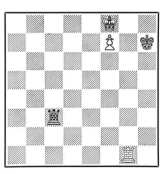

Position 3
Black to play: drawn

Technique, inextricably interwoven with knowledge, is also seen in opening theory. There is an immense amount of this. *Modern Chess Openings* by W. Korn contains 370 closely packed pages of opening variations; exhaustive? – nothing like it. It gives 7 of the 370 pages to Alekhine's Defence; Eales' and Williams' book *Alekhine's Defence* has 140 equally well packed pages on this opening alone. That is reasonably comprehensive – at the time of publication; but it is partly out of date before it appears and the expert will supplement it by studying current master practice – and the master will constantly probe existing analyses to find weaknesses, discover new lines and revive old ones. That is largely knowledge, but technique arises in relating opening play to the ensuing middle and endgames. The master has a deep understanding of the type of middle game that will arise from a given opening variation – so that it is not just a question of learning variations but of knowing the general direction in which one is going. It is hard to illustrate this effectively in a short space; let me take one elementary example – the variation 1. P–K4, P–K3; 2. P–Q4, P–Q4; 3. P–K5 in the French Defence. These moves set the pattern for the whole middle game. White has an advantage in space and he will try to exploit this by building up an attack on the Black King; on the other hand his centre is liable to attack and Black will try to destroy it. Two illustrations – in each case one player plays very badly, the other understands the object of the opening. *A: 1. P–K4, P–K3; 2. P–Q4, P–Q4; 3. P–K5, B–Kt5ch?* This helps White to strengthen his centre and removes the Black Bishop from the defence. *4. P–B3, B–R4; 5. Kt–B3, Kt–K2; 6. B–Q3, QKt–B3; 7. 0–0, 0–0?; 8. BxPch, KxB; 9. Kt–Kt5ch, K–Kt1?* 9. . . . K–Kt3 is better, but will also lose; *10. Q–R5, R–K1; 11. QxPch, K–R1; 12. P–KB4, Kt–B4; 13. Q–Kt6, K–Kt1; 14. R–B3, QKt–K2; 15. Q–B7ch, K–R1; 16. R–R3ch, Kt–R3; 17. RxKtch, PxR; 18. Q–R7 mate. B: 1. P–K4, P–K3; 2. P–Q4, P–Q4; 3. P–K5, P–QB4!, 4. PxP?* He should support the centre by P–QB3. *4. . . . BxP; 5. Kt–QB3, Kt–QB3; 6. B–K2?* He should play B–Q3 to allow the KP to be supported by Q–K2 and, later, R–K1. *6. . . . KKt–K2; 7. B–KKt5.* As will be seen this loses time. *7. . . . Q–B2; 8. B–KB4, Kt–Kt3; 9. B–Kt3, Kt(Kt3)xP.* Black is winning – he has destroyed White's centre and won a pawn. These imaginary games are both examples of opening technique; the winner knows what he has to do and how to set about it – the methodical assault on the centre in *B* is a particularly clear example.

Finally, the will to win: the master has this more strongly than the ordinary player. I have discussed this already in 'The Psychological Struggle' (Section 1) and return to it in the next chapter; here I only want to discuss one aspect – why the strain is so much greater for the master than for the ordinary player. In ordinary club chess, still more in social chess, you do not really have to play to win – you only have to play; go on for a bit and blunders will settle the issue. The better the chess, the less true this is; in top-class chess you must put on pressure if you want to win and this means taking risks. You must approach the precipice of defeat in cold blood and hope that, like Sherlock Holmes, you can push your Professor Moriarty over before he pushes you. It

is this deliberate acceptance of danger, game after game, that is too hard for most players.

Even amongst the professionals – far more determined than the average player or they would not be professionals – very few can stand the strain of trying to win in every game; hence the number of short draws. It is easy to excoriate the offenders – now that I no longer play in tournaments, I like having a go at the criminals myself; it's not so easy when you have to play. My own view is that if a competitor plays hard, interesting chess in most of his games one must accept one or two routine draws in the remainder.

The agreed draw

This matter of the short drawn game generates so much heat and so little light that to finish this discussion of the master game I will give a *cause célèbre* of 1972, the game Hübner *v.* Rogoff in the Students' Olympiad; the occasion was West Germany *v.* USA in the eighth round of the finals. It was an important match – West Germany were well in the running for second place in the Olympiad; Rogoff is an International Master, the 23-year-old Robert Hübner one of the strongest Grandmasters in the Western world. Here is the game:

WHITE R.HÜBNER   BLACK ROGOFF
Opening: Extremely Irregular

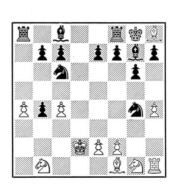

1.	P–QB4	Kt–KB3
2.	Kt–KB3	P–KKt3
3.	Kt–Kt1	B–Kt2
4.	Q–R4	0–0
5.	QxQP?!	QxQ
6.	P–KKt4	QxPch
7.	KxQ	KtxP
8.	P–Kt4	P–QR4
9.	P–QR4	BxR
10.	B–QKt2	Kt–QB3
11.	B–R8!	B–Kt2!
12.	P–R4	PxP

Draw agreed.

To add a further maniacal touch, although the game was agreed drawn it was finally scored as a win for Rogoff. What was the explanation?

Hübner had had two very hard games in rounds 6 and 7 of the event and did not want to play in round 8 – each team has two reserve players; he felt temporarily drained of energy and ideas. His captain, however, insisted that he played – so he did. He played one move and offered a draw. Rogoff accepted; after all, he was Black against a much stronger player. However, the tournament controller refused to accept a one move game and insisted that some more moves were played. To quote Hübner, whose blood was now up, 'I was not yet ready to rattle down some cliché moves in idiotic manner to sell them as chess to the readers of the bulletin and the public, to cover up substance with appearance'. So the game just given was produced, watched with fascination by a large crowd of spectators. But it wasn't only Hübner's blood that was up. The tribunal of arbiters, consisting of the tournament controller (Sajtar) and six others, ruled that both players must apologize and the game be replayed at 7 pm. Rogoff appeared and apologized, but Hübner neither apologized nor appeared. Hübner's clock was started and after an hour's time Rogoff was declared the winner. Next day – somewhat to the general surprise – Hübner turned up as usual and demolished the English top board Botterill in no uncertain style.

As usual in incidents of this kind, everyone was at fault. It was foolish of the German captain Lieb to insist on Hübner's playing; as his score indicates – 5 wins, 1 loss, 2 draws excluding the Rogoff game – he had played hard and successfully for his team and in rounds 6 and 7 he had played for 16 hours and 135 moves. He would not have asked for a rest if he had not needed it – and he had certainly earned it. Moreover he has a nervous streak in his make-up – he withdrew from his match with Petrosian in the World Championship quarterfinals because of the noise – and it was bad judgment on Lieb's part to press him. Once he was playing, however, Hübner ought not to have allowed his personal feelings to cost his side a point. I agree with his view that if you are going to draw without a struggle you should not wrap it up by playing a lot of routine moves first – but the time to make this point was in an individual, not a team event. He must have known that there was a danger of a one-move draw provoking the controller and costing his side a point. However, Sajtar should not have allowed himself to be provoked; Hübner's play and effort had been outstanding and in my view Sajtar should have ignored the length of the game – no rule had been broken. Once loss of face was involved for anyone who gave way, the position was hopeless.

What is the correct attitude to agreed draws? I am sure that it is wrong to try to legislate against them. This is partly because it is not technically feasible. At one time, for instance, there was an attempt to say that no game could be agreed drawn in less than 30 moves, but this was always absurd. Players can cook up games in advance which end in perpetual check in fewer moves; or they can march to and fro until the 30 moves have expired; and some games are quite legitimately drawn in under 30 moves. But a more powerful argument is the same as that against prohibition of alcohol; you can't enforce a law that has the majority against it – and the majority of strong players are against such legislation. The remedy lies with tournament organizers; if players draw too many games without trying, don't invite them to tournaments. For this reason I am all in favour of one-move draws; one can see clearly what is happening. Indeed I would prefer 'no-move' draws. Let the tournament controller announce at the beginning of the round, 'Snooks is tired after his 100-move game against Tomski, and Slivovitz has a hang-over; the game Snooks *v.* Slivovitz has therefore been agreed drawn without play and both gentlemen are now asleep'. We shall then all know where we are and the spectators will have far more interesting material for discussion than Snooks and Slivovitz in their debilitated condition could have provided over the board.

The money side of chess

In 'Profile of a Grandmaster', Larsen explains how he earns his living as a Grandmaster; here I look at the more general questions of amateur and professional in chess and where the money comes from.

Chess is a very satisfactory game in that there is no distinction between amateur and professional – we are thus saved from the dishonest farces that have disfigured games like tennis and continue to distort the Olympic Games. All prizes are money prizes; and all that matters is how well you play. Nevertheless we can in practice distinguish various categories, though they shade into each other. There are the wholetime professionals – the great majority of Grandmasters and a fair number of International Masters; Larsen's account shows the freelance life of a western professional – the communist professional is employed, directly or indirectly, by the State. Next, part-time professionals. Many young players fall into this category – for example Keene and Hartston, the two leading English players. The typical case is that of the university student who works at his academic subject and also as a chess player, earning money in the latter capacity as a chess writer or in tournament prizes;

he is still in the process of finding out whether he wants to be a professional, whether he is good enough and whether he can earn a living at it. Then there are genuine amateurs i.e. players who have no ambition to make chess even a secondary career but are good enough to play in at least some international tournaments. An outstanding example of this group was the late Dr Milan Vidmar (1885–1962) who was Dean of Engineering at Ljubljana University, only played in university vacations and several times gave up chess altogether for a time because of the demands of his work: nevertheless he was a player of true Grandmaster class. It is becoming increasingly hard to succeed at this level as an amateur nowadays but there are still a number of very strong players in this group. Finally, there are chess writers; these may be present or past masters or they may be players who have played little or no top-class chess.

Where does the money come from? In a tournament, for example, players will expect their expenses to be paid as well as reasonable money prizes. There will be a playing hall to be provided and so on; a 16-player tournament with say 8 Grandmasters and 8 other players will cost from £7,000–£15,000. Very little of this will be recouped from spectators or in any other way; it is a net expense to the promoters. In communist countries there is no problem – the government pays; in the West it is mainly a matter of private or local sponsorship – we can best illustrate this by some particular examples.

In Holland every year there is an IBM-sponsored tournament – through computers, a firm like IBM has perhaps a natural interest in chess. In the US – where there is of course a tremendous post-Fischer chess boom – in December 1972 there was the 'Fried Chicken' tournament at San Antonio; Bill Church, the Chairman of Church's Fried Chicken Company is a keen and knowledgeable chessplayer. At Palma de Mallorca there is an annual tournament sponsored by the Tourist Department. In England, there is the annual Hastings Christmas congress; the traditional 10-player Premier event sponsored by the Hastings corporation has now been increased to a 16-player event largely paid for by the financier J.D.Slater, a keen player and generous patron of chess. The new Teesside corporation has also started to finance one major event annually; and – an example of a 'special occasion' – Bath sponsored the 1973 finals of the European Team Championship as part of 'Monarchy 1,000'. (It is perhaps a little strange that the chess celebration of 1,000 years of monarchy in England should have been by eight teams, five of which were communist.) National

chess organizations and, in England, the 'Friends of Chess' (an organization for promoting international events), help sometimes to get these events under way but the bulk of the money comes from sponsorship of one of the types described above. National federations, and sometimes governments, also help in such relatively minor ways as paying travelling expenses for their own players.

Simultaneous exhibitions – where a master plays a number of games at once – are matters of local initiative. When a master plays, say, at Hastings he will usually give a series of displays afterwards; local clubs, or groups of clubs, that would like a display invite him – in England a Grandmaster might get £1 a board for a 40-board display, in the USA substantially more (see 'Profile of a Grandmaster'. Chess books are steady sellers – with a sharp rise since the Fischer/Spassky match; but it would perhaps be ill-omened for me to say too much on this subject.

From general to particular

In this chapter I have given a general picture of the international chess community and players. It is a community keenly conscious of its own identity, in which one is a chessplayer first with everything else – nationality, colour, class – far behind. It is a strenuous life, nervously exhausting, with 30 to 40 years of competitive chess for its leading exponents. Poorly paid in comparison with the professions or a physical sport, it is probably a better living than an artist's; and it has the artist's compensation and justification of being a creative activity. In the next section, I try to put some flesh on these dryish bones by looking in detail at one great player – Larsen.

Solutions to the positions

Position No. 1 is drawn by 1. . . . R–R1ch, 2. K–Q7, R–R2ch; 3. K–Q6, R–R3ch. As soon as White tries to escape perpetual check by going to the QB or KKt file, Black plays his Rook onto the K file winning the KP and drawing the game.

Position No. 2 is lost for Black. 1. . . . R–Kt1ch; 2. K–Q7, R–Kt2ch; 3. K–Q6, R–Kt1 (3. . . . R–Kt3ch; 4. K–B7, R–K3; 5. K–Q7 winning); 4. K–B7, R–QR1; 5. R–QR1!, R–K1 (5. . . . RxR; 6. P–K8 = Q and wins); 6. K–Q7 and wins (6. . . . K–B2; 7. R–B1ch).

Position No. 3 is drawn after 1. . . . R–B1ch; 2. K–K7, R–B2ch; 3. K–K6, R–B1; 4. K–Q7, R–QKt1; 5. R–QKt1, R–QR1!; 6. R–QR1, R–QKt1 and White cannot make headway (7. K–K7, R–Kt2ch, etc).

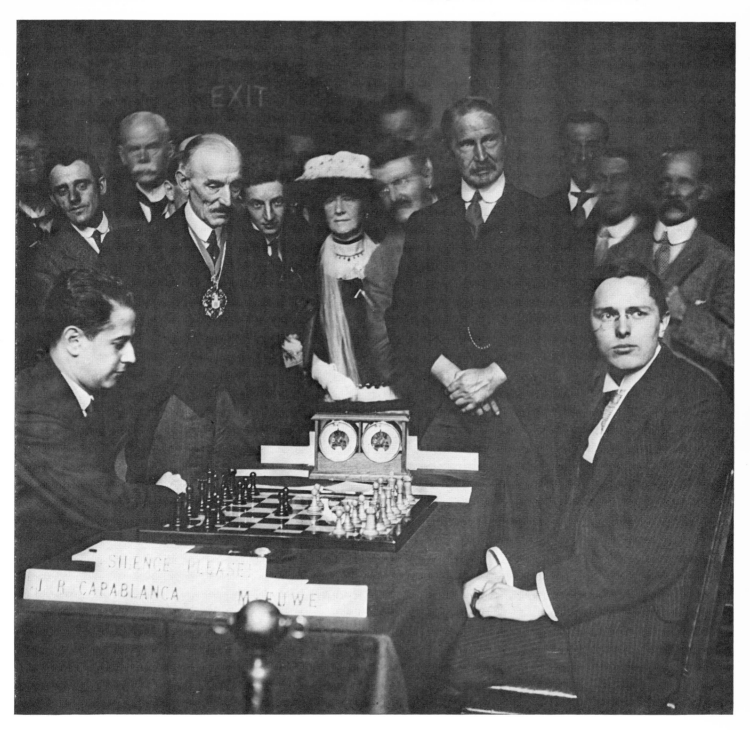

The decision

First, I asked Larsen when he made the decision to become a professional, whether he had ever thought of having a dual profession like Botvinnik (who is an engineer and a chess professional), and about his financial problems in the early years and his rather uneven form in the years 1956–1964 before he consolidated his position as a leading Grandmaster.

'It is hard to say when I decided to become a professional because I didn't make the decision suddenly. I remember that when I became a Grandmaster they wrote in the Danish chess magazine that I had said – and I probably had – that I did not intend to become a chess professional. The first year after I became a Grandmaster I really worked at my engineering studies but after that I worked very little on them and slowly gave them up. Then came the military service – I had avoided that as long as possible, but couldn't any longer when I was 26. I was two years in the army and after that, when I came out, one of the first things that happened was that I came equal 1st in the Interzonal. If there was a time that I decided, it was just after that–but it was not really a decision, it was something I drifted into.

'The last year I was in the army I was a sergeant and I had normal pay; it was the first time in my life that I had a regular income. No – I didn't find it too hard because I was living "poor student" style. I remember having difficulties with the tax authorities in 1959 because they couldn't believe that I had lived on £200 a year – but my demands were not so fantastic! I would not have liked the idea of a double career like Botvinnik – it would not have been easy to manage and I didn't ever like the idea of being just an employee.' The value Larsen attaches to personal independence and freedom came up many times in the interview.

Over the years from 1956 to 1964, while he was deciding, Larsen was also learning. 'I connect my uneven results over these years with the fact that I came from a small country. We have no other Grandmasters and I cannot, like a Moscow master, go into the Central Chess Club and play with ten other Grandmasters. So I didn't start in all tournaments with the same intention. Some I wanted to win, others I regarded more as training tournaments – and some after a bad start I decided that I had better regard as training tournaments! The most typical example is Beverwijk 1959 which was soon after the Portoroz Interzonal where I had done very badly. After that I didn't care at all; I didn't mind what place I took – I just wanted to play as sharply as possible. I played two good games only and those were the only two I won [Larsen scored 4/9, but won the same event in 1960 and in 1961.] That was a training tournament.'

Earning a living

By the age of 30 Larsen was a committed professional player. He was married and could not live indefinitely 'poor student style'. I asked him how he earned his living as a Grandmaster.

'I have three main sources of income – tournaments, exhibitions and writing. Taking tournaments, 80 games a year – say four major tournaments and one minor one – is enough. I have played much more, in 1967, 1968 and 1970 for example, but you feel it when you play too much. Normally I will be away from home for five or six months a year for tournaments. I do not prepare for special tournaments or opponents (except for a match, that is different) – I am not scared or nervous enough – but I am preparing, in general, all the time. Except sometimes when I am travelling, I think about and work at chess almost every day. Nowadays you get paid very well for exhibitions in the States – normal has been $5 a board for, say, 40 boards and recently people paid $20 a board in Mexico (though I didn't get it all) for a 20-board display. So I give a number there. I write chess books, and articles for newspapers and I do many annotations for chess magazines. I said once that I got a third of my income from tournaments, a third from exhibitions and a third from writing but that is a very rough average – it varies very much from year to year. I make over £5,000 in a year, less than £10,000.

'Now things are changing very much. It is no problem now for a Grandmaster in the United States to make $20,000 a year There could be regular chess on TV in the US with such things as a professional league and so on. Until now, however, there have been very few players in the West – perhaps only Fischer, myself and maybe Benko – who have done better financially than if they had been headmaster of a school [like the British player H.E.Atkins whom we had been discussing]. But it is a nice career because you are very much your own boss.'

I then asked Larsen whether giving exhibitions or writing about chess affected his play. 'Exhibitions do not matter; they have nothing to do with the chess you play in tournaments. But writing is much more dangerous. The worst case was when I wrote my *50 Selected Games* [Larsen's *Selected Games of Chess*; Bell – a superb collection]. My wife brought the English MS to the post office just the day I left for Puerto Rico. At Puerto Rico, I had original ideas – that was not the trouble – but in some games I suddenly realized that I had played stupidly and my opponent had played stupidly and that this game should never be published – and then I lost all interest and played terribly. I became too much of a perfectionist! I lost many games because of this.'

A note on tournament prizes may be of interest. Larsen got £500 for his 1st at Teeside in 1972, £350 for his 1st at Hastings 1972/3, just over £100 for his 8th place at San Antonio (where the top three got almost £1,000 each – a higher than average prize). He also often gets an appearance fee, which is sometimes more than his prize.

What makes a Grandmaster?

'You can't say any one thing – except hard work. There's a lot of hard work; it may not be hard work for Fischer since he became champion but I'm sure that he has worked very hard in the past. And you must concentrate and fight; some people are not fighters and some cannot concentrate enough on anything. Good health and physical condition are important too. One should take regular exercise; I ought to – I don't know what – but I don't. A terrible thing is that when I travel I get over-weight – this terrible stomach! – living in hotels. One must eat well because it is not good to get tired in tournaments – but it is difficult to pick the right food in hotels, because it isn't there. And nervous stamina? Yes; I have a lot of that you know. I can often be like an elephant; nothing really upsets me. A lot of problems in life – I think time will solve them; I'm not very worried. If I was, I should never have been a chess master; I would have been an engineer. Parents and friends saw it as a terrible problem; I had never finished my studies, though I had been a bright student – but I didn't see it as a problem.'

And courage; where does Larsen get the courage to fight and always to play to win? 'The main thing is not to be afraid of losing. Why should I be afraid? Although chess is my profession and a very important part of my life, if I lose I know two things: first, it is only a game, and second, by taking the risks I do I will win more than I lose. For some masters losing at chess is almost like dying; for me this is absolutely not so. It is not too hard to get the energy to try to win so long as you are in good health and like to play – most players have this; but some of them dare not risk anything because the fear of losing is so terrible to them. It happens very often, at all stages of the game, that there is a choice between safety and a draw or taking a risk to win. In such cases I would normally take the risk. However, although I am famous for taking risks, I don't usually take very much of a risk; unlike Tal – who doesn't care whether his position is good or bad if only it is complicated enough – I don't like bad positions.'

What about the technical qualities – analytic power, positional judgment, creative ability? 'If you haven't got creative ideas, sooner or later you get tired of being a professional. It must be terrible to be playing a lot of chess and feel that you are never finding anything new – you could certainly have a nicer job somewhere else. Analytic power and positional insight vary very much for different Grandmasters. Smyslov and Petrosian never liked to analyse complex positions very much, Tal obviously does it very well and Korchnoi's whole play is based on analysis. If you are Smyslov or Petrosian then you have such positional understanding that you can avoid many complications and dangers and the need for so much analysis. Analytical power improves very much with practice; you learn to find what is critical in a position, what is worth analysing – you see which pieces are active, where the weak points are. When you don't know what to analyse, you sit there for a long time, picking variations almost at random. Tal and Korchnoi were probably born with a greater gift for analysis than I was and I was born with a greater gift than Smyslov or Petrosian; and in positional insight it is the other way round. Korchnoi is fantastic at calculating complex variations, especially when he is hard pressed; but he must analyse because his judgment when he doesn't calculate is very bad – he has to get through a lot of variations before he knows what's happening. Of course many things that worry the ordinary player are not problems at all for a Grandmaster; but in the difficult positions Spassky has said "Korchnoi is always wrong". Maybe a strong point of Fischer is that he is good both at analysis and in judgment – though Tal can calculate better and possibly Korchnoi also.'

On the creative side Larsen's views are interesting though not everyone would agree with them wholly. Steinitz, Réti, Nimzovich (whom Larsen rates as the chief influence on his early years as a player), Botvinnik (in his early years), Bronstein, Tal (and I think himself) he would rate as creative; but not Lasker, Capablanca, Alekhine, Keres or Fischer. Take Keres for example. 'Bronstein has influenced me – maybe Keres, but not so much; I like Keres's book but I do not admire Keres as a chess artist. Keres is not an artist, he is a practical player. As a young player he was practical in a different way; his brilliancies were all rather conventional. I doubt that he has ever tried to be an artist and if he has he gave it up in the Second World War – and also gave up the hope of becoming World Champion. I mean the following: Keres said to me once, "Sometimes I sit for 20 minutes and I know that some spectators are thinking that now there is something very deep coming: you know what's happening? I can't find any ideas and I am taking a nap – except for snoring and closing my eyes." A player like Bronstein would never do that; he would be trying all the time.'

Finally technique: 'Donald Byrne, at Majorca 1968, said to me that I was a real professional; I could win games even when I was in bad form. It is true; you can do it then by technique. In the Zonal tournament at Halle 1963, I was playing terribly (I was doing military service at the time) – but I came second. I only played two enterprising games, but I just used my opponent's time pressure. Sometimes however bad form shows in lack of patience, caused by tiredness, and then it is not so easy to win by technique; that is something horrible – then you lose games you never should lose.'

So, summing up, hard work is essential, good health and nerves almost equally so – and to win tournaments one must master the fear of losing games. Technically, a mixture of creative ideas, positional insight and analytic power is needed; these are mixed in very different proportions in different players but, naturally, all great players by ordinary standards have all three. And when all else fails, his technical skill and knowledge will at least produce a respectable result – provided he is not seriously overtired; for this a rest from chess is the only answer.

The Soviet Union and the West

Larsen is far from being an admirer of the Soviet chess scene and is remarkably sceptical about many of their claims, especially as regards tournament preparation. I mentioned to him the thoroughness and detail of Soviet preparation as described, for example, in *Soviet Chess* (D.J.Richards, O.U.P.) and in *Grandmaster Geller at the Chessboard*. These observations triggered off quite an outburst. 'I have heard a lot of nonsense about that [Geller's account of 'dossiers']; nowadays in fact the Russians are complaining that the players from other countries are much better prepared. Maybe someone in the Soviet Union has some files but the Russian Grandmasters have no access to them. Part of the claims in Geller's book are psychology. It has been very common in the last few years for Soviet Grandmasters to complain how bad the organization was – that they could never get to see all these foreign tournament bulletins, magazines and books that their Federation was receiving. Polugaievsky wrote

on this after Busum 1969 – discussing his game with Hecht, he said that he had never seen any of Hecht's games and was impressed by how many of his games Hecht [a West German International Master] knew. Korchnoi has said the same thing – that the foreigners know their games much better than they know the foreigners'. I don't believe all these stories of the Soviet study; they brag about these things. I think this is inner politics in the Soviet Union; you have to make it clear that you are a hard-working man. Kotov writes about all the many games you must study with at least one hour for each game; you cannot measure chess work in tons [at one time, Larsen tells me, the Russians measured not only steel and grain output by tonnage but also furniture production – and firms 'behind plan' caught up by producing very heavy furniture] – so the best they can do is to explain it as so many working hours.

'No, I wouldn't trade my independence for any extra security as a chess professional in the USSR. They are very tied up and often made very nervous by their huge organization, the Chess Federation, the Physiculture Committee and all that. At least I'm very independent and if the Chess Federation doesn't like something I do – well, it doesn't hurt me very much.'

To add a personal opinion on this, my guess would be that the truth lies somewhere between Larsen's view and the official Soviet doctrine. Certainly the position of the chess professional has been in the past a good deal better in the USSR than in the West, and Soviet preparation and study was more thorough and systematic. But in the last 20 years the West has learnt a lot and conditions for the Western professional have improved; conversely I think that the Russian establishment has become too much of a bureaucracy and Larsen is probably right in saying that there is a great deal of humbug about its claims.

The only time he has played in the USSR since 1963 was (unsuccessfully) in the 1973 Interzonals; this however is for financial not ideological reasons. As Larsen succinctly puts it, 'Prizes in Soviet tournaments are normally in roubles, which my mortgage company does not accept.'

The use of 'seconds'

In important matches nowadays most players have seconds who help them in their preparation and in adjournment analysis. It is typical of their independent, individualistic natures that neither Fischer nor Larsen have much use for such assistance. Here is Larsen on the subject.

'If there is time enough for both adjournment analysis and

sleep, I find seconds only useful as life guards (keeping disturbances away), shoe shiners and errand boys. I would not like to rely on analysis by somebody else. I do not know if Fischer analysed with Lombardy [his second in the World Championship match with Spassky]. In my opinion, the typical second tends to become something like a compromise politician: when he has a difficult problem (opening or adjournment) he will be satisfied with a solution which will not be criticized, though it may not be absolutely best.'

Past and present

One of the questions I asked Larsen was the old one of how the great players of the past compared with those of the present; in particular, how Lasker would do against the present world-class players and how Larsen himself would do if he were transported back with his present knowledge to the 1920s.

'Lasker? He would lose terribly; he would always find himself in types of position he had never seen before – because of course none of us would play a simple Queen's Gambit or a Steinitz Defence to the Lopez against him. It is true that he had no difficulty against the hypermoderns in 1924, though he expected it. He said to Maroczy before the tournament, "We have nothing to do here; these people have invented all these new things and we don't know them" – then he won the tournament. But the best theorists then were not the best players – Réti, for example, was weak tactically. No, I think he would lose terribly to the ten best players of today. If he could get into positions with which he was familiar – then of course he would be a great player; but I think he would not be able to. Even Alekhine would have to study for a year first; I am not sure, but I believe the man had never seen an exchange sacrifice on c3 in the Sicilian. Imagine that!

'If I were put back in the early 1920s, it would be easy, very easy to be World Champion. There would be many draws but in enough of the games I would get opponents into positions they didn't understand. Most people find this arrogant – but now we know so much more. If we take positions they understand, we are not better; but we know more types of position. It is a matter of selecting the right openings. Of course, the 1920s was a period of breakthrough in ideas; it would be much easier still if you went back to the early 1900s. The first real uncertainty is with Alekhine; he didn't want to play the new openings – he didn't like them – but he worked hard at them and he developed. Alekhine was not basically creative – he was a practical player,

but he learnt from others. Not Capablanca – he had difficulty with the new openings in his later years.'

A clearcut verdict with which I would agree. An interesting implication is that you cannot compare strength by comparing a great game of the past with one of the present; you have to consider how, without acquiring the extra knowledge, past players would cope with the modern styles. No-one is saying that the old players were less talented, but they knew less.

The World Championships

I asked Larsen about various aspects of this – his views about the Fischer/Spassky match, about his own chances if he played Fischer again and about the organization of the World Championships.

'The Fischer/Spassky match was not a bad match – although these title matches are never good. People forget that because they remember the best games. And there were two or three very good games in the Fischer/Spassky match. Spassky I think was caught very much off balance by all that happened at the beginning of the match. One thing that was very much criticized in the Russian press was that Fischer had not come to the nice official opening of the match with the President and the Government and everybody present; and I think that is also how Spassky felt. He thought that this should be a fine event at a high level and here was this naughty boy ruining it by the way he was behaving; and that probably took away some of his desire to play the match. But I agree that it is puzzling that he took so long to recover; Spassky used to be very tough psychologically which was why I thought he would win the match. First I was not sure that Fischer would play and then if he did I thought something would happen and then he would lose his mind! Of course Spassky did recover after game 10 – but it was too late; he was already three points behind and tired.

'In a return match I would give Spassky no chance; the strain on him would be even worse. I don't believe what Spassky said after the match – that now he really wanted the title. Soon after he became World Champion he came to dislike it – and he will remember that. He had many disappointments as champion. The Russians didn't take him very seriously as World Champion – which I find very strange. He got less money than Botvinnik and Petrosian; he didn't get at once as nice a flat and this was a great disappointment to him. Also one of the things that I considered important before the match was that Fischer had never beaten him – Spassky had played with him like the wise old uncle with the child; but now he is not the wise old uncle any more.

'Also it will mean a lot to Spassky how much support he gets at home – and I don't think he does get it; he gets a lot of Western support as a very sportsmanlike loser – but that is being sent down to the second category and then being a nice chap down there. In Russia, first it seems that they are not interested in a return match and secondly everybody now looks to Karpov; except possibly for one or two Grandmasters, nobody there thinks Spassky has a chance – and he will not be independent of this.

'In spite of my 6–0 defeat at Denver, I think that I would have a better chance than Spassky. It is true that I am a better tournament than match player but I think that I am learning to play matches. At Denver it was very hot and dry and this climate did not suit me. Yes, I think that I would have a chance in another match with Fischer; I do not think he is technically superior. After all, he is only 3–2 up against me in other games.

'I did not find Fischer's personality particularly disturbing but I don't like the way in which all the rules and the whole organization of a match are made for him. For instance, it has never in the history of chess been considered disturbing that you walk up and down on the stage; but Fischer doesn't like it, so now suddenly there is a room behind the stage in which you can walk – they don't say who tells you when it is your move! I don't think that Fischer is more affected by bad conditions than other players; but he protests more. But it was not the organization at Denver that affected me – it was the climate. Who knows now whether Fischer will ever play any more matches: but if I did play him I would have a good chance.

'As regards the organization of the World Championship I would like the Zonal tournaments done away with and it is ridiculous to have as many players as at present in the Interzonal because half of them have no ambitions – they are not trying to become World Champion. I think that it would be very easy to have a World Championship and a Candidates Tournament every second year. One could use ELO ratings for selection, or, better, a committee which used the ELO ratings when there was nothing special against them. Select 16 players – 4 will be surprised and pleased that they are considered as World Championship candidates and nearly all the others will certainly be the right choices; everyone will be satisfied – except the little countries which want a system which will include their players in a World Championship. In the Olympiads I did not play this year because I am in principle against individual ELO ratings for

games in international team tournaments. It does not hurt me personally but they should not count because the situation is different in team events; you must play for the team score. But these little countries whose players never go abroad like their players to have a rating – so they love it!

'The trouble is that FIDE is a very weak organization. It has no money – and therefore makes no money. If it had had the money, it would have put up the prizes and directly sponsored the Fischer/Spassky match and then sold TV rights and so on and made money. The membership fees for affiliated countries are ridiculously small and the FIDE income is only about 87,000 guilders [£10,000]. I know the trouble – it is a currency problem; the communist countries with large membership have severe restrictions on paying out foreign money. It is very difficult. Then there are the problems with the small countries; a country with 80 playing members has one vote just like the USSR and so you get some strange decisions. At the last congress you know there was the scandal of the Interzonals [where the number of competitors was increased to allow more players in from the weaker zones – who had not the faintest chance of any success].'

I agree with almost everything Larsen says in this section – except that I rate his chance of beating Fischer lower than he does! But one must believe in one's self to be a great player. He is absolutely right in all he says about FIDE; the vanity of the small countries – their wish to appear to have strong masters and World Championship candidates even if anyone with any knowledge can see at once its complete unreality – has in a number of ways distorted both the individual and the team championships.

The English scene
I asked Larsen his impressions of chess and chessplayers in this country; although he disclaimed any great knowledge he had some interesting criticisms to make.

'I don't know chess in this country very well, but to me England is a strange chess country; you are still an island. The immediate interest in an international tournament is not impressive and I have the feeling that many of the organizers have never seen another international tournament and just do it in their own way; and spectators are too noisy. At Hastings about a quarter of all male spectators seem to rattle coins in their pockets – even if they sit in the first row. In Yugoslavia they will applaud if Tal sacrifices his Queen – that is different!

On the other hand the sale of chess books in England is fantastic; it must be as well organized as the sale of alcohol.

'In England chess writing is a special thing; English players write when they are 20 – it is too young. It is very bad for their chess. In other countries they do not become writers so early. You know Donner [the Dutch Grandmaster] said to me once, "Those young English players, do you know what they want to do? They want to refute the Grünfeld; they want to refute the Najdorf. Imagine!" That never makes a good player. This is not exactly a criticism of them – writing is a help in earning a living; but it is a criticism of them as potential Grandmasters.

'Then it has been explained to me many times how necessary it is to be out of club rooms in London at 10 p.m., so you play three-hour sessions; it is very bad. No one in Denmark, even in the 4th category, plays three-hour sessions: it is far too little. Here you play 30-move sessions and then adjudication; this reduces fighting spirit and you don't learn to play endings.

'But it is good in England that you are now becoming again one of the leading countries in mounting international tournaments. You know, I have the feeling that it really hurts you not to have a Grandmaster. What should you do? It is hard to say. Of your leading players, Hartston should play more; with Keene – I don't know. He could still be a very good Grandmaster, but it takes some breakthrough and I don't know how to achieve it. He has a style like Petrosian and I think that he has studied more per year he has played than Petrosian; but Petrosian made the breakthrough and Keene has not yet. In general, there has been this joke you know that English players are always offering draws; this is a bad habit that can spread from a very few leading players and affect even the very young.'

Overall, Larsen clearly has a mixed and slightly puzzled reaction to the chess scene here. Impressed by the number and sale of chess books and by the international activity, he is surprised by the relatively small direct response to tournaments and by a certain amateurishness in us as players and spectators. I think that there is a good deal in his criticisms; I also think that the increased activity may lead to a cure.

Summing up

I asked Larsen whether on balance he was glad that he had become a professional; what he got out of it, whether (as even playing as an amateur I used to feel) he felt more intensely alive when playing chess, and whether he thought chess interfered unduly with his personal life.

'Being a professional you are very much your own boss and that is very important for me. If you feel you are playing interesting, creative and original chess then – why ask what you get out of it? No one asks a painter or a violinist – it is accepted; why ask the chess player? More intensely alive? Of course you are – you are more intensely alive whenever you are doing something you do well and have to concentrate on. You express yourself . . . that is a very misused word, perhaps you express yourself when you drink coffee, but maybe – O.K. – you are expressing yourself in some way. Excitement, of course; and there is something else – ambition. This ambition; it is very difficult for me to imagine giving up something that I did so well when I was 12 that the adults were amazed – when should I have given it up or why? Of course I could have done it as an amateur instead; I could have been an engineer, a school-teacher, a politician, a journalist – maybe even an author. I think that I could have made a mediocre author – but that is not interesting to me; why should I have stopped what I did best?

'Does it interfere with family life? Of course I travel a lot, but we have no children and sometimes my wife travels with me. Interfere! It interferes very much with family life if a man leaves home at 8 o'clock and comes home at 6 in the evening tired. Chess interferes in a different way but I cannot imagine that it interferes more or even as much as the kind of work that a lot of professors or research workers do at the university – and some politicians have no family life at all. Then if you are good you can prove it very quickly and that is very nice; you don't doubt yourself. Compare it with an artist or a scientist; even the scientist may work for years without knowing whether it will lead to anything and all these artists who are only recognized after they are dead – that is very hard. It is very nice to get recognition early – that it is there at once. Of course, it is true that recognition is what has been missing for chess as a whole, in the US for example – and it is this that Fischer has suddenly got.

Did he find that people regarded being a chessplayer as something freakish – and did it ever worry him that a chess-player's peak came early in life, so that in the forties one is already going downhill?

'I've never felt that people have regarded me as a freak because I am a chessplayer; I wouldn't have cared if they had – I don't mind what people think – but in fact I have never had that experience. But it would have happened in the States; not only because people don't understand chess but because it doesn't make enough money. A man who is capable of being a chess master could do something else and make a million – at least that's what they think, though it's not always true.

'Do I worry about my play when I'm 50? I think about it – but it doesn't worry me very much. I shall probably be the strongest 50-year-old ever. Yes, that is a typical piece of optimism and it may not come true – that is largely a health problem. But I shall be one of the strongest – and I think that I shall win more tournaments than anyone else has done at 50.'

What advice would he give a young player (I mentioned the 19-year-old Michael Stean as an example) if he were to ask him about becoming a professional?

'Advice? I would not advise someone whether to become a professional or not – I don't give people that kind of advice; a man must make up his own mind. But if he had decided to become one then I would certainly tell him that the most essential thing is to fight – and treat the first five years as training. Don't accept a draw when Petrosian offers it – and don't worry if you lose afterwards. It is a worse defeat to accept a draw prematurely than to lose – that they must get used to. Writing? That is a difficult problem, because it will help him to earn a living, but too much is bad for play. But don't take a premature draw. Never!'

Finally I asked Larsen, 'Have you ever had any regrets about your choice of a career?' He replied without hesitation, 'No, I have never had any.' I believed him. I finish this section with one of his victories in the 1964 Interzonal tournament.

WHITE B. LARSEN   BLACK L. PORTISCH
French Defence (*Interzonal, Amsterdam, 1964*)
(Notes in quotation marks are by Larsen in *Larsen's Selected Games of Chess*)

1.	P–K4	P–K3
2.	P–Q4	P–Q4
3.	Kt–QB3	B–Kt5
4.	PxP	PxP
5.	Q–B3!?	

An excellent example of a tournament surprise. Q–B3 is not particularly good – Larsen never played it again in a tournament – because of the line 5. . . . Q–K2ch! and if 6. B–K3 then not 6. . . . BxKtch; 7. PxB, Q–R6; 8. K–Q2! with a good game but 6. . . . Kt–KB3; 7. B–Q3, P–B4! (Mestrović–Marić, Yugoslavia 1967) and Black stands well. But 5. Q–B3 was a completely new move when played and it is very hard when surprised to find

the best line over the board given, as here, a large choice; 5. . . . Kt–K2, 5. . . . B–K3, 5. . . . P–QB4, 5. . . . Kt–QB3 all had to be considered. As Larsen says, 'Portisch had enough to think about!'

5.	...	Kt–QB3
6.	B–QKt5	Kt–K2
7.	B–KB4	0–0
8.	0–0–0	Kt–R4?

'A premature attack, as far as I can see. But afterwards we are all so very wise . . . To me 8. . . . B–K3 looks like the right move.'

9.	KKt–K2	P–QB3
10.	B–Q3	P–QKt4
11.	P–KR4!	Kt–B5
12.	P–R5	P–B3

'Why does not Black play 12. . . . Q–R4 or 12. . . . P–R4? Because of the threat 13. P–R6, P–Kt3; 14. B–B7!, QxB; 15. Q–B6 and wins.'

13.	P–KKt4	Q–R4

'Here Portisch probably overlooked an important defensive resource for White. Afterwards 13. . . . P–R4 was recommended but after, for instance, 14. Q–Kt3, P–R5; 15. P–Kt5, P–KB4; 16. BxKt, QPxB; 17. P–R3 Black is faced with almost the same problems as in the game.'

14.	BxKt	QPxB
15.	P–R3!	BxKt

15. . . . BxRP?; 16. PxB, QxPch; 17. K–Q2, P–Kt5; 18. R–R1!, PxKtch; 19. KtxP, Q–Kt5; 20. KR–QKt1 winning the Queen – the resource mentioned in the previous note.

16.	KtxB	Q–Q1
17.	KR–K1	

And not 17. KtxP, Q–Q4!; 18. QxQ, KtxQ; 19. Kt–B7, KtxB; 20. KtxR, Kt–Q4 with advantage to Black.

17.	...	P–R4

Here Larsen points out that after the move suggested by commentators, 17. . . . Kt–Q4, White plays 18. KtxKt, QxKt; 19. QxQ, PxQ; 20. P–KB3 with much the better ending. 'In some variations the White King goes to QB3, threatening to march right into the Black position. This must be prevented with . . . P–QR4, but then this pawn becomes vulnerable.' In general, at Grandmaster level a player will accept a middle game danger rather than go into an inferior ending where his defeat although much slower is also more sure.

18.	Q–Kt3	R–R2
19.	P–R6!	

Forcing a weakening of the dark squares.

19.	. . .	P–Kt3
20.	B–Q6	R–K1

20. . . . R–KB2; 21. R–K2 followed by QR–K1 will also lose.

21.	Q–B4!	K–B2

Or 21. . . . Kt–Q4; 22. KtxKt, PxKt; 23. QxP!, R–KB2! (23. . . . QxQ; 24. RxRch, K–B2; 25. R–B8ch, K–K3; 26. R–K1ch winning easily); 24. Q–R4! with a pawn up and the better position.

22.	B–K5	P–KB4

22. . . . Kt–Q4; 23. KtxKt, PxKt; 24. BxP! White now has the same complete command of the dark squares as we saw in the Steinitz–Blackburne game (see page 58). The rest is easy – Larsen finds the quickest method.

23.	B–Kt8	R–Kt2
24.	Q–K5!	R–Kt1
25.	P–Kt5	P–Kt5

Or 25. . . . Kt–Q4; 26. KtxKt, PxKt; 27. B–Q6! followed by QxQPch.

26.	Q–B6ch	K–K1
27.	QxBPch	K–B2

'Or 27. . . . Q–Q2; 28. RxKtch, KxR; 29. Q–B6ch. Or 27. . . . R–Q2; 28. Kt–Q5. Or 27. . . . K–B1; 28. B–Q6, PxKt; 29. RxKt, RxR; 30. R–K1.'

28.	Q–B6ch	K–K1
29.	P–Q5	R–B1

'After 29. . . . PxKt; 30. P–Q6 Black has no reasonable move.'

30.	Q–B6ch	Q–Q2

'Or 30. . . . K–B2; 31. QxBP'.

31.	B–Q6	R–KB2

'Or 31. . . . QxQ; 32. PxQ, R–R2; 33. Kt–Q5, R–KB2; 34. P–B7.'

32.	BxKt	PxKt

32. . . . RxB; 33. RxRch, KxR; 34. Q–B6ch, K–K1; 35. R–K1ch or 32. . . . QxQ; 33. B–B5 dis ch and White will come out at least a piece ahead.

33.	B–Kt4ch	Resigns

33. . . . K–Q1; 34. BxPch, R–B2; 35. BxRch, QxB; 36. R or Q–K8 mate.

CURIOUS CHESS PROBLEMS.
XIII.

THE following curious position is given by Damiano.

White to mate in four moves, without being allowed to move his King.

BLACK.

WHITE.

JOHN W. PARKER, PUBLISHER WEST STRAND, LONDON,

Chapter 10: The Amateur game

In the previous section we have dealt essentially with professional chess – the all-out struggle, almost as merciless to the winner as to the loser, to reach and remain at the top. Here we look at all the various forms which amateur chess can take. 'Chess for fun' does not imply that one is not serious; both correspondence chess and the composition of problems and endgame studies are activities which, while he is engaged on them, the player or composer takes very seriously indeed – but they are leisure activities rather than ways of earning a living. They may be more important to the practitioner than his job – this is often true of hobbies; but they are not his profession. In this sense – and not in the sense that the activity is trivial – they are chess for fun and not for blood.

Before considering variants of chess, what about the game itself played socially, in club matches, in the weak classes of tournament; how does such chess differ from serious tournament chess and how should one play to get the most enjoyment from it?

Strategy, technique and opening knowledge are all now of minor importance; games will be decided at best by a good tactical stroke – at worst by blunder and counter-blunder combined with a war of attrition by the player who has blundered away least material. For what it's worth, here is my advice on how to get the most out of chess at this level.

First, find as many different opponents as you can. Many social players play only with one opponent; when you do this you get into a rut – you play the same opening over and over again and win or lose in a few stereotyped ways. It is hard to develop or find anything new if you play like this. The best opponent is one who is slightly better than you are; this makes you struggle to improve. To play much stronger opponents, however, is a waste of your time and theirs, and is too discouraging; you can never gain self-confidence or develop any ideas of your own – get such players to give you lessons, don't play them.

Play strictly to the rules i.e. touch and move. Apart from the fact that few things are more irritating than the player who fingers every piece in turn, transfers his men to new squares, peers all round them and then puts them back (hopefully, on the correct square) you will never learn to concentrate properly and order your thoughts if you do this. Above all, never take moves back and never allow your opponent to do so; as well as encouraging carelessness this breeds ill-feeling – for the time inevitably comes when you don't want a move taken back (see the reference to Canute on page 41 for an extreme example).

Choose openings that you can understand. The old-fashioned openings, unless you are a strong player, are the best – King's Gambit, Vienna, Scotch, Danish, Giuoco Piano, Evans. Their objectives – rapid development, open lines, occupation of the centre and attack on the King – are the natural ones; that is why these openings were played by the older players. The fact that against the knowledge and technique of a modern master they are too straightforward to lead to an advantage is irrelevant so far as the ordinary player is concerned. The rule to follow is very simple; don't go on to more advanced openings until you reach a level at which the simpler ones are inadequate.

In the middle game (and in the opening) play to win; never reject a move because it leads to complications and you are therefore afraid to risk it – if you think it is right, play it. In that way you get much more interest – and you learn.

Don't despise the endgame; as long as there is any life in the game, don't abandon it as a draw. That is not to say that you should continue in hopeless positions; if at your level of play you have no chance, resign.

Finally, read about the game. Presumably you do if you've got here, so this advice may seem redundant. However, this is general chess reading; if you are a weak player read one of the many good basic books on the game – and it is always worth taking a magazine such as *The British Chess Magazine* (9 Market St, St Leonards on Sea, England), *Chess* (Sutton Coldfield, England) or *Chess Life and Review* (U.S. Chess Federation, 479 Broadway, Newburgh, NY 12550, USA).

The time scales of chess: from lightning to correspondence
Perhaps the simplest form of variation of the game is to change the time-limit. The standard tournament rate is 40 moves in $2\frac{1}{2}$ hours (40 each in 5 hours); it often surprises me that there is no slower time-limit and I would have thought there was some merit in a substantially slower rate for the Candidates and World Championship matches. Two things one could do would be (*a*) to make it, say, 30 moves in $2\frac{1}{2}$ hours, (*b*) to have (as in GO) a time limit for the whole game – perhaps 8 hours each player.

In weekend tournaments and in club matches the time limit is faster; 24 moves an hour is a normal rate in club matches and some events are even played as fast as 30 moves an hour. Coming down to play of a different order of speed there are two kinds; 5-minute or 10-minute games where the player has 5 or 10 minutes for the entire game and 5- or 10-second chess, where a buzzer is sounded every 5 or 10 seconds and the player must move. In my opinion the second form is much inferior for two reasons; it is better to give the player discretion to divide his time, however small, as best he can – and at 5-second chess too many players cheat by using a second (or more) after the buzzer has gone in completing their move. Another advantage of the 5-minute type is that it lends itself to handicapping; indeed I think reducing the available time is the best form of handicap in chess and the only one that does not spoil the game. To play with 1 minute (for the whole game) against the opponent's 15 is probably equivalent to conceding odds of a Rook. The present World Champion, Fischer, is also the best 5-minute player in the world: after the USSR *v*. The Rest of the World match in 1970 (won $20\frac{1}{2}$–$19\frac{1}{2}$ by the USSR) a 5-minute tournament was held which Fischer won with the staggering score of 19 out of 22 (Won 17, Lost 1, Drawn 4) with the next three places occupied by Tal $14\frac{1}{2}$, Korchnoi 14 and Petrosian $13\frac{1}{2}$ (Spassky did not play).

If you enjoy off-hand play then I strongly recommend using a clock. You can use it, as just mentioned, as a method of handicapping; play with an adjustable time handicap, transferring time after each game from the winner to the loser until a balance is reached. Next you can control the time the game takes; nothing is more maddening than to sit down for a 'quick' game and suddenly find that your opponent (I would not suggest that the reader would behave like this) having got an unexpected advantage starts to play very very slowly. Finally it tightens the game – it may be a quick game but it prevents it being a slack one; this makes it both more enjoyable and better practice.

There is one form of chess in which play is very much slower than in any over-the-board play: correspondence chess. In international play, the normal time limit is 10 moves in 30 days, i.e. 30 days excluding time in the post. If one is playing a game with an East European (the Communist post is a leisurely affair) 4 days in transit is very quick; so you have a schedule such as D-day start thinking, D+3 post letter, D+7 it reaches opponent, D+10 he replies, D+14 you receive reply – one move each in two weeks. 2–3 years is quite normal for a game. Indeed at the moment of writing I am playing top board in a friendly match Cheltenham (England) *v*. Sochi (USSR). Friendly it may be, but no-one can say that the moves are played without due deliberation. It is six-a-side, two games each; there is no time limit and, as we send all the moves together, our armies move at the pace of the slowest soldier. I won one of the games very quickly – in well under 3 years; in the other I have been on the defensive for 4 years but in the course of the next six months I expect to equalize. One of our team went round the world by sea during the match and only got two moves behind the rest of us.

Does this sound a little tedious? It isn't. If you play 10 correspondence games at a time (many addicts play more) you receive about one move a day – and the time soon comes when far from being impatient you rather hope for a postal strike. Indeed a curious phenomenon can be observed with some opponents – that the more difficult the position the longer it seems to take your letters to reach them; in my experience this effect is particularly marked in Bulgaria – any serious threat on my part seemed to paralyse the Bulgarian postal service to such an extent that I began to feel nervous about dislocating the entire Bulgarian economy and bringing the country to a standstill.

Correspondence (or postal) chess will teach you a lot about your inherent limitations as a player. You have, effectively, all the time you want; you surround yourself with books and magazines with all the latest opening theory; you analyse endlessly, moving the pieces about as much as you like; you are under no physical or nervous strain. And do you play the correct moves? You do not. Partly because despite all the books there may be some new wrinkle you did not know and partly because you still make oversights in analysis. But the real reason brings us back to the innate differences between the master and the ordinary player; some ideas never occur to you however long you think and in the positions where you cannot analyse to a decisive conclusion but have to make a judgment, you judge wrong.

How does C.C. compare with O.T.B.*? It has some advantages, some disadvantages. Its central disadvantage is that it is only half a game; it does not make anything like the demands on character, willpower, nervous stamina that O.T.B. play does – it is a much more partial struggle. On the other hand, you are much less likely to spoil a game by a blunder in C.C.; it is much less strain on the memory; and if you lack the opportunity for local O.T.B. play and cannot afford the time for tournaments, C.C. is a natural alternative. The two groups for whom I would particularly recommend C.C. are (1) those who dislike, or cannot stand, the strain of O.T.B. play (many older players come in this category), (2) those who lack the opportunity for O.T.B. play. Young and ambitious players should stick to O.T.B.

Perhaps the best of all C.C. players is the American Hans Berliner; he won the 1965–68 World C.C. Championship with the remarkable score of 14/16 (W12, D4, L0), three points ahead of Hybl and Husak (both Czechoslovakia), and then retired. In numbers of good players, the USSR leads here as in O.T.B., though not so decisively; but in quality at the very top it is interesting that the two greatest modern players – Fischer in O.T.B. and Berliner in C.C. – are both Americans. I give one of Berliner's games from the 1965/8 event.

WHITE H. BERLINER   BLACK S. NYMAN
Benoni Defence (World Correspondence Championship, 1965–8)

The comments on this game are based on Berliner's notes in 'The Correspondence Chess World Championship' by H. Berliner and K. Messere. Here is an extract from Berliner's introduction setting the scene for the game.

'Strategy is the name of the game in the world of postal chess. . . . Even at the highest levels of over-the-board chess a clever tactician can time and again elude his doom by being alert. . . In correspondence chess this does not happen. With proper strategical decision-making a small advantage can be nurtured and expanded step by step. . . My opponent in this game makes the mistake of adopting a somewhat inferior, passive defence. As the coils tighten round him he loses his composure and the game.

'There are several important opening decisions to be made which affect the harmonious co-operation of the pieces. Later there are two major middle-game decisions: how to break on the Queen-side, and where to place the White Queen.

'Black . . . fails to understand that his Knights are the backbone of the defence and when the first tactical volley is fired he fails to find his one slight hope of salvation.'

1.	P–Q4	Kt–KB3
2.	P–QB4	P–B4
3.	P–Q5	P–K4

Berliner thinks that this line, played for some years by Petrosian, is unsatisfactory for Black.

4.	Kt–QB3	P–Q3
5.	P–K4	P–KKt3
6.	B–Q3	B–Kt2
7.	KKt–K2	0–0
8.	P–B3	Kt–R3
9.	P–KR4	Kt–B2
10.	B–Kt5	P–KR3

Otherwise White plays Q–Q2, B–R6 and P–R5.

11.	B–K3	B–Q2
12.	Q–Q2	K–R2?

'12. . . . P–KR4 was necessary, after which White still had the two lever actions P–KKt4 and P–QKt4 to rely on for a later break.' It is interesting that such a natural move as K–R2 should be wrong.

13.	P–R5!	P–KKt4

13. ... Kt x P?; 14. P–KKt4 and 13. ... P x P?; 14. Kt–Kt3 are both bad.

14.   **P–R3!**

The main action will be on the Queen's side and White gets ready to play P–QKt4 before Black can do so.

14.   ...   **P–Kt3**

15.   **P–KKt4**

White now has (a) a safe home for his King on the K side, (b) the possibility of later K-side action. As Berliner says, a White Knight can reach KB5 while Black cannot get a Knight to his KB5.

15.   ...   Kt–Kt1

16.   P–Kt4   K–R1

17.   K–B2   Q–B3

18.   K–Kt2   KR–Kt1

19.   KR–QKt1   Q–Q1

20.   R–R2   Q–QB1

21.   B–QB2   B–B1

22.   R(2)–Kt2

White now envisages two possible plans after an ultimate exchange by KtPxP, QPxP. One is to advance P–QR4, intending P–R5, but this he thinks can be met by P–QR4 by Black whose backward pawn on Kt3 will be defensible; the other is to play for P–Q6 with tactical threats on the Q and QKt files. He decides that the latter will be better and now makes a series of moves to improve his position further before exchanging on QB5.

22.   ...   Kt–K1

23.   Q–Q3   Kt(Kt1)–B3

24.   Kt–Kt3   Kt–Kt1

25.   B–B2   P–B3?

White had intended Kt–B5 and B–KKt3 with pressure on the KP in order to provoke P–B3; now however Black plays it voluntarily thus depriving his Knights of KB3 and further reducing their manoeuvring power.

26.   Kt–B5   Kt–K2

27.   Kt–K3   Q–B2

28.   Q–Q1!

'Threatening to invade the weak white squares on the Queen-side from QR4 after an exchange of Bishops.' It is very difficult in practice to defend these cramped positions.

28.   ...   K–R2

29.   B–QR4   Kt–B1

30.   Kt–B5   Kt–Kt2

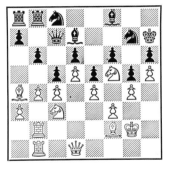

31.   P x P   B x B?

Best was 31. ... QPxP against which Berliner gives 32. P–Q6!, KtxQP; 33. Kt–Q5, BxB; 34. KtxQ, BxQ; 35. KtxKt(Q6), B–R5 (best); 36. Kt(6)–Kt5!, Kt–K1!; 37. KtxR, RxKt; 38. Kt–B3, B–B3; 39. Kt–Q5, Kt–Q3; 40. R–QB1, BxKt; 41. BPxB, Kt–B1; 42. P–R4, P–R4; 43. R(B1)–QKt1, R–R3; 44. P–Q6!, BxP; 45. R–Q2, R–R2; 46. RxB!, KtxR; 47. RxP, Kt–B5; 48. R–Kt5, R–B2; 49. K–B1 with fine winning chances. He also gives a number of subsidiary variations – a striking example of how deeply the C.C. master analyses. Interesting to see that White's 31st move is the first capture by either side.

32.   P x KtP!   Q x BP

32. ... PxP; 33. KtxB, KtxKt was rather better.

33.   Kt x B   P x P

34.   R–Kt4   Q–B2

35.   Kt x Kt   B x Kt

36.   Q–Kt3   P–Kt4

37.   Kt–B3!

37. RxP, RxR; 38. QxR, Q–B7 gives Black more play.

37.   ...   Kt–R2

38.   Kt x P   Kt x Kt

39.   R x Kt   R x R

40.   Q x R   Q–B7

40. ... RxP; 41. Q–K8! followed by 42. R–Kt8 winning.

41.   R–Kt4!   Q–R7

42.   Q–Q7   Q x P

43.   R–Kt7   R–KKt1

44.   Q–K7   Q–R1

44. ... K–R1; 45. R–Q7.

45.   R–Q7   Q–KB1

46.   Q–K6   Resigns

White just takes the QP, maintains his stranglehold and advances the passed pawn at his leisure.

Chapter 11: Variants of the game

'There are more things in heaven and earth, Horatio, than are dreamt of in your philosophy'   *Hamlet*

We can divide these into three groups: (*a*) Alternative forms of chess in other countries due to a different development from the original Indian game, (*b*) Attempts to improve and replace the Western game (*c*) Variants for fun. I consider these in turn.

Alternative forms in other countries
As we have seen the original game was considerably modified over the centuries since it first reached Europe and there were also a number of minor variations within the Western game itself. These have now all disappeared through international competition and modern Western chess is now firmly established as a world-wide game. However in several Eastern countries chess developed in different ways and even where the European game is known the local form is still played. I know of four distinct forms – Chinese, Burmese, Siamese and Japanese – and there may well be others.

Of these four games, Japanese chess, or Shogi, seems to me by far the most interesting and the only one that is a serious competitor to European chess; it is also the most popular – there are said to be 10,000,000 Shogi players in Japan. (There are also said to be 10,000,000 GO players – and now the Japanese have taken up Western chess as well; I hope there is enough population to go round. All these figures seem to me highly suspect.) Instead therefore of describing all four games I will concentrate on Shogi.

Shogi

Distinctive features
Shogi is played on a 9 × 9 board, each side having 20 men – see the diagram on page 102 for the initial set-up. The pieces are flat with the character for the piece printed on the face (rather like a pocket or magnetic set in our game); there is no distinction in colour – all the men are printed in Black – and one distinguishes 'Black' from 'White' simply by the direction in which the piece is pointed. On the back of most of the pieces there is another piece printed in red whose function I will describe later.

The object of the game is the same as in our chess – to checkmate the enemy King; there are however four major differences from the European game.

(*i*) The total available strength is considerably less; the strongest pieces are the Rook and Bishop and there is only one of each. Taking the European pawn as 1 unit and excluding the

Kings, I make the initial strengths 41 in European chess, 30 in Japanese – even without the Queen, the force is slightly greater in the Western game.

(*ii*) The Japanese pawn not only moves forward one square at a time (there is no initial double move), it also takes in the same way. If this applied in our game, then when each side had a pawn on K4 the pawns would be mutually *en prise*; on the other hand after 1. P–K4, P–Q4 the pawns would not be attacking each other. This is not a minor point – it affects the whole nature of the game, because you cannot get the semi-permanent pawn formation which is the underlying framework of the position in our game. The Japanese game has a much less rigid structure than ours – it's an invertebrate game.

(*iii*) Most of the pieces can be promoted if they reach the back three rows of enemy territory. Promotion is optional except under certain circumstances in which it is compulsory. The gain in strength is by no means so great as in our chess. When a piece is promoted it is turned over, all promotable pieces having a red character giving the piece's new name and value on the back.

(*iv*) When a piece is captured it is not put back in the box; it goes into a 'reserve base' held by the captor and he can re-introduce it as his own piece into the game whenever he likes by using his move to place the piece on any vacant square on the board. This makes a fundamental difference to the entire game; the total force is available throughout and there is no endgame – just an endless middle game. For example, in championship game Chyama (10-dan, champion, Black) *v.* Masuda (9-dan, challenger, White) when White resigned on move 61 after almost 18 hours play, he was threatened with an unavoidable mate; at this time White had 16 pieces on the board, 5 in his reserve base – Black had 13 on the board, 6 in the reserve base.

The net effect of these differences – (*ii*) and (*iv*) are the vital ones – is that the game is much more tactical, less positional, than the Western game; there is no question of exploiting small positional weaknesses, partly because the absence of a fixed pawn structure makes these much more transitory, partly because the force never gets reduced and so small material advantages are unimportant. It is the safety of the King that counts. For this reason I think that it is a game worth learning and playing; it is not just a variant of our chess – it is a game with a wholly different flavour.

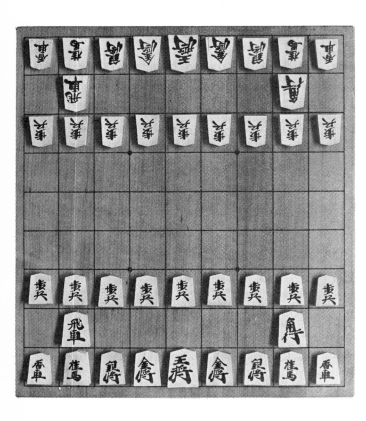

The Moves

The pieces, their European equivalents if any, their moves and their promoted forms are as follows:

Piece	European equivalent	Relative value (FU=1)	Move	Promoted form
1 GYOKU 'Jewelled General'	King	–	As King	–
1 HISHA 'Flying Chariot'	Rook	9	As Rook	RYU (Moves as Rook+King)
1 KAKU 'Angle-going'	Bishop	8	As Bishop	UMA (Moves as Bishop+King)
2 KIN 'Gold General'	–	5	(one square only)	
2 GIN 'Silver General'	–	5	(one square only)	NARI-GIN Moves as KIN
2 KEI 'Honourable Horse'	Much weaker form of Knight	4	(Knight move but only forwards and only two possible squares)	NARI-KEI Moves as KIN
2 KYO 'Pikeman'	Much weaker form of Rook	3	Forwards only (not backwards or sideways) with Rook move	NARI-KYO Moves as KIN
9 FU 'Soldier'	Pawn	1	Moves as Pawn (no double move) but captures as it moves, not diagonally	TO-KIN Moves as KIN

Notes

(*i*) The expression 'Rook+King' means that the RYU can move one square in any direction or move like a Rook. The addition of the King's move is even more valuable to the UMA which, unlike the Bishop, can thus change the colour of the squares on which it operates.

(*ii*) Since GIN, KEI, KYO and FU all promote to KIN it seems strange at first sight that they receive different names when promoted. The reason is that if captured they will reappear on the board in their original, unpromoted form – so it makes a difference whether you capture a TO–KIN or a NARA–KEI.

(*iii*) The KYO can jump as the Knight can, i.e. it is not impeded by intervening pieces, but it can only go to squares two ahead and one to the side, not to the squares one ahead and two to the side.

(*iv*) The relative values are taken from *How to Play Shogi* by the Japan Shogi Federation, so they should be right – but I find them a little surprising. The ratio of 9:8 for HISHA to KAKU compares with 10:7 for Rook to Bishop in our game and I am surprised that the KEI rates as high as 4: no doubt the ease of promotion affects the values.

Promotion

A man may be promoted as soon as it enters the enemy territory (his back three rows), or at the end of any move which starts in enemy territory. The promotion is part of the move; you make the move and then (if you wish to promote) turn the piece over, whereupon it operates with its promoted value until captured. Normally, promotion is optional; however when a piece which can only move forwards – FU, KEI or KYO – has reached a square from which it cannot advance further it must be promoted. This implies that FU and KYO must be promoted on reaching the ninth rank, KEI on reaching 8th or 9th.

Re-entry

Re-entry is the process of putting a captured enemy man back on the board as one of your own. As stated above you can, with certain restrictions, re-enter a piece onto any vacant square, such re-entry constituting a move. The restrictions are:

(*i*) You cannot re-enter a FU on a file on which you already have an unpromoted FU. I imagine the reason to be this: since (unlike the pawn) a FU takes as it moves, it can never change file – thus it is impossible to have 'doubled FU' of your own and so the rules will not allow you to achieve this through re-entry. There is however no objection to the re-entry of a FU on the same file as a TO-KIN (promoted FU).

(*ii*) You cannot re-enter a KEI, KYO or FU on a square from which it has no possible future move; this is clearly linked with the rule about promotion.

(*iii*) You may not re-enter a FU on a square on which it gives mate on the move. This is a curious restriction as a FU is allowed to give mate in the normal course of affairs, and other pieces may be re-entered to give mate on the move.

Notation

The files are numbered 9 8 7 6 5 4 3 2 1 (i.e. 1 is at the right). The ranks are numbered I, II . . . . . . IX starting from the top; Black moves first and plays from the bottom, i.e. IX is Black's back rank. The symbols used are move, '–'; capture, ':'; re-enter, ' < '; promote '*'; check, '+'. The reserve base is called R.B.

A game

To tempt readers a little to learn the game, here is a game between Mrs Mieko Ishibashi (2 dan) and Miss Akiko Takoshima (2 dan). As I had some difficulty in playing through the game correctly, readers will hardly expect me to offer any technical comments; I have, however, abbreviated those in *How to Play Shogi*. The game gives me a vague impression – I am incapable of any more precise judgment – of being average club standard.

Apart from the intrinsic interest, if you ever have to teach anyone to play Western chess I suggest that you try to understand Shogi for another reason. It will show you just how hard it is to learn to play chess. Tackling Shogi I found considerable difficulty initially in remembering all the different moves, had no idea what to do and little idea of what was happening; and that was starting from a base of complete familiarity with a similar game. It was a salutary experience.

BLACK MRS ISHIBASHI   WHITE MISS TAKOSHIMA
Opening: Unknown (to me)
Tokyo, July 2nd, 1962

(In recording the moves, I have used A, B, C . . . I for the ranks instead of Roman numerals.)

1.	FU–7F	FU–3D

Good first moves, focusing the power of each KAKU against the enemy zone.

2.	FU–2F	FU–4D
3.	FU–2E	KAKU–3C

Otherwise 4. FU–2D, forcing an exchange of FU and bringing the Black HISHA into active play.

4.	GIN–4H	FU–5D
5.	FU–5F	GIN–4B
6.	KIN(4I)–5H	HISHA–5B
7.	GYOKU–6H	GIN–5C
8.	GIN–5C	KIN–3B
9.	GYOKU–7H	GYOKU–6B
10.	GIN(7I)–6H	GYOKU–7B
11.	GIN–7G	GIN–6D
12.	GIN–4F	

Each side protects GYOKU with KIN and GIN. When the GIN on the HISHA side is advanced to the front, it will be time to start attacks.

12.	. . .	KIN–4C

13.	FU–3F	FU–5E
14.	FU:5E	FU–4E!

A brilliant move. After the FU sacrifice, the White KAKU begins its attack on the Black HISHA.

15.	GIN:4E	KAKU:5E
16.	HISHA–1H	KEI–3C
17.	GIN–5F	KAKU:7G*+

A profitable exchange, getting both GIN for the KAKU.

18.	KAKU:7G	HISHA:5F
19.	KAKU < 3B	

The first re-entry, threatening the White KIN on 4C.

19.	. . .	KIN–4B
20.	FU < 5G	HISHA:3F
21.	FU < 3G	HISHA–2F
22.	KAKU:2C*	HISHA–2I*

Capturing the KEI and promoting the HISHA; White has the upper hand.

23.	KAKU:3C	KIN:3C
24.	UMA:3C	KEI < 8F+

'KEI has been re-entered as a sacrifice so that White may continue attacking.' I think that the point is that when the FU on 8G takes this, the square 8G is vacated for another White piece to re-enter.

25.	FU:8F	GIN < 8G+
26.	GYOKU–6H?	

He should play 26. GYOKU: 8G; then after 26. . . . RYU:6I; 27. GIN < 7H protecting GYOKU and KEI.

26.	. . .	KAKU < 7I+
27.	KIN:7I	RYU:7I+
28.	Resigns	

Because after 28. GYOKU: 7I White plays 28. . . . KIN < 7H mate.

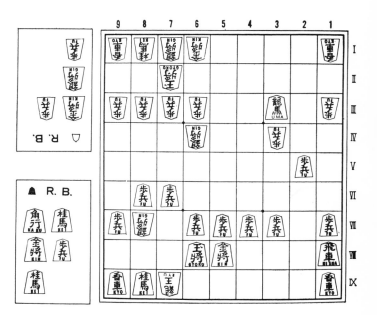

Attempts to improve

These attempts have one of three ideas underlying them: (*a*) 'The game is played out', (*b*) 'It is too dominated by opening theory', (*c*) 'Greater complication is a good thing in itself'. It is worth considering the validity of the ideas first and then the remedies.

The most famous exponent of the first idea was Capablanca; his perfect technique combined with lack of adventurousness in the openings did for a time make it appear as if perhaps chess was becoming like draughts and that the time was approaching when a great player – except by an occasional blunder – would never lose a game. Even in Capablanca's prime this was not quite true and his defeat (6–3, 25 drawn) by Alekhine showed that he himself was not invulnerable. Since his time, the theory has become much less plausible; post-war players have shown how much more scope there is, especially in openings, than Capablanca realized.

The second idea is one with which I have more sympathy; it is irritating for a gifted player who lacks the time to study the theory to be hopelessly beaten in the opening without his opponent having to think at all. But when one looks at the objection closely it doesn't really hold up. The opening is the most obvious but by no means the only part of the game where technique counts; it comes in the middle game as well and still more in the ending. The fact is that in any activity the professional – the man who works at it – will beat the amateur; if he can't, then it's a trivial occupation.

I find the attitude expressed in (*c*) rather irritating, the more so as the desire for extra complications is often expressed by those who are only too clearly unable to cope with those that already exist. Still, it is not wholly unreasonable; present day chess is a great improvement on the Arab game and was produced by increasing the powers of some pieces and thus making the game more complicated. My view is that such changes should only rarely be made and that there is so much skill and knowledge now invested in Western chess that one should be particularly hesitant to change. It is by no means obvious that greater complication is an improvement; the immediate effect is largely bad – the finer points of the old game are destroyed and you are starting again at a primitive level. This comes back to the first point – is chess played out? If it is, then change it; if not, greater complication will mean a lot of trouble for less than nothing.

(I am talking here of proposals to replace the existing game, not of variations for off-hand play.)

Turning to the kinds of change that could be made, the smallest is that of minor changes in the rules. There is only one which seems to me worth consideration; that is the stalemate rule. It is rather strange that stalemate should count as a draw; if you reduce an opponent to a state where he has no legal move, you might well feel that you had beaten him. To get your opponent into *Zugzwang* – a state in which the opponent, although not immediately threatened, has to make a fatal move – is regarded as a particularly elegant way of winning; and stalemate is very like an extreme form of *Zugzwang*. On the other hand, the fact that stalemate is a draw leads to interesting endgame theory and occasionally to attractive combinations; so it has some empirical justification. One has to weigh this against the natural logic of the game and the fact that if stalemate were a win the proportion of drawn games would be reduced and a finer discrimination made between players. There would be a good deal to be said for going back to the old idea and treating stalemate as an inferior form of win – on the grounds that if you can checkmate in the ending you can almost always give stalemate as well, but not conversely – and score say $\frac{3}{4}$–$\frac{1}{4}$ for a stalemate victory.

A much more drastic change would be to play randomized chess; this has often been suggested, amongst others by the mathematician Dr I.J.Good. White's pieces are placed on his back row in an order decided by lot and the corresponding Black pieces opposite them; the only restriction is that a player's Bishops must be placed on different coloured squares. There are 1,440 essentially different initial arrangements under this scheme. This is a method of destroying opening theory, while not destroying the opening. I have played randomized chess quite a number of times and my feeling is that you throw a good deal away and don't get much back. In destroying opening theory, you seriously damage middle game strategy which largely arises from the openings; and in my experience no hitherto mute inglorious Morphys now produce randomized masterpieces – everyone plays worse and, by and large, the same players win. It's fun to play for a change but it is not in the foreseeable future a replacement for chess.

The next level of change is to enlarge the board and introduce new pieces. This is by no means a new idea; the great Mongul emperor, Tamburlaine, played 'Great Chess' on an 11×10 board – there seems to be a characteristic touch of megalomania in this. An interesting early European modification, mentioned by A.S.M.Dickens in *A Guide to Fairy Chess*, is The Courier Game which was played in parts of Germany from 1200 to the nineteenth century – a very long life for a variant form. This was played on a 12 × 8 board; the four extra pieces were two Couriers, a Sneak and a Man. When it was introduced the Bishop and Queen had their old moves; the Courier had the modern Bishop move – so for over 600 years there was a form of chess in which the old and new Bishops were used side by side. To complete the picture of the Courier game, the Man moved like the King and the Sneak moved one square along rank or file. The most popular new pieces, however, are not those with such humble powers as the Man or Sneak; they are the Princess (with move of B+Kt), the Empress (R+Kt) and that bogeyman of the big board, combining the moves of Queen and Knight – the Omnipotent Queen, Terror, General or Amazon. A modern monstrosity calculated to strike fear into the heart even of an Amazon is the Atomic Bomb invented by Nassouh bey Taher of Transjordan in 1949. A pawn can promote to an Atomic Bomb and then leap to any desired square where it immediately explodes destroying itself and everything in the immediate vicinity; should it destroy the enemy King, then the piece of next highest rank becomes King. Presumably an H-Bomb piece would destroy all the pieces – and the board.

None of these variants with new pieces and enlarged boards has attracted any serious attention in modern times as a possible rival to the orthodox game; more interest has been shown in them as offering new forms of chess problem. I would be surprised if any of them were to replace the present game in the next 50 years. On the whole I think that they are rather uninteresting; the logic of an expanded game would be just the same as that of our own chess and with the new game it would be just a question of working back to where we are now – developing new opening theory along the same lines and so on.

Finally, there is 3-dimensional chess; this seems to me too difficult ever to be likely to replace 2-dimensional chess and I therefore discuss it as a variant to be played for occasional amusement. It may seem strange to say that a form is too difficult for serious play but suitable for amusement, but it is so. In 3-dimensional chess there is some fun in keeping track of what's happening and in manipulating the pieces correctly, but I don't see any deep theory of the game being developed.

Summing up, I see neither the need nor the likelihood for drastic changes in the foreseeable future; there is a case for a change in the stalemate rule and I would not be surprised to see this take place. If a major change is needed then I would prefer to see one which did not involve new pieces, but a modification of our use of the present men. Randomized chess is one possibility; another would be to introduce some of the Shogi ideas – e.g. some form of replacement of captured men. But I must say that I am well content with chess as it is.

Variants for fun

There are three ways in which one can vary the game, (a) different objectives, (b) new pieces and boards, (c) new rules. Group (c) is by far the most interesting; I propose therefore to dispose rapidly of (a) and (b) and consider (c) in more detail.

Losing Chess

This is the only form of (a) that I know; players try to lose rather than win. The King is taken like any other piece; capture is compulsory, but when there is a choice of captures you can make which you choose; stalemate can be played as a win or draw as you prefer. The most deadly piece (to its owner) is the Bishop; the Queen is less dangerous because it can usually arrange to capture a protected piece and thus get recaptured, but if a Bishop once starts capturing it can often be made to take almost the whole opposing army. Here is an example.
1. P–KKt3, P–KB4; 2. B–Kt2?? Now the game is over. 2. . . . P–QKt3; 3. BxR, B–Kt2; 4. BxB, Kt–QR3; 5. BxKt, Q–B1; 6. BxQ, K–B2; 7. BxP, P–KR4; 8. BxP, K–K3; 9. BxK, R–R2; 10. BxKt, P–K4; 11. BxR, P–R5; 12. PxP, P–Kt3; 13. BxP, P–K5; 14. BxP, P–B3; 15. BxP, P–Kt4; 16. BxP, P–R3; 17. BxP, B–R6; 18. KtxB. A limited game, amusing to play occasionally.

3-Dimensional Chess

This is the only one of the many forms using new pieces or boards that is worth detailed description. The explanation given here is of the standard form (if there can be said to be a standard form) as described by T.R.Dawson.

It is played on, or in, a 5 × 5 × 5 cube; you can think of this as five boards, each of 25 squares, superimposed on each other like five floors in a hotel. I shall call these A, B, C, D, E and use the algebraic notation for each board, i.e. the files are lettered a, b, c, d, e and the ranks numbered 1, 2, 3, 4, 5. Each player has

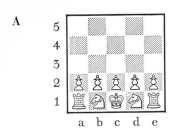

3-Dimensional Chess

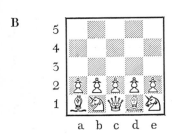

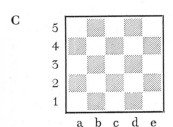

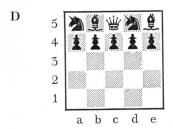

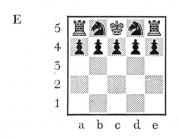

King, Queen, two Rooks, two Bishops, two Knights, two Unicorns and ten pawns. The moves are as follows:

Rook. Within one of the boards A to E, like an ordinary Rook; also straight up and down, like a lift. In notation, put the rook on Aa1 (i.e. in a corner): it can go to Ab1, Ac1, Ad1, Ae1 or to Aa2, Aa3, Aa4, Aa5 or to Ba1, Ca1, Da1, Ea1.

Bishop. The 2-dimensional Bishop move is extended in a similar way to that in which the Rook's move was extended. Put a Bishop on Ab1; within the A board it can move to Aa2 or to Ac2, d3 or e4. It can also move 'upwards' to Ba1 or to Bc1, Cd1 or De1 or to Bb2, Cc3, Db4 or Eb5. Like the Rook it always moves in a horizontal or vertical plane; within any such plane it makes normal Bishop moves.

Unicorn. The Unicorn, on the other hand, uses all three dimensions in its move – it does not move in a horizontal or vertical plane but from corner to corner of the cubical array. Put a Unicorn on Aa1; it can go to Bb2, Cc3, Dd4 or Ee5. Or put it on Bb2; then it can go along the main diagonal to Aa1, Cc3, Dd4 or Ee5 – it can also go to Aa3, Ac1, Ac3, Ca1, Ca3, Cc1. One way of 'seeing' its move is this; wherever it stands, imagine a cube with the Unicorn in the centre square of the cube – then it can move in the direction of any of the eight corners of the cube.

Queen. This combines the moves of Rook, Bishop and Unicorn.

King. One square in any direction (including the Unicorn's).

Knight. Analogous extension of the ordinary Knight's power to that of the Bishop and Rook. A Knight on Ac1, for example can go to Aa2, Ab3, Ad3 or Ae2; to Ba1, Cb1, Cd1 or Be1; or to Bc3, Cc2.

Pawn. The White pawns start on the A or B second rank; they queen on the E fifth rank. They move vertically or horizontally towards their queening squares, i.e. a White pawn on Cc2 could move to Cc3 or to Dc2 but not to Cd2 or Cb2 since these latter moves would not be towards the queening squares. Captures are made by diagonal Bishop type (not Unicorn) moves, again towards the queening square. Thus a pawn on Cc2 could capture on Cb3, Cd3, Db2, Dd2, Dc3 but not on Dc1.

The initial set-up is as shown in the diagrams.

I have not yet tried to play this game, but it seems to me about as good a form of 3-D chess as one is likely to get. While it is theoretically possible to play it on 5 boards side by side, the visualization required would be difficult; it would be worth while making a frame to allow the boards to stand above each other so that one could 'see' the moves, as in 'Total Chess' below.

Below:
Charles Beatty with his wife, author Joan Grant, demonstrate 'Total Chess' in 1946. A man may move to any square vertical to the one which he could have occupied on the flat; and may not move into or across the vertical projection of a pawn. Another variation on 3-dimensional chess

Kriegspiel

Coming now to group (*c*), one of the best of all chess variants is Kriegspiel, an excellent game in its own right. Kriegspiel is a mixture of chess and poker; I remember playing it with Oswald Jacoby, the American international bridge master and expert in all card games. We were about equal; my superiority in chess was counterbalanced by his at poker.

The game needs two players and an umpire. Neither player is told the other player's moves but he is given certain clues, described below, about the enemy position. The umpire – much the most enviable role – keeps the correct combined position on a board of his own and imparts such information to the players as they are allowed to have.

The available sources of information are as follows:

(*a*) Illegal moves. If you try to make a move and it is legal, then you must play it; if it is not legal then you try something else. Suppose a game began 1. P–K3, P–KB3 (no reason why this should be bad at Kriegspiel); 2. B–B4 (a risky move) and Black tries 2. . . . K–B2. The umpire says 'illegal', and Black knows that this square is covered, probably by a Bishop on B4; he might therefore play 2. . . . P–QKt4 hoping next move to take the Bishop.

(*b*) Pawn captures. A player may ask if he can capture anything with a pawn. If the answer is 'yes' then he must try at least one capture – and he must not try one that he knows to be impossible. For example White plays 1. P–K4, Black replies, White says 'Are there any?', the Umpire says 'Yes'. Now White knows that the only possible captures are 2. PxQP and 2. PxBP, so he must try one of these. If that one fails he can then do what he likes. Go back now to our example in (*a*). Looking at it from Black's view point the game goes 1. ?, P–KB3; 2. ?, Black tries K–B2. Umpire says 'no'. Now there are only two ways this square could be attacked; from a Bishop on QB4 or from a Knight on KKt5 or K5 (1. Kt–KB3, P–KB3; 2. Kt–K5 or Kt5). Black says 'Are there any?'; if the answer is 'yes', he takes the Knight. If 'no', he plays P–QKt4.

(*c*) Captures in general. A player may only ask about possible pawn captures, but both players are told when a capture is made and what square it is on, but not what has been captured nor what has made the capture.

(*d*) Checks will be announced and the nature of the check, i.e. check from a Knight, check on the rank, or check on the file and in the case of diagonal checks whether it is on the shorter or longer of the two diagonals on which the King stands. In the case of a double check he will announce the nature of each check: for example *White* R on K1, B on K2, *Black* K on K1 – White plays B–R5 double check and the umpire says 'Black is in check on the file and on the short diagonal'.

To illustrate the various points, we can look at the whole of the imaginary game of which we gave the first two moves above.

| 1. | P–K3 | P–KB3 |
| 2. | B–B4 | |

Black attempts to play 2. . . . K–B2. *Umpire* No. *Black* Any? *Umpire* No. *Black* (to himself) He's played B–B4; here's a chance to win a piece.

| 2. | ... | P–QKt4 |

White (to himself) What was that illegal move he tried [he will have heard the umpire's 'No']? There are only the following possibilities; that he played 1. . . . P–QB4 and was trying P–B5 or that he played 1. P–KB3 or KB4 and was trying K–B2. He doesn't usually play his pawns two squares first move at Kriegspiel – there's a good chance he played P–KB3. Also that pawn capture he tried would fit in very well with P–KB3 since then he would hope it was my Knight that was stopping K–B2. In that case he discovered that my Bishop is on B4; I'd better move it. I have an idea – I might even mate him, if I've judged his psychology right.

| 3. | B–Q3 | |

Black Any? *Umpire* No. *Black* (to himself) Pity. Still, now his Bishop's moved, his KKtP is unprotected; I might catch the Rook in the corner.

| 3. | ... | B–Kt2 |

White (to himself) Yes, that 'any' meant that he was trying for my Bishop. If I know Black, he'll have played P–QKt4 rather than P–Q4 and now he'll have played B–Kt2, after my Rook; just his kind of idea. If I was sure, I could play Q–R5ch and mate him – but he may have anticipated just this and played 3. . . . P–Kt3 waiting for Q–R5; how can I find out? I know!

| 4. | P–KKt3! | |

Black (to himself) Do I really want to take on KKt2? He's a cunning devil and he may have played K–B1 in which case

BxKtP will just lose a piece. Well at least it can't do me any harm to try and take the Rook in the corner though I'm sure I can't. [Plays]

4. ... BxR

Umpire Black has captured on his KR8. *Black* (to himself) Good heavens – the man's a raving lunatic. *White* (to himself) If only my guess about 1. ... P–KB3 is right, I've won the Kriegspiel all-time brilliancy prize. Here goes anyway.

5. Q–R5ch

Umpire Black is in check on the short diagonal. *White* (to himself) That's one hurdle over; now it's just a question of whether he played P–KB3 or P–KB4. *Black* (to himself) What's going on now? [Tries K–B2.] *Umpire* No. *Black* tries RP capturing on Kt3. *Umpire* No. *Black* tries P–KKt3. *Umpire* Yes.

5. ... P–KKt3

White (to himself) Now comes the moment of truth; is his KBP in the way of my Bishop or not? Tries BxKtP. *Umpire* White has captured on his KKt6 and Black is in check on the short diagonal. *White* (overcome with excitement) MATE IN TWO!

6. BxPch

Black Oh.

6. ... PxB

Umpire Black has recaptured.

7. QxP mate

I don't pretend that as a game this is in any way typical – but the method of reasoning is typical. Although unsuccessful in this case, note in particular Black's use of his King to obtain information.

Two minor comments on the rules:

(a) You need not ask about pawn captures and when you make a pawn capture it is not announced that it is with a pawn. Take the opening 1. P–K4, P–K3; 2. P–QB4, Kt–KB3; 3. Kt–QB3, P–Q4. *White* Any? *Umpire* Try. White plays 4. BPxP. *Umpire* White has captured on his Q5. *Black* Plays (without question) 4. ... KPxP. *Umpire* Black has captured on his Q4. *White* Any? *Umpire* Try. *White* tries PxKBP. *Umpire* No. *White* plays 5. KtxP. *Umpire* White has captured on his Q5.

As will be clear, Black cannot know which of White's captures are with pawns and which are not. This is an important point since if you can mislead an opponent about the file on which a pawn stands you may be able to queen it later on.

(b) You may not ask 'Are there any?' if you know (know, not think) that there are none. For example, if you have lost all your pawns then you may not ask 'Any?' in order to deceive the opponent.

I cannot leave this section without mentioning a truly remarkable book of Kriegspiel problems, *Are There Any?* by G.F.Anderson (Stroud News and Journal, Stroud, Glos., £1). In these, the assumption is that White has somehow or other guessed the position correctly and now has to force mate in a given number of moves. I give two examples; the first to enable readers to understand the difficulties and how to overcome them – the second to try and solve. Suppose Position No. 1 was an ordinary 2-move problem, there would be many solutions, e.g. 1. P–Kt7. Now 1. ... P–Kt6; 2. RxP or QxP or 1. ... B–Q5; 2. R along the rank. 1. ... B–K6; 2. Q–Q5. 1. ... B any other move; 2. R along rank or Q–Q5. The difficulty is that since we don't know what Black will have played we can't tell which of our moves will be mate. We get round this as follows. Against any Bishop move except B–Q5, Q–Q5 will be mate: so play 1. K–R8! Now 1. ... B–Q5 is check and will be announced as such; then 2. R–K5 is mate. If there is no announcement, then try 2. R–Kt3. That will only be possible if Black has played 1. ... P–Kt6; and if it is possible, it's mate. If it is not possible then the Bishop has moved somewhere other than Q5, so play 2. Q–Q5 mate. Note the importance of trying the moves in the right order; you must dispose of the P–Kt6 possibility before playing Q–Q5.

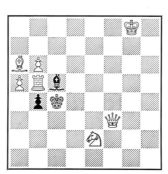

Kriegspiel No. 1

White to play and mate in 2 moves

The second position is a little harder – for the really hard ones, go to Anderson's book. If it were Black's move, there would be no problem; he would have to play 1. . . . P–Q7 or 1. . . . Kt moves. So one would try Q–B5 which would be mate if it was legal; if not legal then the Black Knight has moved, so play Kt–B4 mate. Now try to solve it before reading further.

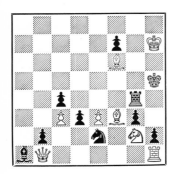

Kriegspiel No. 2

White to play
and mate in 2 moves

The solution is 1. R–QB1! If Black's reply is a capture on his QB8, try 2. Q–QKt5 – this will be mate if possible; if it is impossible play Kt–B4 mate. Equally if Black captures on his QB6, play Kt–B4. If no capture, ask 'Any?' If answer is 'Yes', this means the Knight must have played to Q5 or KB5. White must try a pawn capture, but he does not wish to make one, so he tries a capture on QKt4; this will be impossible, so then play Kt–B4 mate. If the answer to 'Any'? is 'No', try 2. Q–KB5; this will be mate if legal. If not legal, we have now reduced Black to two possibilities – Kt–Kt8 and P–R8, promoting. So try R–R1; if legal, it will be mate. If not legal, then Black must have moved Kt–Kt8, so play Kt–B4 mate! If the White Rook does not go to QB1 originally, White will be unable to distinguish between Kt–Kt8 and Kt–B8, hence the key move. I found these problems fascinating illustrations of logical deduction.

Four-handed Chess

This is another excellent game, which combinative players will particularly enjoy. You need a special board, but it is not hard to make one. The board has an 8×8 centre and four flaps of 3×8 round the four sides (see diagram); each of the four players has a complete set of men which are placed on the back two rows of his flap. If we call the players (in clockwise order) A, B, C and D then they play in turn in this order and A and C are partners against B and D. The object of the game is to mate both opponents; when one player is mated he is put into suspended animation – he misses his turn and his pieces exert no influence on the game. They do not even give check, nor can they be captured. The moment the checkmate is relieved, however, they spring to life (I deal later with some implications of this). A player must get out of check on his own move and may not leave it to his partner to rescue him; thus if D checks A, A is not allowed to say 'C moves before D moves again, so I will leave it to him to rescue me'. Finally, pawns queen on the opponents' back rank, not on the partner's, i.e. A's pawns queen on the B or D back rank. Since this involves a series of captures, in practice pawns never queen at all and their value is purely defensive. Pawns may leap over their partner's pawns and when they reach the partner's back rank move backwards until they get back to their home base. I have never seen any pawn get anywhere near the partner's back rank and regard this provision as entirely academic.

The most distinctive feature of the game is that of combined attack launched by the partners against one of the opponents. Take, for example, the apparently harmless opening *A* 1. P–K3, *B* 1. P–K3, *C* 1. P–QB3, *D* 1. P–K3? After this blunder, *D* is immediately mated! *A* 2. QxPch!, *B* 2. any, *C* 2. QxP double check and mate. Notice that had B played 1. P–QB3, this combination would not have succeeded; in that case *A* 2. QxPch is met by *B* 2. QxPch!, *C* 2. KxQ, *D* 2. BxQ.

Other points worth noting are (*a*) that on the much bigger board the short-stepping Knights are relatively less valuable than in ordinary chess, (*b*) the tremendous power of a major piece in the centre of the board, (*c*) that it pays to try to unbalance the opponents' forces. For example, in the unlikely event of your ever reaching an ending, if A has K and R, B K and 2 Rs, C K and R, D K only, then A and C have an obvious advantage. D is virtually useless, so A and C between them have the same force as B and two moves to his one. The kind of thing that will happen is this; C attacks one of B's Rooks with his own, D makes a useless move, A gives B check, B gets out of check. Next round,

C takes B's Rook, D makes a useless move, A checks B again, B gets out of check and has lost a Rook. (*d*) It is very useful to be able to check the player who moves immediately after you; in this way you can control the sudden double attack against your partner – see the mating example above.

Returning to the question of the player who has been mated, various points arise. If an opponent relieves the mate, he may not do so with capture; in the example above (1. P–K3, P–K3, P–QB3, P–K3; 2. QxPch, any, QxP mate, no move), A is not allowed to relieve the mate by 3. QxQ. He may however play 3. Q to D's Q3 relieving it and C – if not checked by B – could then play QxB, restoring the mate. There is, however, a curious logical flaw in the rules as I have seen them stated as regards playing into check by a mated player. Suppose D is mated and A plays into a position where his King is attacked by one of D's frozen pieces; now B relieves the mate – then A has been put into an illegal position, because he is in check to a player who is going to play before he does! The rule ought I think to be that only the player playing immediately before the mated player can go into a potential check in this way. If C plays into check by the mated D, then even if B relieves the mate, C can get out of check before D plays!

I hope that you will not be put off by this piece of legalistic nitpicking – Four-handed is a really splendid game, exciting and entertaining. Even more than most partnership games it can of course be quite maddening, but there is a simple remedy not available at bridge; play both hands yourself – it's a marvellous double dummy game.

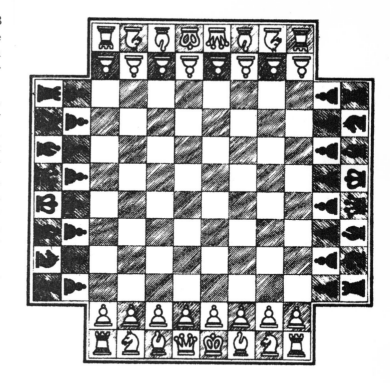

Blitz

Kriegspiel and Four-handed are the best variants, but I also enjoy Blitz – it too is an excellent combinative game. Here White has one move, then Black has two, White has three . . . and so on. If you give check your turn stops immediately and you must get out of check on the first move. Here is a sample.

1. P–K4. 1. . . . P–Q3, Kt–QB3. 2. Kt–KB3, Kt–QB3, B–B4. 2. . . . B–Kt5, BxKt, BxQ, BxP? 3. Kt–Q5, Kt–B4, Kt–Kt6, Kt–K5, BxP mate – or 3. P–KKt4, P–Kt5, P–Kt6, B–K6, PxP mate. Black left his King too congested – very dangerous in this game: he should move his Queen on the last of his four moves, e.g. Q–Kt1. Then White could play 3. KxB, P–K5, PxP, PxBP, PxQ=Qch, Black 3. . . . RxQ, P–B4, P–B5, P–B6, PxP, PxR=Qch and now mate by 4. K–K2, B–K6, P–Q4, P–Q5, PxKt, P–B7, PxR=Q mate.

Alice Chess

A baffling and amusing variant. In it, there are two boards and when you make a move you play from one board onto the other. You do this as follows: you play the move on the board on which the man starts and you then transfer it to the corresponding square on the other board which must be vacant for the move to be legal. The pieces all start in their normal positions on Board 1. The following may make the idea clear: 1. P–K4 (1)–(2), P–Q4 (1)–(2). Now White's KP and Black's QP are attacking each other on Board 2. 2. Kt–QB3 (1)–(2), Q x P (1)–(2). Notice (*a*) that Black's last move was not check, because the Queen finished on Board 2; (*b*) that it was quite safe, because all the guardians of the White QP were on Board 1. 3. P x P (2)–(1); the White pawn suddenly reappears on Board 1! Notice by the way that pieces are protected by men on the other board; the Black Queen on Board 2 is not seriously threatening the Knight, since if 3. . . . Q x Kt? (2)–(1) the Black Queen reappears on its QB6 on Board 1 and is at once taken.

As in ordinary chess, a player is mated if he is in check and has no way out – and some very unexpected mates arise. For example: 1. P–K4 (1)–(2), P–Q3 (1)–(2); 2. B–B4 (1)–(2), Kt–QB3 (1)–(2)??; 3. B–Kt5 (2)–(1) mate! Why? First of all, Black cannot interpose – if for example he attempts 3. . . . B–Q2 the Bishop unfortunately disappears onto Board 2 and he has no piece on Board 2 which he can move so that it reappears on Q2 or QB3 on Board 1: and Black cannot play K–Q2 (1)–(2) because the first part of the move is illegal on Board 1.

If you want to try this game, there is something to be said for using one board only, provided you have two clearly distinguishable sets of chess men. Use one set to indicate 'I am on Board 1' the other to say 'I am on Board 2' – and remember that each set can move through squares occupied by the other but not onto squares occupied by them. Whenever you complete a move, replace the man by its 'pair' in the other set.

Other forms

Those I have already given are my favourites; here are a few more out of the large number of others. The *Pocket Knight* has an element of Shogi in it; each player has an extra Knight in his pocket and can use a move when he likes to place it on any vacant square. Once on the board, it functions thereafter as a normal Knight. Interesting to play once or twice. In *Two Move Chess* each player has two moves at a time – check ends the turn and a player must get out of check on his first move. Less good

than Blitz. In *No-Capture Chess*, a man can only be taken if the capture gives mate; once you have a little experience, almost all games are drawn.

Finally, in *Refusal Chess*, each player has the right at each move to refuse to accept the first move tried by his opponent, but must accept the second. If Black cannot escape from check he is mated. Quite an interesting variant in several ways. For example, take Scholar's Mate. 1. P–K4, P–K4; 2. B–B4, B–B4; 3. Q–R5, Kt–QB3. Can White mate next move? He plays 4. Q x BP mate – Black refuses it; so he plays 4. B x P mate. Why mate? Because when Black tries to play 4. . . . K–K2 White refuses it.

The Rival: GO

'. . . the elaborate frivolity of chess . . . where the pieces have different and bizarre actions, with various and variable values, what is only complex is mistaken for what is profound'
Edgar Allan Poe, *The Murders in the Rue Morgue*, 1841

'GO UCHI WA OYA NO SHINI ME NI MO AWANU'
'a man playing GO would not stop even to be present at his parent's death-bed'   *Japanese saying*

It may equally annoy both chess players and GO players to see GO described in a book on chess; the chess players because it is not chess, the GO players that their great game should be mentioned in passing. My own view is that all chess players should know about the only board game that can rival theirs in depth and also surpass it in age – and that GO players should welcome a little extra publicity in the West.

In the famous passage from which the quotation is extracted, Poe is comparing chess unfavourably with draughts; in so doing he merely reveals his ignorance and incompetence as a chess player since the rest of the passage shows that his level of play was such that almost all his games were decided by blunders. However, more or less by accident he has stumbled on a point which, while not important in a comparison between chess and draughts (too limited a game to stand such comparison), is relevant as between chess and GO.

Other things being equal, simplicity of rules and structure is a merit in a game; and in GO we have a game which is as profound as chess and of the simplest possible structure. In 'The Nature of

Chess' I remarked that if a board game of the chess type were played on Sirius all the detail would be different; if a game like GO were played there it might well be identical.

In GO there is only one kind of piece and that never moves; the contrast with chess could hardly be greater. So far as I know there has been no major change in the rules since the invention of the game 4,000 years ago. Like chess, it is a war game; but whereas chess symbolizes a romantic-type war, dominated by the great men on either side and ending with the surrender of the King, GO is the war of the common soldier – all men are equal and the object of the game is the capture of territory. Mao Tse-tung was a keen GO player and an American author, Scott A. Boorman, in *The Protracted Game* has tried to show that Mao's strategy in the Chinese Civil War (1945–9) was based on the strategy of GO; I do not myself think that he makes his case but it is an interesting comment on GO that he should even try.

The GO board is a 19 × 19 lattice; the board is empty to begin with and the players play 'stones' alternately onto any vacant point they choose; one player has Black stones, one White, Black moving first. Pieces of one colour are connected when they are next to each other along the horizontal or vertical lines of the lattice; in this way you can build up a connected group. A group (or single piece) is surrounded when it has no access along the lines of the lattice to any vacant square (i.e. when it cannot 'breathe'). GO Plate 1 illustrates this. Diagrams I–III show a single man surrounded; note that in III the Black man at S18 is not connected to the man at T19. In diagram IV White is not surrounded; in V and VI we see a connected group surrounded. VII shows a connected group of White men, VIII an unconnected group of Black men. IX shows a group that is not surrounded because it can 'breathe' at M11, N11, O11. In diagram X, White has just played M5 and completed surrounding the Black group which will therefore be removed; notice that if Black had played last (e.g. at L5) it would be the White group of three that was surrounded.

There are certain situations in which a connected group is absolutely safe; the essential is to have two independent breathing points or 'eyes'. Plate 2, diagram II is an example. The White group is connected and Black cannot surround it without

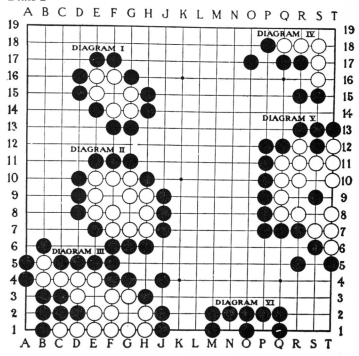

Plate 1

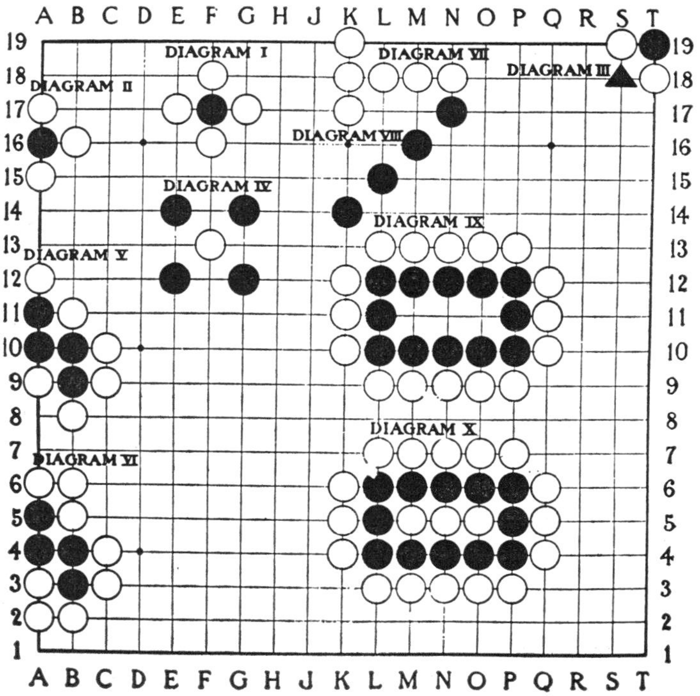

Plate 2

filling F9 and G8 – but if he plays at F9, since that does not complete the surrounding, the stone would automatically be removed as being itself surrounded. Diagram I is obviously unsafe; Black plays at F15 and takes the group. In diagram VI the Black group is safe; however in III and V, White is lost. In IV, White can save the group by playing immediately at T19 and in no other way. Try to work out III, IV and V for yourself.

The difficulty of GO is partly strategic, partly tactical. The strategic problem can be crudely described as follows: how densely need you occupy an area to conquer it, i.e. to make sure that if the enemy invades it you can surround and destroy his men. Occupy it too lightly and he will capture some of it; occupy it too heavily and he will conquer a larger area somewhere else while you are doing so. Tactical complications arise as follows: when an action takes place in one part of the board it is rarely completed – players will suddenly leave it and start play elsewhere. In the middle game therefore the board is covered with unfinished encounters, incomplete groups; there are always possibilities of joining such groups together. The other type of combination is the sacrifice of a small group in order to use the time to expand one's territory elsewhere.

Plate 3 shows the position after 80 moves in a championship game; the numbers show the order in which the moves were played – Black to R16 was the first move, White to R4 the second and so on. Black's 71 is surrounded, his 11 will be; White's group 52, 50, 58, 56 is about to be lost.

One major advantage of GO compared with chess is that it is easier for players of widely differing strengths to enjoy a game against each other. At chess, the odds of a Queen or Rook distorts the game, because the player receiving the odds can adopt the strategy of offering exchange of pieces. At GO odds of nine stones (i.e. Black puts nine stones on the board before White plays) does not alter the essential nature of the game at all.

I hope that this very brief sketch – by a very weak player! – may interest you in the only serious rival to chess.

If you want to learn how to play GO, get:

The Game of GO (Arthur Smith, Charles E. Tuttle Co., Rutland, Vermont) or *Basic Techniques of* GO (Haruyama and Nagahara, Ishi Press GO Series, Box 1021 Berkeley 1, California USA or 8 Bowls Close, Stanmore, Middlesex, England).

Plates 1 & 2 are from *The Game of* GO; plate 3 from *The Master of* GO (Tuttle.)

Plate 3

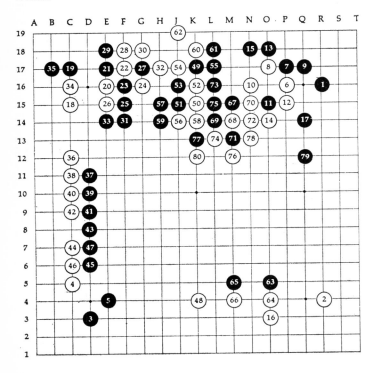

Chapter 2: Problems and endgame studies

'I could be bounded in a nutshell and count myself a king of
infinite space'   *Hamlet*

Bad writing is strewn with the corpses of analogies; let me add another decaying body to the refuse heap. Suppose one were to criticize the lines 'Hail to thee, blithe spirit, Bird thou never wert' on the grounds that the skylark was certainly a bird, that it was difficult to attach any exact anatomical or other meaning to 'blithe spirit' and that in so far as one could it was at best doubtful whether the skylark would qualify as one. Wouldn't you feel that the critic had slightly missed the point – that he was applying irrelevant tests to the poem?

The chess player who in his ignorance says of a problem, 'What an absurd position; no players would ever get into it', or 'Why didn't Black resign long ago – I've no patience with this rubbish', is exactly such a critic. He is looking in a problem for something it was not intended to supply; and naturally he doesn't find it. This type of criticism is sometimes put in an even more absurd form, 'Chess problems are so artificial'. Artificial! That a chess player can say this with a straight face – the only natural method of winning at chess (often adopted in the old days) is to take up the board and brain the opponent with it. You might as well have Laurel and Hardy attack the Marx Brothers on grounds of lack of realism.

Look at problems for what they are; a mixture of puzzle and art form. It is probably best first to enjoy them as puzzles; when you have struggled to solve them you will begin to see what else they contain besides – indeed if you never see them as anything but puzzles, you can still get a lot of pleasure from them. Endgame studies, being much closer to the game, are more naturally congenial to players; some readers may therefore find it better to come to problems via studies, though that would not be my approach – I find the complete change offered by problems more refreshing.

In this chapter, besides a brief account of problems and studies, I give twenty positions. Before reading the solutions in the text, try to solve them; even if you don't succeed, you will get a much better grasp of the positions in this way and therefore a better appreciation. Expert readers will probably feel that I have done their subject scant justice and, in particular, that I have not given examples to show the complexity and depth of the best modern problems and studies. This is undoubtedly true; my reason is that such examples would be out of place in an introduction of this kind, whose main aim is to persuade readers that there is, in problems and studies, a whole new field of chess to enjoy. If I succeed in this, then readers can extend their knowledge from some of the works listed at the end of the book.

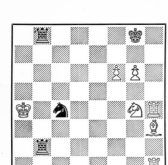

1. 'The Maiden's Problem'
(from the lost AS-SULI *ms*,
ninth century AD)

*White to play and mate in six
moves* (*old style Bishop*).

2. Abu'n-Na'am
(from the lost AL-AOLI *ms*,
ninth century)

*White to play and mate in
three moves*

Early Problems

Chess problems sprang from the game in much the same way as literature sprang from everyday life; partly as story telling, partly as heroic exaggeration – or, if you prefer it, as a mixture of lying and boasting. Our first two problems, both from the ninth century, illustrate this.

In the first problem – White to play and mate in six moves – remember that the Bishop has the old, not the modern move, i.e. it can move two squares only, but it can jump an intervening piece. Thus, in the diagram the Bishop has two moves, B–B5 and B–B1; B–Kt2 is not a possible move. The story of 'The Maiden's Problem' or 'Dilaram's Mate' is that White, a confirmed gambler, had staked his favourite wife, Dilaram, on the game. In the diagrammed position he is threatened with mate by either R–R1 or R–R7. What should he do? Dilaram – a better player evidently than her husband – looking at the board from behind the harem screen cried 'Sacrifice your Rooks, Oh Prince, and save Dilaram; forward with your Bishop and your Pawn and with the Knight deal death'; and it was hardly surprising that White was now able to find the winning line. *1. R–R8ch, K x R; 2. B–B5 dis ch, R–R7; 3. R x Rch, K–Kt1; 4. R–R8ch, K x R; 5. P–Kt7ch, K–Kt1; 6. Kt–R6 mate.*

(In passing, if the Bishop were the modern piece it would be mate in 4 by 1. R–R8ch, K x R; 2. B–Kt2ch, K–Kt1; 3. B–Q5ch, K–B1; 4. R–R8 mate.)

The second position shows the other element in early composition; there is a note to the position which says, 'This happened to Abu'n-Na'am and he used to boast of it', the solution being *1. Kt–R5ch, R x Kt; 2. R x Ktch, K x R; 3. R–K6 mate.* As Weenink justly remarks in *The Chess Problem* (my account of the early history is based on this admirable book), 'that [the position] is largely "composed" is clear from the strong attack of the Black force. White would have been mated on the previous move, if the position had been approached in the course of a game.' In both these positions we see a feature that characterizes all early problems, that if White does not give mate he will immediately be mated himself. There are two reasons for this – one aesthetic and one practical. The aesthetic one is the 'heroic' element – the same love for victory against hopeless odds which permeates early story-telling; the practical one is that, as Weenink says, the counter-threats are the chief element in establishing the soundness of the problem – it must be check, check all the way or the sky will fall on White. This effect of restricting White's choice is precisely the one which the modern problem does its utmost to avoid.

In mediaeval times a third strand, a very curious one, came in; the problem was used by the 'con man' – a chess equivalent of the three card trick. Look at diagram 3; no, the omission of the White King is not a printer's error, but a vital part of the confidence trick. The operator sets up the position as shown and asks the victim to bet whether or not White can mate in two moves. Now this position with the four Knights on the diagonal was well known and there is a mate by *1. R–B2ch, Kt x R; 2. Kt–Kt3*. If the customer says 'no mate', it is too simple; the mate is shown and the stake collected. If however he knows the position and bets that there is a mate, then the reply was 'How stupid of me (or 'by my halidom' or whatever was current), I've forgotten the White King' – which is then casually added on KKt4. White plays 1. *R–B2ch* to be met by 1. . . . *Kt x Rch* and again the stake is collected. Next day, they meet again and the operator appears to have forgotten the previous encounter. The victim, with feeble cunning, asks for the White King to be added – and it is put on KR3; noting that 1. . . . Kt x R would again be check after 1. R–B2ch, he now bets 'no mate in two'. But alas – *1. R x Kt!* and mate is unavoidable. Should the limit to the better's gullibility still not have been reached, a Black pawn is inserted on its QB5; now, with K on KR3, *1. R x Kt* is met by *1. . . . P–B6!* and there is no mate. Still more punishment requested? Then the Black pawn is put on QB6, not QB5, with White's King still on KR3. *1. R x Kt!* now does force mate, as Black must move and any move is fatal.

Curiously enough, this ignoble genre had some good features technically. Because the problems had to be easily grasped, the mates were short – and the shortening of problems was in the long run a benefit because it allowed the idea of a number of alternative lines (impracticable in longer problems) to be introduced; also it tended to lead to unnecessary pieces that played no part in the problem being removed.

Sam Loyd

Lying, boasting and cheating – these were the humble beginnings of the modern problem. There was comparatively little technical advance until the nineteenth century, when a gradual change began to take place. Before going on to the moderns it is worth looking at two problems by one of the

3. 'CIVIS BONONIÆ *ms*' (probably about 1300)

White to play and – perhaps – mate in two moves

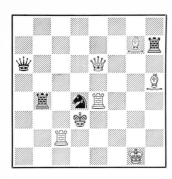

4. S. LOYD (*Leslie's Illustrated Newspapers*, 1856)

White to play and mate in four moves

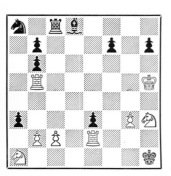

5. S. LOYD (*London Era*, 1861) 'Excelsior'

White to play and mate in five moves

greatest of all composers, Sam Loyd, who to some extent bridged the gap between old and new.*

First, No. 4 – a striking 'old style' problem composed by Loyd at the age of 15. The solution is *1. R x Ktch!, K x R* (1. . . . R x R; 2. Q–K2 mate); *2. R–Q2ch!, K x R* (2. . . . K–Kt8 or B8; 3. Q–K1); *3. Q–K1ch!, K x Q* (3. . . . K–Q6; 4. Q–K2 mate or 3. . . . K–B7; 4. Q–Q1 mate); *4. B–B3 mate.* Fundamentally, this is like the old Arab problems; it is checking throughout and must be because of Black's counterchecks. However, even in this problem by a 15-year-old we see some advance on the Arabs; there are subsidiary variations, the solution is less obvious, the position does not pretend to be a game position and it is altogether more sophisticated.

The second Loyd problem is an extraordinary tour-de-force and is a remarkable example of the chess problem as a specialized form of puzzle. For its background, here is Loyd himself. 'It was quite an impromptu to catch old Dennis Julien, the problemist, with. He used to wager that he could analyse any position, so as to tell which piece the principal mate was accomplished with. So I offered to make a problem, which he was to analyse and tell which piece did *not* give the mate. He at once selected the Queen's Knight pawn as the most improbable piece, but the solution will show you which of us paid for the dinner.' The solution is *1. P–QKt4!* (threatening 2. R–Q5 and 3. R–Q1 mate; 1. R–Q5 is defeated by 1. . . . R–B4!), *R–B4ch* (best); *2. P x R, P–R7*; *3. P–B6* (threat 4. R–KB5), *B–B2* (to meet R–KB5 with B–B5); *4. P x P, any move; 5. P x Kt ⇌ Q mate.* Here we can see features of the modern problem coming in. First, the quiet, non-checking moves; only the final move in the main variation is a check – this at once, by increasing the choice of possible Black replies, makes the problem both more difficult and less limited. Equally significant, there is no surplus fat in the position; every man on each side is necessary. Why have a Black pawn on KR2 for instance? Because otherwise 1. P–QKt4 will be met by 1. . . . B moves and 2. . . . R–R1ch. And the White Knight on QR1? This inept-looking officer has two vital functions; to meet 1. . . . R x P with 2. Kt x R and (in the main line) after 2. . . . P–R7 to prevent the pawn queening. But we are only halfway

---

*Sam Loyd was born in Philadelphia in 1841 and died in Elisabeth, New Jersey, in 1911; he was an expert solver and composer of puzzles of all sorts. His notepaper heading – an autobiography in itself – reads 'Sam Loyd, Journalist and Advertising Expert, Original Games, Novelties, Supplements, Souvenirs, etc. for Newspapers . . . Author of the famous *Get Off the Earth Mystery, Trick Donkeys, 15 Block Puzzle, Pigs in Clover, Parcheesi*, etc., etc.' He was also a good but not outstanding player.

to a modern problem; a brilliant puzzle, staggering one by its ingenuity – but nothing more. To see what else there can be, take our sixth example, by the Czech composer, Miroslav Havel.

The Modern Problem

The solution to this three-mover is *1. Kt–R5*. Now Black has four possible moves: *P–B5, K–Q2, K–B4 and K–Q4. A. 1. . . . P–B5; 2. Kt–B6, K–B4; 3. R–QB1 mate. B. 1. . . . K–Q2; 2. Kt–Q4, K–K2; 3. R–Kt7 mate. C. 1. . . . K–B4; 2. R–B1ch, K–Q4; 3. Kt(5)–B4 mate. D. 1. . . . K–Q4; 2. Q–B7, K–K3; 3. Kt(2)–B4 mate.* For the first time the word 'beauty' might occur to us; why? Well, first there is an extraordinary feeling of space and quiet about the problem; the Black King seems able to go where he likes free from any interference by White. This is allied with an impression of delicacy and subtlety arising from the indirectness of the threats. 'The spider's touch, how infinitely fine, Feels on each thread and lives along the line.' Then there is the economy of the problem. Look at the four mating positions. In A, B and C all the White force (except the King in A and B) is needed to control the nine squares of the Black King's field and no square is controlled more than once; such mates are called models. D is not a model mate because the White Rook is not involved, but it is 'pure', i.e. no square in the King's field is guarded more than once. Finally, there is a striking geometrical connection between the mating positions in A and B; in essence the B position is the same as A turned through a right angle.

This problem is different in kind from the earlier ones. Even the most barefaced Abu'n-Na'am would not boast of having played this in a game – and no Dilaram would have to advise her husband on how to win as White. The position has nothing to do with the game; and even the puzzle element, dominant in Loyd's five-mover, is quite secondary here – though the problem is not easy to solve. The aim of the problem is aesthetic – its difficulty is only relevant in the contribution it makes to the overall effect on the solver. For the first time in these examples we see a modern problem; neither a story, nor a puzzle but a small-scale work of art.

There are, however, important elements in a modern problem which hardly appear at all in Havel's three-mover. Elegant though the play and mating positions are, it has little formal structure; for this reason it is a type of problem in which the ideas are rather quickly exhausted – after a while you begin to feel that there is nothing new to do. The Bohemian school, of which Havel was the greatest exponent, has exhausted the type.

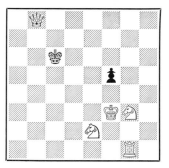

6. M.HAVEL (*Vynalezy A. Pokroky, 1904*)

White to play and mate in three moves

7. A.ELLERMAN (First Prize, *Guidelli Memorial Tourney*, 1925)

White to play and mate in two moves

8. PROF. R.C.O.MATTHEWS (First prize, *The Problemist*, 1951)

White to play and mate in three moves

To see what is meant by structure, look at problem 7; this was thought by the great English composer Comins Mansfield to be the finest two-move problem ever made.

The key-move is *1. R–Q7*, threatening 2. Q–KB4 mate, to which Black has six possible defences. First there are three variations with the Black Queen. A. *1. . . . Q–Q5; 2. Kt–Q6.* B. *1. . . . Q–K4; 2. Kt–B5.* C. *1. . . . Q–R1ch; 2. Kt–Q8.* All these defences unpin the White Knight, which discovers mate from the Bishop on a different square for each Queen move; notice in A and B, how the fact that the Black Queen blocks one of the King's possible flight squares allows White in turn to cut off a Rook's guard on the square. Then we have two more 'self-block' variations: D. *1. . . . R–Q5; 2. R–K7.* E. *1. . . . B–B6; 2. Q–Q3.* The sixth variation is F. *1. . . . B–B7; 2. QxQB* bringing in yet another geometrical idea – line opening and closing. B–B7 opens the rank for 2. QxQB and at the same time closes the second rank to the Black Queen, so that 2. QxQB cannot be met by 2. . . . Q–KKt7. Finally, why does the White Rook have to play to Q7 on the first move; why not R–Q8 or R–Q1? If 1. R–Q8 then 1. . . . Q–KB7! and since White cannot now play Kt–Q8 there is no mate; and if 1. R–Q1 then 1. . . . Q–Q7!

We can see what a strong geometrical, structural pattern this problem has. Unpinning, discoveries, self-blocking, line opening and closing – these are all geometrical ideas; and the number of these ideas and the ways of combining them opened a very wide field to the composer. However, we are still not at the end of even this sketchy account.

Problem 8 shows a new logical idea; that of 'changed mates' which can be superimposed on the geometrical and combinative ideas in Ellerman's masterpiece. To explain it we have first to explain set play. Suppose that in Problem 8 (by Professor

R.C.O.Matthews, one of the leading English composers), White was allowed to pass his first move and force Black to play instead, then he would win as follows. If Black moves either Knight he is immediately mated (by QR–B1 or B–Q3); he must then move his Queen, but at the same time the Queen must guard her QR6 and K6 against Kt–R3 or Kt–K3. There are only two squares from which she can do this, QR2 and K2. If 1. . . . Q–R2 then White plays 2. B–Kt4! (not 2. B–Q4?, Q–K2), and Black can no longer guard the two vital squares since if 2. . . . Q–K2 then 3. Kt–R3 mate. If 1. . . . Q–K2 then 2. B–Q4! (not 2. B–Kt4?, Q–R2), Q–R2; 3. Kt–K3 mate. Now this play which assumes that White misses his first move is called the set play – because it is inherent, so to speak, in the position as set up. But White must move – and there is no move which preserves the status quo; if there had not been a Black pawn on KR5 White could have preserved it by K–R2 – and a very dull problem would result. White's key move in fact is *1. Kt–Q7!* threatening *2. KtxQ.* As before Black can reply 1. . . . Q–R2 or 1. . . . Q–K2. If *1. . . . Q–R2* then *2. B–Q4!* (not now 2. B–Kt4?, P–B3!) and if *1. . . . Q–K2* then *2. B–Kt4!* (2. B–Q4?, P–B3!). And there is the uninteresting line 1. . . . QxKt; 2. BxQ.

Now compare the set and actual play and we have the following complete solution:

Set play: *1. . . . Q–R2; 2. B–Kt4!* (2. B–Q4?, Q–K2!) etc.
   1. . . . Q–K2; 2. B–Q4! (2. B–Kt4?, Q–R2!) etc.
Actual play: *1. Kt–Q7!, Q–R2; 2. B–Q4!* (2. B–Kt4?, P–B3!)
   1. . . . Q–K2; 2. B–Kt4! (2. B–Q4?, P–B3!)

the White second moves being interchanged between set and actual play. Apart from the 'changed mate' aspect, this is a 'focal' problem, the two foci being the squares QR3 and K3, both of which the Black Queen must try to protect.

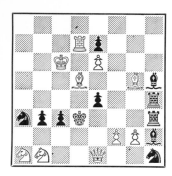

9. C.MANSFIELD
(First Prize,
Die Schwalbe, 1956)

*White to play and mate
in two moves*

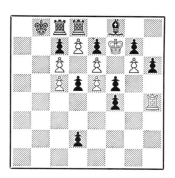

10. DR O.T.BLATHY
(*Vielugige Schachaufgoren*,
1890)

*White to play and mate
in 102 moves*

Problem No. 9 is our final example of a new idea in the modern problem – that of 'virtual play', an extension of the changed mate theme just described. One of the many geometrical themes in problems is that of playing a piece onto the intersection of the lines of action of an enemy Rook and Bishop, so that if one of the pieces captures, it interferes with the other. In Problem 9 we might, for example, play 1. P–Kt4, threatening both Q×KtP mate and Q–Q1 mate with the play 1. . . . . B×P; 2. Q×KP mate and 1. . . . . R×P; 2. Q–Q1 mate. Unfortunately, however, 1. P–KKt4 is defeated by 1. . . . . Kt×P! guarding both threats. What about 1. P–KKt3? This cuts off the other Rook and Bishop; 1. . . . R×P; 2. B×KtP mate and 1. . . . B×P; 2. Q–K3. But 1. . . . . Kt–B7! saves the day. Or 1. P–B4? 1. . . . . B×P; 2. Q×KP. 1. . . . R×P; 2. B×KtP; no, 1. . . . P–K6! Finally try *1. P–B3!* 1. . . . R×P; 2. Q–Q1; 1. . . . B×P; 2. Q–K3. Can Black defend against both these threats? Yes, by 1. . . . . R–B5 or 1. . . . . B–B5; but *1. . . . . R–B5; 2. B×KtP* and *1. . . . . B–B5; 2. Q×KP*. Now we can set out the complete solution.

1. P–Kt4?, threat Q×KP or Q–Q1, defeated by *1. . . . Kt×P!*
1. P–Kt3?, threat B×KtP or Q–K3, defeated by *1. . . . Kt–B7!*
1. P–B4?, threat Q×KP or B×KtP, defeated by *1. . . . P–K6!*
1. P–B3!, threat Q–Q1 or Q–K3, *1. . . . R–B5; 2. B×KtP.*
                                1. . . . B–B5; 2. Q×KP.

The three unsuccessful tries, P–Kt4, P–Kt3 and P–B4, give the virtual play; the mates that would occur if these moves solved the problem. The true solution has the same ideas as the tries and the various defences bring in all the four mates that were threatened in the tries. The analogy with music is evident; we have three presentations of the theme in the threats and play after the three tries, brought together in the fourth presentation with the true key move.

The Wilder Shores
'Though this be madness, yet there is method in 't'
Polonius in *Hamlet*

This completes our brief account of the main lines of development of the problem. Any problemist will realize how sketchy and partial it is; I hope, however, that it will be enough to make some readers at least want to know more about the subject. Before leaving problems, I will say something still more briefly about developments outside the main stream.

One type which I mention more as a curiosity than for any other reason is the long-range problem of which Problem No. 10 is an example – White to play and mate in one hundred and two moves. All these problems have the same basic idea and once you have mastered it they are easy to solve.

In the diagrammed position play *1. R–R1, K–R2; 2. R–R1ch, K–Kt1*. Now, if you imagine the Black pawns on Q4, Q7, B4, B5 and R3 removed and give Black the move, he has to commit suicide by R×P or R–K1. However, the pawns are there and it is White's move; he dare not leave the back rank with his Rook (because of P–Q8=Q) and if he moves along it then he frees the Black King. So he plays the following manoeuvre: *3. K–Kt8, R–K1; 4. K–R8, R(K1)–Q1* (R(B1)–Q1 comes to the same thing); *5. K–R7, R–K1; 6. K–Kt8, R(K1)–Q1; 7. K–B7.* Now we have returned to the position five moves earlier, but with Black not White to move; so he is forced to use up one of his spare pawn moves, e.g. by *7. . . . P–B6*. White then repeats his King manoeuvre gradually forcing the Black pawns to advance until – at move 57 – one of them must queen. Then we have *57. . . . P–Q8=Q; 58. R×Q, K–R2; 59. R–R1ch, K–Kt1; 60. K–Kt8.* One after another the Black pawns must immolate themselves

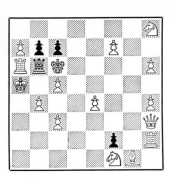

11. H.W.BETTMANN
(First prize, *Babson Memorial Tourney*, 1923)

White to play and force Black to mate him in three moves

and by move 96 the last one has gone. The problem then ends with *97. R–R1ch, K–Kt1; 98. R–R2, RxP; 99. KPxR, R–Q1; 100. P–K6, R–B1; 101. PxR=Qch, KxQ; 102. R–R8 mate.* (In *Ultimate Themes*, T.R.Dawson mentions that, using a 10 x 10 board, J.N.Babson contributed a direct mate in 1,900 moves for the *British Chess Magazine* Christmas issue 1893; this monstrosity was cooked in 1,896 moves, subsequently revised to 1,866).

Then there are problems in which the conditions differ in some way from those of ordinary chess; these are grouped together under the somewhat unfortunate name of Fairy Chess. Those which simply introduce new pieces I find rather dull – a more interesting group are those with different objectives: two types of these are fairly well known – selfmates and helpmates. In selfmates, White compels Black to mate him; Problem 11 is a remarkable example of this class. White's aim is fairly clear – he wants to compel Black to play RxR mate; but the solution is extraordinary. The first move is *1. P–R8=B;* this pins the QKtP without protecting the Rook on R6, as 1. P–R8=Q would do. Now we have the four variations. A. *1. . . . PxB=Q; 2. P–B8=Q!, QxPch or QxKt; 3. P–Kt5ch, QxP mate.* If 2. . . . Q any other move, White captures it and Black must play his only legal move, *3. . . . RxR mate.* B. *1. . . . PxB=R; 2. P–B8=R!, RxKt; 3. RxR, RxR mate.* Not, however, 2. P–B8=Q?, RxKt!; 3. Q (either) xR and the R on R6 is protected. C. *1. . . . PxB=B; 2. P–B8=B!* (2. P–B8=Q, R or Kt?, BxP!) *BxP; 3. BxB, RxR mate.* D. *1. . . . PxB=Kt; 2. P–B8=Kt!* (2. P–B8=Q?, KtxQ!, 3. RxKt, K–Q2) *KtxQ; 3. RxKt, RxR mate.*

In helpmates the players cooperate in getting Black mated; problem No. 12 is a good example, again by that master of problems of every type, Sam Loyd.

You must envisage a mating position and then see if you can get there. The solution (Black plays first) is *1. K–B3, R–QR8; 2. K–Kt2, B–Kt8; 3. K–R1, B–K5 double check and mate.*

Finally, there are retrograde analysis problems. The convention in problems is that the position must be legal, i.e. it must be possible to reach it from the initial game position – the moves to do so need not be probable (the position usually excludes this) but they must be in accordance with the rules of chess.

Problem No. 13 is a good example by the high priest of Fairy Chess, the late T.R.Dawson. There are two stages to its solution, the first easy, the second a little harder. The first question is, 'What could Black's last move have been?'; the second and

12. S.LOYD (*Chess Monthly*, November, 1860)

Black to play and help White to mate him in three moves

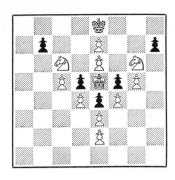

13. T.R.DAWSON (*Falkirk Herald*, 1914)

White to play and mate in two moves

harder question, 'Why is there only one possible answer and not two?' A quick examination shows that Black's last move must have been either P(B2)–B4 or P(Q2)–Q4; to either of these White replies PxP *en passant* followed by P–B7 or P–Q7 mate. But which of these moves was played? Unexpectedly, we are able to find out. For the White pawns to have reached their present positions they must have made ten captures; so, as Black has only lost ten pieces altogether, they must all have been taken by White pawns. So Black's QB must have emerged from its home square, QB1 – otherwise no White pawn could have got at it; therefore Black's QP moved earlier in the game – and so his last move must have been not P(Q2)–Q4 but P(B2)–B4 and the solution is *1. KtP x P* en passant!

Retrograde analysis provides excellent puzzles and J.G. Mauldon, Professor of Mathematics at Amherst College, Mass., USA has composed a number of very fine problems of this type for Christmas competitions in my *Sunday Times* columns; I have collaborated in the minor role of writing up a story to go with them. I give an example of our combined efforts at the end of this chapter.

Endgame Studies

Endgame studies are much closer to the game than problems and players who foolishly regard problems as beneath their notice are often interested in studies. A problem is to a game as poetry is to life; a study is to a game as a detective story is to a police court report. In a study we see idealized game positions – the ideas are those of a game, but stripped of all irrelevant material and shown in a concentrated form. What one gets from such studies is a feeling of the immense potential of the game – the difficulty and subtlety that can lie hidden in the simplest position and the extraordinary power of individual pieces in special positions.

Positions 14–16 are examples of 'hidden depth'. What could be more completely hopeless than White's position in No. 14? He can never take Black's KtP because the BP or RP will queen; so all Black has to do is capture the White pawn and come across with the King. Many players would resign if they were White – and yet the position is a draw! *1. K–Kt6, K–Kt3; 2. K x P, P–B4* (*2. . . . P–R4; 3. K x P* leads to a similar finish); *3. K–B6, P–B5; 4. K–K5, P–B6; 5. K–Q6, P–B7; 6. P–B7, P=Q; 7. P=Q,* drawing. Or *1. . . . P–R4; 2. K x KtP!* (*2. K x RP?, K–Kt3* and wins), *P–R5; 3. K x P* and now (*a*) *3. . . . P–R6; 4. K–K6, P–R7; 5. P–B7* and draws, (*b*) *3. . . . K–Kt3; 4. K–K5!* and either catches the Black pawn or queens his own. One can hardly believe this even when one sees it.

Position 15 has a curious history, given in full in A.J. Roycroft's excellent book on endgame studies, *Test Tube Chess*. Move the Black King to some square on the King's side, say KR3, and White wins as follows: *1. P–B7, R–Q3ch; 2. K–Kt5, R–Q4ch; 3. K–Kt4, R–Q5ch; 4. K–Kt3, R–Q6ch; 5. K–B2* followed by queening the pawn and the Q *v*. R ending is a standard win for

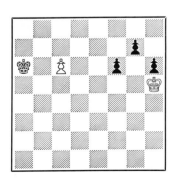

14. R.RÉTI ('*Endspielstudien*', 1928)

White to play; what result?

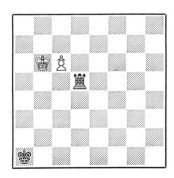

15. 'The Saavedra Study'
G.E.BARBIER and F.SAAVEDRA
(*Glasgow Weekly Citizen*, 1895)

White to play; what result?

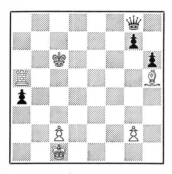

16. H. MATTISON (*Rigaer Rundschach*, 1914)

White to play and win

17. H. RINCK (*Deutsche Schachzeitung*, 1903)

White to play and win

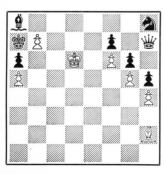

18. A. A. TROITZKY (*Novoye Vremya*, 1896)

White to play and draw

19. A. O. HERBSTMANN (*Izvestia*, 1926)

White to play and draw

the player with the Queen. Note that White must not play too soon to the QB file, e.g. 3. K–B4?, R–Q8!; 4. P–B8=Q?, R–B8ch and Black wins. So far, nothing out of the ordinary. However Barbier pointed out that if you put the Black King on QR8 as in the diagram, Black would draw after *5. K–B2* by *5. . . . R–Q5!; 6. P–B8=Q* (6. K–B3, R–Q8), *R–B5ch!; 7. Q x R* stalemate. Why then is it called the Saavedra study? Because Saavedra, a reader of the *Glasgow Weekly Citizen*, pointed out that after all White won – *5. . . . R–Q5!; 6. P–B8=R!!* (threat 7. R–R8ch), *R–QR5; 7. K–Kt6!* and the double threat of 8. R–B1 mate and 8. KxR is decisive. An extraordinary example of an accidental composition.

What do you make of position 16? One's first instinct is to play B–K3ch followed by B–B5, make Black give up his Rook for the KP and then win with the extra B and P. Unfortunately they don't win; B and RP of the 'wrong colour' (i.e. queening on a square of different colour from the Bishop) only draw, because the Black King cannot be driven out of the corner. How then does White win? By *1. B–K3ch, K–Kt2; 2. P–K7, R x P* (threat R–R1); *3. B–R7!, R–R8!; 4. K–B4, R–B8ch; 5. B–B2!* (5. K–K4?, KxB and Black wins), *R x Bch; 6. K–K3, R–B8; 7. K–K2* and the pawn queens. I wonder how many Grandmasters could play this apparently simple position correctly over the board.

Positions 17 and 18 illustrate the powers of individual pieces. In position 17, the White Rook and Bishop trap the Black Queen on an open board. *1. R–R8!, Q–R7!* (1. . . . QxR; 2. B–B3ch – the reason why Q–R2 is bad will soon appear, and other Queen moves lose at once); *2. R x P!, Q–Kt1* (2. . . . QxR; 3. B–K8ch); *3. R–R8, Q–R2; 4. B–Kt6!* and the Queen is lost. Not difficult – but very surprising.

Position 18 shows an even more striking virtuoso performance by the White Knight. 1. R–Q5! and now (*a*) *1. . . . KxR; 2. Kt–B5, K–K5; 3. K–Q2!* and draws, (*b*) *1. . . . P–B8=Q; 2. R–Q4ch!, KxR; 3. Kt–B5ch* and wherever the King goes Black's Queen is lost.

Finally, chess studies have their element of fantasy just as much as problems. First, position 19, a Bishop contra mundum. White draws by *1. P–Kt8=Qch!, K x Q; 2. K–Q7 dis ch, K–R2; 3. B–Kt1ch, K–Kt2; 4. B–B5!, Q–Kt1; 5. B–B8!!* and the game is drawn. If the Black King moves, White checks him until he goes back to Kt2 and then returns to B8 with the Bishop. If 5. . . . Q–R2 then 6. B–B5 and we are as we were; and 5. . . . QxB is stalemate! If chess players had an ecclesiastical vote, that Bishop would be Pope.

20. G.M.KASPARYAN (3rd Prize, *Moscow*, 1967)

White to play and draw

Position 20 is by one of the leading modern composers. *1. Kt–B4*, threatening (*a*) 2. Kt–Kt6ch and 3. KtxQ, (*b*) 2. Kt–K6ch and 3. P–B8=Qch. So *1. . . . K–Kt2*. Now *2. P–B8= Qch!*, *BxQ* (*2. . . . KxQ; 3. Kt–Kt6ch and 4. KtxQ); 3. P–R8=Qch!!*, *QxQ (3. . . . KxQ; 4. Kt–Kt6ch); 4. Kt–R5ch, K–Kt1 or R2 dis ch; 5. Kt–B6ch, K–Kt2; 6. Kt–R5ch* and draws. This might quite literally be said to be a perpetual check and a half.

And now, to end this chapter, the Mauldon Christmas puzzle. In tackling this, there are two things to do: first to discover all the possible positions – then to satisfy yourself that they are legal, i.e. could be reached in an actual game.

The Mauldon Puzzle

'1972 has been an exciting year for chess in our part of the world. Traditionally the conservative village of Markston supplies the local chess champion, young Horace Spatchcock being their leading man at present. Judge of our surprise when Markston's great rivals, the brash Yonkers, not generally addicted to chess, suddenly produced "Loopy" Fizzer. Markston sent over old "Tiger" Peters, their former champion, to play Loopy but the Tiger came back badly mauled and there was nothing for it but for Spatchcock to tackle Fizzer himself.

Well, Fizzer's famous victory is local history now and I won't go into all the troubles we had – how the match had to be played at Coldbury Hamlet, how it would all have fallen through if Squire Thatcher hadn't put up an extra fiver prize money, how Fizzer had all the 75 watt bulbs replaced by 100 watts and then played in dark glasses throughout, and so on. Anyway, they played, and the diagram shows the lunchtime position in one of the games with Spatchcock to move.

Now even Fizzer and Spatchcock make mistakes, and as they were going out of the room to lunch, we heard the following snatch of conversation. Fizzer: "Your move, huh?" Spatchcock: "Yes. You know, Loopy, I could have checkmated you on my last move." Fizzer: "Yeah, Horace, fancy missing that. Sometimes you miss a mate with a Queen but it wasn't one of those." None of us had seen any of the previous play (we didn't even know whether Spatchcock was White or Black), so we tried to work out from the lunchtime position and this conversation what the position must have been when Spatchcock missed the mate. One of our difficulties was that the White pawn shown as on the line between K2 and KB2 must have been shifted slightly as the players got up, so that we could not tell which of these two squares it was on (though we were sure that its correct square was either K2 or KB2) – so we had to consider both possibilities. We spent hours on the position; one of us thought he could work out which square the pawn was on and what the missed mate must have been – others disagreed with him in one way or another.

In fact, how many possibilities (for the position when Spatchcock missed the mate) were there in the light of our information – and what were they?'

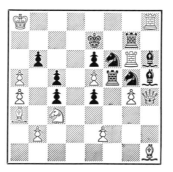

The Mauldon Puzzle

Solution to Professor Mauldon's Puzzle

'There are seven legal positions which satisfy the conditions.

(*a*) With White pawn on K2: two solutions, in each of which Spatchcock is White. 1. The position when Spatchcock, as White, missed the mate was K4R2/p3k1r1/1N2pnRb/, the rest the same as the basic position. White can play 1. B x BP mate, but actually the game went 1. R–R8, P x Kt giving the basic position. 2. Position K6R/4kpr1/1p2bnRb/P1pPPrnb/, rest the same: Black has just played P(B2)–B4. White can play 1. P x P e.p. mate, but the game went 1. P x B, BP x P – basic position. One of the two Black Bishops on a white square must of course be a promoted pawn.

(*b*) With White pawn on KB2: five solutions. 3–6. As 1 above, but Black's KR1 can be vacant or be occupied by a Rook, Knight or Queen, but not by a Bishop. 7. This is the only solution in which Spatchcock is Black. Position K3k2r/6rR/, rest the same as basic. Black, not having previously moved his King, plays 1. . . . 0–0 mate; the game went 1. . . . K–K2 dis ch; 2. R x R – basic position.

These seven positions are all legal and Professor Mauldon has constructed games in outline to show how each of them can be reached.

Position 7 with White P on K2 is also legal, but can be reached only by the promotion, without capturing, of either White's QP or KBP and either of these possibilities implies that the Black King has moved and therefore castling is impossible. Position 2 with White P on KB2 is illegal since it would require that, after at most one pawn-file-change on each side, the King's pawns must have dodged round each other. Other potential 'solutions' are excluded by the fact that they similarly involve the collision of the two KRPs or else require too many pawn captures. All positions in which Spatchcock's missed mate was with a Queen are ruled out by Fizzer's remark: "... Sometimes you miss a mate with a Queen but it wasn't one of those".'

Section 5 : The Iconography of chess

Chapter 13 : Chess and visual Art

Chapter 14 : Chess and Literature

Pawn .   Rook .   Knight .   Bishop.   Queen .   King.

Chapter 13: Chess and visual Art

'All chess players are artists'   Marcel Duchamp

In an earlier chapter we looked at the theoretical question, 'Is Chess an Art?' In this section we look at the connections in practice between chess and various forms of art. At first sight it is surprising that we have chapters on chess and visual art and on chess and literature, but none on chess and music – for undoubtedly it is music that most resembles chess and there have been a number of people who have excelled in both. Philidor is the outstanding example, and Prokofiev was a keen player; the famous violinists Menuhin and Oistrakh are both addicts. Amongst chess players Taimanov is a concert pianist, Smyslov a talented singer. The brilliantly gifted Yugoslav, Fuderer, could have been a professional pianist or chess player – and became a scientist. These are just a few of many cases; only mathematics is more closely connected with chess than music.

But we cannot express any of the aspects of chess directly in music in the way that we can in painting and literature – so music does not feature in this section. It is in the more concrete arts that the abstractions of chess find a different form of expression.

Chess touches and intersects with visual art at many points and in many ways. In this chapter we try through the illustrations to show some of these ways; basically this is a chapter to be looked at rather than read. However, a summary of the main types of interaction may, I hope, add something to readers' enjoyment of the illustrations.

The most immediate point of contact lies in the chess sets themselves. A well-designed set is a beautiful object and we enjoy looking at it; the *Directoire* 18th-century French set (previous page) and the standard modern Staunton pattern sets are examples of this.

It is curious that many people who dislike abstract art will look with pleasure at, say, a Staunton set, in which the designs of the pieces are highly abstract representations – look for instance at the King and Queen – whereas the more modern pieces, which show the nature of the moves in their design, seem to us more abstract – but are actually more concrete.

Chess sets, like other human artefacts, carry with them various overtones which add extra depth to the pleasure we take in their appearance. Age is the most obvious – for example the recent Russian finds (page 38) of what may be the oldest of all

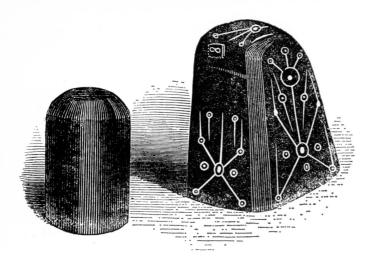

Above: the 'Warrington' men, 11th century
Below: Nigerian Chessmen, 1972

known chess pieces, or the Warrington men – but not the only one. Chess has always been regarded not only as a game, but as a symbol, an *eidolon*, of life and war. This is reflected in many ways – amongst them, the design of sets. In the 18th and 19th centuries particularly, sets were made to illustrate political, military or social conflicts. One set shows Louis XVI and Marie Antoinette with Lafayette as a Bishop, opposed by George III and Queen Charlotte with Clive and Cornwallis as Bishops; and there are Indian sets depicting the struggles between the early East India Company and the native states. Coming to more modern times, in the first flush of revolutionary enthusiasm in Russia there were sets showing the struggle between capitalist and communist societies; the capitalist pawns were all bound in chains in contrast to the free workers who constituted the communist pawns. Such sets could I suppose never become really popular because of the awkwardness when the wrong side won. Finally, we have sets such as the Nigerian one shown below, where the pieces have no propaganda purpose but simply show the local people. I find this a set of great freshness and charm.

As well as chess pieces being used as art objects in their own right, they are frequently used as incidental 'props' in paintings. They can be used purely as decorative objects – like apples or

guitars; or the game itself can be used as a focus for some kinds of human emotion. If you want to show the characters and feelings of people in a situation of conflict and to concentrate attention on the individuals and not the issue, a game of chess is an excellent way of doing so. Look for example at the Cruikshank drawing: a number of the less admirable emotions are vividly portrayed – but because the cause of these feelings is not essentially important, the whole tone of the picture is lightened. It is comedy, not tragedy. Chess is used in a similar way in political cartoons: by transferring the conflict from real life to the chess board, one lightens the effect without blunting the impact.

Chess also figures in art – mostly bad art – as a form of reportage. A typical example of this is the painting of the match between Leonardo and Lopez at the court of Philip II. It is an indifferent painting – but we can't help being interested. It happened and it was drama. Similarly no chess player can fail to enjoy the picture of Staunton playing St. Amant (page 140). In modern times, another form of visual reportage is the postage stamp with chess as its subject; the pioneer was Bulgaria in 1947 and about a hundred of these minuscule objects have now been produced by countries scattered all over the world.

So far, none of the examples we have considered have much to do with the content and nature of chess itself. We come a little closer to this when we look at chess as an allegory of life, which gives a number of contacts between chess and art, visual and literary.

Many of the early books on chess are not really about chess at all; they are 'moralities', using chess as an analogy. The most famous of these was written in 1275 by a Dominican friar, Jacobus de Cessolis and translated from the French by Caxton 200 years later as *The Game and Playe of the Chesse* (see jacket). Anyone looking for technical instruction would be sorely disappointed: the book is a social homily. It is amusing to see his allocation of the pawns to occupations; KRP – husbandmen, KKtP – smiths, KBP – drapers and notaries, KP – merchants, QP – physicians, QBP – innkeepers, QKtP – city guards and (why this unwarranted slur on a harmless pawn?) QRP – ribalds and gamblers. But at a higher level than this rather pedestrian affair, chess has persistently been regarded as a picture of the struggle of the human being with forces beyond his control. In earlier times, one of the most popular fables was that of man playing the devil for his soul; the devil, about to give mate, finds that the mating move forms the pieces into the shape of the cross, is therefore unable to play the move and loses. In

Above: 'Game of Chess' by George Cruikshank, 1835
Below: 'A Chess match at the Court of Spain'
by Luigi Mussini 1813–88

Above: McKnight Kauffer's design for 'Death', Checkmate, *1937*
Below: Ingmar Bergman's The Seventh Seal, *1957*

more modern days, man's struggle against death is a typical theme. Two outstanding examples are the ballet *Checkmate* (composer Sir Arthur Bliss – Master of the Queen's Musick – and choreographer Ninette de Valois), and the Ingmar Bergman film *The Seventh Seal*.

In *Checkmate* (first performed on 15th June 1937 at Sadler's Wells) Red and Black represent Love and Death; in a hopeless struggle, the Red King is stripped of all his defenders and finally, senile and helpless, is struck down by the Black Queen. At one moment in the game, the Red Knight has the Black Queen at his mercy but is overcome by her beauty and cannot kill her (a touch that would surely have Freud's approval). Bergman must I think have known the ballet and it may have influenced his film, the basic idea of which is said to have come from a mediaeval painting of Death as a chess player. Here a Swedish knight, his faith shaken by the horrors of the plague, challenges Death to a game of chess with his life as the stake. By thus engaging Death's attention he saves others, but ultimately loses the game and his own life – and fails to discover from Death the meaning of existence.

In this use of chess in art, we are still not looking at chess as itself an art form but we are perhaps approaching it; something of the nature of chess itself is used when it is employed as an allegory. Before coming to the central question, however, let me dispose of one visual aspect which does not fit easily into a general plan: chess used as an image and an idea in advertising.

There are three ways in which chess is used in advertising. The first is chess as a status symbol – a sign of gracious living (alas, how little the advertiser knows of the average club player nowadays – hooked on this diabolical game, he has not the time, the inclination or the necessary qualities for gracious living); the players in these advertisements can only play while smoking the finest Havanas and drinking the best Scotch – though judging from some of the positions they get into, they might do better to be a little more abstemious. This form of advertisement underlies a paradox about chess; it used to be a court game and confined to the upper classes – now from a social viewpoint it has split into two games. Serious chess is a classless game, the players are mainly young and even the amateurs play (or try to play) in professional style; surroundings and conditions (though improving) tend to be poor. Social chess, i.e. chess played at home by the middle aged as a relaxation, is still an upper-middle-class game; so perhaps these advertisements are not so wide of the mark after all. Next we have what is probably only a temporary phenomenon; chess as a 'with it' activity, an 'in-game'. Here the players are much younger than in the first type of advertisement; up to the minute in all they do, they have learnt the latest game by following Fischer/Spassky. I fear that these ephemeral creatures have now moved on to backgammon – though no doubt when Fischer plays Karpov in 1975 or 1978 they (or rather their successors) will be back again. Finally there is a new type of advertisement, of which an example can be seen on the right, the chessplayer as the wise man. I found this advertisement very interesting. If one just looks on the surface, one says 'here's the expert, the Man who Knows Better' advising the ordinary chap (eyes, pipe, glasses, sweater; the kindly superbrain all over). But if you are a chess player it's a lot more interesting. It's quite a sensible position – it might be from a real game. And where is the White Queen going? It looks like R6 – but then the Black King takes it. 1. Q–R6ch, KxQ; 2. PxP dis ch – is this a brilliancy? It is – from a game P.Schmidt *v.* A.N.Other and it is mate in nine moves, with sacrifice of Q, R, B and Kt. Yes indeed – if this can happen, how safe is your money or anything else? I believe that this form of 'wise man' advertisement will increase; and it is interesting to see that in general in chess advertisements much more trouble is taken to avoid absurd positions, putting the board the wrong way round (though this still happens, it no longer occurs 50% of the time) and other errors of the type that can only occur if the advertiser is wholly ignorant of the game and indifferent to its players.

Finally, what about chess not as a vehicle for visual art but as an art itself? So far as I know, there has only been one man who was both an important visual artist and a fine chess player – Marcel Duchamp. He played four times in the Olympiads for France and although he did badly, that was not so much from lack of natural ability as from lack of technique and will to win. As an artist he was the forerunner of much in modern art and one of the greatest creative figures – some would say the greatest – in 20th-century art. In Duchamp, a man whose interests were equally divided between chess and art, we have someone uniquely qualified to speak; in these paragraphs I try to give a summary of his views.

Duchamp was deeply opposed to what we may call the 'connoisseur' view of art – art as a series of beautiful objects with a hierarchy of values and grades of desirability set up partly by tradition, partly by the artist's name and partly by the current auction room prices. He thought that this attitude corrupted art and artists. His beliefs led him to experiment with un-

Advertisement, UK *1972*

Above: Tournament poster designed by Duchamp

Below: 'King and Queen surrounded by Swift Nudes', 1912

conventional media and to use original, even outlandish, forms. He presented as art works ready-made objects – such as a coat rack – where there was no artistic association with the past. His opposition to the material art object as a possession to be prized led him towards the idea of abstracting art from its physical body, almost to the extent of rendering it wholly immaterial. Chess, with its abstract beauty lying in the mind, and its physical representation on the chess board being in equally abstract symbols, wholly unconnected with the visual objects of real life, had therefore a strong appeal to him; he felt that in some way visual art ought to be like this. At the same time he was aware of the fundamental contradiction within chess, viewed in this light; that while chess may sometimes be a form of art, it is always a game. To have ideas you must think like an artist; but to win you must be a technician, a scientist and a fighter – above all an opportunist. At any moment one must be ready to jettison one's whole plan in order to fork the enemy King and Queen. He had therefore an ambivalent attitude to chess; in its ideal form chess was an art and all chess players were artists – in practice the picture was muddied by the inevitable materialism of any game. I suspect (without knowing) that Tal would have been his ideal modern player and Anderssen his hero from the past. Let Duchamp himself have the final word in this chapter; he is speaking at the August 1952 banquet of the New York Chess Association. We needn't agree with him, but we must respect his opinion.

'Objectively, a game of chess looks very much like a pen-and-ink drawing, with the difference, however, that the chess player paints with black-and-white forms already prepared instead of inventing forms as does the artist. The design thus formed on the chessboard has apparently no visual aesthetic value, and is more like a score for music, which can be played again and again. Beauty in chess does not seem to be a visual experience as in painting. Beauty in chess is closer to beauty in poetry; the chess pieces are the block alphabet which shapes thoughts; and these thoughts, although making a visual design on the chessboard express their beauty *abstractly*, like a poem. Actually, I believe that every chess player experiences a mixture of two aesthetic pleasures, first the abstract image akin to the poetic idea of writing, second the sensuous pleasure of the ideographic execution of that idea on the chessboard. From my close contacts with artists and chess players I have come to the personal conclusion that while all artists are not chess players, all chess players are artists.'

Chapter 14: Chess and Literature

'. . . In this game, the Devil says 'Check!' when a man falls into sin; and unless he quickly covers the check by turning to repentance, The Devil says 'Mate!' and carries him off to Hell, whence there is no escape'.

Innocent Morality (12th or 13th century)

As mentioned in the chapter 'Chess and visual Art' chess as an analogue of life gives perhaps the earliest link between chess and the arts – both visual art and literature. The quotation above is an example – an agreeable mixture of the ingenious and the naïve. Leaving aside these mementos of the past, what forms does chess in literature take today?

One must I think exclude the vast army of purely technical works – books on openings, middle games, endings, collections of games and so on – even when, as sometimes happens, these are really well written. The writer's object is instructional and the reader reacts accordingly.

There is however a shadowy no man's land, occupied largely by Réti, where the writer has a dual object. Réti's *Modern Ideas in Chess*, in its description of the development of style, has a technical object; but the brilliance of his descriptions (e.g. of Capablanca as a representative of Americanism in chess) justify us in calling it literature as well. Someone who knows little or nothing of chess can enjoy and admire much of this book. A number of attempts were made to rival Réti in writing on the Fischer/Spassky match, but these seldom if ever got above the level of good journalism; think what Réti would have made of the opportunity! The account by G.H.Diggle of the Staunton/St.Amant match, which I give, while not quite in the Réti class, is certainly good enough to be a worthy representative of this category.

Another slightly obscure group is that of the 'Bedside Book' – technically based to some extent, it is a pot-pourri meant for dipping into at random. Some examples: Irving Chernev's *The Chess Player's Companion* – short stories on chess, anecdotes, positions, entertaining games; Dr Schumer's delightful *Chesslets* with (amongst other things) games annotated by quotations – including a game from the Olympiads with each of the quotations in a different language; and Terence Tiller's *Chess Treasury of the Air*, brilliantly subtitled, *My Husband and I* – with a White Queen on the cover. Not literature – and yet not 'not literature' – if I make myself clear.

Turning to what is undeniably literature, to a true writer the fascination of chess lies in the psychology of the player and the effect of chess on him. The outstanding work here is Vladimir Nabokov's *The Defence*, a study of a master obsessed and finally destroyed by chess. Other examples are Stefan Zweig's *The Royal Game* and Ellison's *Master Prim*; I give extracts from both of these. *The Dragon Variation* by Anthony Glyn is a study of the exploitation of chess players by the Press and by patrons with more money than sense; it also brings out the cold self-absorbed nature of a certain type of player – of chess leaving no room for anything else. Kester Svendson's *The Last Round* is a short story showing the veteran master's dreams fulfilled in a way that too seldom happens in real life.

There is an interesting paradox here which I touch on again when discussing the Zweig story; the better writers are less near the truth than the worse ones. As a novel, *The Defence* is in a quite different class from Ellison's or Glyn's; yet their chess players are more like the real article. This is an observation rather than a criticism; let me put it differently. Ellison and Glyn are coming as near as they can to giving you a photograph (this is especially true of Ellison). Nabokov and Zweig are painting a picture – and not one that is purely representational; not abstract, but perhaps post-impressionist. In the end one gets more from the better writers; but it is worth understanding the difference in approach.

Finally, there is chess in fantasy and science fiction. The chess automaton is a favourite theme of which Ambrose Bierce's *Moxon's Master* is a classic example. *Professor Pownall's Oversight* by H.R.Wakefield, with its curious mixture of dream and reality, its feeling of obsession and fate, is one of my favourite chess stories. Equally so is Lord Dunsany's light-hearted fantasy *The Three Sailors' Gambit* where the three sailors with their crystal ball purchased – for the usual price – from the devil, make mincemeat of all opposition. C.L.Harness's *The Chess Players* – the story of a chessplaying rat – is an S.F. satire on chess players that has an uncomfortable ring of truth; the players are not interested in the fact that the rat can play – only in how well he plays.

And last of all *A Quiet Game of Chess*, at the extreme end of the spectrum; decide for yourselves about this.

I have not attempted anything like an exhaustive list of chess novels and stories in literature; my hope is merely to have mentioned enough to make you look for yourselves.

Staunton versus Saint-Amant, 1843 *by G.H.Diggle*

(First published in 'The British Chess Magazine',
November and December 1943)

*I have included this for two reasons. First because Mr Diggle –
who has written only too little – is one of the best writers on
chess that I know; in this brilliant account he reproduces perfectly
the flavour of the period. The other reason is the extraordinary
resemblance between this encounter and the Fischer/Spassky
match.*

*In the 1840s, France had a chess dominance which, if not as
securely based, had lasted far longer than the modern Soviet
supremacy; for 100 years France had been the accepted leader,
and Staunton's victory was as dramatic an incident in chess
history as Fischer's overthrow of Spassky. Then there was the
general rivalry between France and England; Waterloo was only
28 years away and there was a satisfaction that spread far
outside purely chess circles. Newspapers that had never before
reported a chess match groped their way into the encounter as
best they could.*

*But more than just these general resemblances was the
striking similarity of the course of the match. Staunton's
devastating start (7 wins and a draw in the first 8 games); his
victory after 89 moves in the 12th game, 'a great struggle of
many vicissitudes' – Diggle might be describing the great 13th
game in the Fischer/Spassky match; and then St. Amant's
recovery. He crushed Staunton in their famous 13th game – the
description of this could be that of the 'poisoned pawn' 11th game
in which Spassky destroyed Fischer. And finally Staunton's
victory – by what score? 13–8, as compared with $12\frac{1}{2}$–$8\frac{1}{2}$ in the
modern match.*

*The differences are as interesting as the likenesses; read
Diggle's account of the conditions of the match. No adjournments
(not even for food), no restrictions on spectators; what would
Fischer say?*

They were giants in those days.

'This memorable encounter which,' in the words of the victor,
'excited a degree of interest perhaps unparalleled in the history
of any similar contest, took place in Paris in November and
December, 1843.' Staunton has been criticized for always calling
it 'The Great Chess Match between England and France,' but
the struggle really was worthy of this title. For nearly a century
previous the French had been, as a chess-playing nation,
traditionally supreme. This supremacy, established by Philidor,
had been maintained successively by Deschapelles (though in a
somewhat shadowy manner), by La Bourdonnais (far more
decisively), and (up to 1843) by St. Amant himself. And it was
this supremacy that was the real thing at stake in the two fateful
months one hundred years ago, when the 'Sceptre of Philidor'
was wrested from the last of his successors by an Englishman.

Nor was the 'unparalleled interest' any mere grandiloquent
figment of Staunton's pen. Overwhelming evidence survives as
to how genuinely the contest fired the public imagination on
both sides of the Channel. We have the recollections of such men
as Wayte and Tomlinson, who were both young players when
the match took place. 'In the chess clubs of this country,' writes
the latter, 'the greatest excitement prevailed; and the games, as
and when received, were played over and over.' Nor was the fer-
ment confined to the very few of our cities which boasted such a
club at that time. Chess came to life in all sorts of obscure haunts
and shallows in the provinces. From all over the country converts
sprang up and vociferously demanded 'The Games of the Grand
Match.' Prior to this emergency, no English newspaper, with
the sole exception of Bell's 'Life in London,' had ever heard of
chess. But now the Press (editors and compositors alike) rose to
the occasion. The moves were copied (with a surprisingly small
crop of errors) from Galignani's 'Messenger,' with which
enterprising periodical they had been supplied in the first place
by no less a person than St. Amant himself. Some of our bolder
journalists even ventured to favour their readers with a few
brief comments on each game printed. Thus we read how in the
second game, 'Mr. Staunton skilfully posted several pieces in
readiness for the mate,' and how in the fifth 'Monsieur St.
Amant's men were too bunched together' so that he 'could not
play his full game.' It was enlightened by such expositions as
these that our fashionable forefathers, in many a rural drawing-
room and study, set out their ungainly chessmen and stumbled
heavily through the moves.

Such was the state of erudition of the Press and of the public
when Howard Staunton and Pierre Charles Fournié de Saint-

Amant faced each other in what was virtually the first set match for the Chess Championship of the World. But what of the higher chess circles of London and Paris? What of the champions themselves? The result of their struggle is well known – yet posterity has paid strangely little attention to the actual games. They have been passed over as dull, tuneless, and obsolete affairs with no claim to remembrance now. This estimate, originally put forth in bad faith by the enemies of Staunton, has been repeated from time to time by loose writers of later generations who have pretended they have taken the trouble to see for themselves, and who might have learnt something had they really done so. For these games amply repay examination. Fought out in a tense atmosphere, and under conditions which would have appalled a modern master, many of them are not only splendid struggles in themselves, but taken in the order played have all the interest of a drama. In no championship match since has a challenger achieved such devastating success at the start, or a champion made such a remarkable stand at the finish. At the end of the eighth game we see St. Amant, and at the end of the twentieth (though to a lesser extent) Staunton, almost 'down and out,' only to rise again. Alphonse Delannoy, describing the scene at the Cercle des Echecs towards the end of the match, speaks of 'long hours, whole days of doubt, despair, joy, hope and illusions, with the spectators as indefatigable as the players.'

The match was for £100 a side, four games to be played each week, and the winner of the first eleven to be declared the victor. So far the conditions resemble those which would prevail in a championship match to-day. But here the parallel ends. In these humanitarian days of the chess clock and the sealed move, our masters are safeguarded against having to fight 'from morn till midnight' at a stretch. Moreover, spectators, if admitted into the arena at all, must hold their breath at a respectful distance. Even the all-powerful Press may only creep about on tiptoe just inside the ropes. But our rival heroes of 1843 were not allowed (and apparently did not expect) any such consideration. Each game, under the terms of the match, began at 11 o'clock in the morning. Once started, it had to be played out to a finish in one sitting. No adjournment was allowed 'except in case of severe illness,' and there was no time-limit for moves whatsoever. Another hardship (as Mr P.W.Sergeant points out in 'Championship Chess') lay in the fact that 'there was no protection of the players.' Far from being carefully insulated with board and men, the two champions were grievously beset hour after hour

with eager onlookers restricted as to number only by the capacity of the clubroom and as to noise entirely by their own discretion.

These conditions were a rigorous challenge even to such giants of a rugged age as were Staunton and St. Amant. Again and again the two champions, having fought without respite throughout the day, were faced late in the evening with a crucial endgame to be played out in surroundings which (to quote Staunton's second, Captain Wilson), 'had become insupportable through the lighting of the lamps, and the crowding in of more and more spectators who had come to see the finish.' 'During the playing of the nineteenth game' (if we are to believe Bell's 'Life'), 'Such was the anxiety of the public to witness the skill of Mr Staunton and the heroic resistance of St. Amant, that both parties suffered terribly from the heat, and gendarmes had to be posted at the club doors to refuse further admittance.' Nevertheless 'both parties' (St. Amant at 43, Staunton ten years younger) stood up to it splendidly. Only two breakdowns due to exhaustion (games 9 and 11) can be traced – Staunton is the unlucky player in both cases. And the extraordinary thing is that (judging from Captain Wilson's records of 'the longest times consumed by the players in deliberation on their moves') neither of them made any attempt early in a game to avoid hard work in order to conserve his energies for a crowning effort later on. For example, in the fourteenth game, which lasted till midnight, Staunton at the very outset, with every piece still on the board, devotes twenty minutes to a most elaborate offer of a pawn, which St. Amant rejects, but only after thirty minutes' 'long and intense deliberation.' Incidentally, Captain Wilson's figures show that St. Amant was much the slower player. 'But,' said Staunton, when discussing his opponent with Tomlinson fifteen years later, 'his conception was slow. He did not take more time than was necessary. I never met a man with such powers of endurance. He seemed as fresh at the end of fourteen hours as when he sat down.' Staunton also told Tomlinson that the only refreshment his opponent took throughout the long sittings was 'coffee, and snuff in profusion'; he himself relied on 'tea, and light things.'

On November 14th, 1843, the contest began with St. Amant strong favourite. The prowess of the aristocratic wine merchant was well known. Indisputably the strongest player in France, he had twice visited England, contended with the chief players of both the London and the Westminster Chess Clubs, and (in the words of Walker) 'beaten us all round.' Now, seated ready for the first game in his own stronghold of Paris, surrounded by friends and admirers, and even with the busts of his predecessors, Philidor and La Bourdonnais, surveying the scene from the background, he must have looked a monarch not easy to dethrone. For all that the challenger, on his arrival at the Cercle des Echecs with his two seconds (Captain Wilson and Mr Worrel) made a striking impression on the Parisians. 'When I saw that massive forehead,' writes one of them (Monsieur Doazan), 'I prophesied no easy victory for us.'

The forebodings of M. Doazan were soon to be confirmed in staggering manner. As is well known, the match began with an avalanche of victories for the Englishman. In the very first game we find him outplaying his opponent completely, and throughout the next fortnight he simply sweeps all before him until by November 28th he is actually leading by seven games to nil, with one solitary draw (the third game). The second and fourth games are, as Wayte says, excellent examples of Staunton's style in his best day – the advantage he seizes in the opening is never let go, and the win comes each time in 30 moves. The fifth game is a tremendous fight, with St. Amant in

the concluding stages obviously straining every nerve to bring off his first win, only to be frustrated at the very end by Staunton's masterly pawn play. After a sitting of nine and a half hours the Frenchman is compelled to resign once more. 'The excitement of the spectators,' says Bell's 'Life,' 'was perfectly indescribable on seeing their favourite, St. Amant, so thoroughly defeated.'

On the evening following this game the President of the Paris Chess Club, General Guingret, gives a 'magnificent banquet, worthy of Lucullus,' at which he entertains both champions, their seconds, and all the chess notabilities of Paris. Even the great Deschapelles himself condescends to be present, and his health is proposed by Staunton in a speech (says Delannoy) 'revealing to us all M. Staunton not merely as a great master of chess, but as a man of culture and wit.' Other toasts proposed are those of 'King Louis Philippe,' 'Victoria Reine d'Angleterre,' 'Every player of chess, whatever his nationality and whatever his playing strength,' 'General Guingret,' 'Howard Staunton,' and 'St. Amant, who will soon become himself once more.'

When the struggle is resumed, however, the landslide continues. In both his next two victories Staunton makes valuable contributions to chess opening theory which have left their mark to this day. In the sixth game as first player he begins with a new move (1. P–QB4) – known ever after in consequence as 'The English Opening'; in the seventh (he has declined a Queen's Gambit) he 'strikingly demonstrates the power of the QB when posted at QKt2' – a mode of development never before taken seriously in Paris, where fianchettoed Bishops were derisively nicknamed 'the little chapels'. 'When our latest moderns,' writes Mr J.H.Blake, 'open out with P–QKt3 and B–Kt2, they must thank Staunton for having rescued that manoeuvre from the faddists of his time, and shown it to have high theoretical value when placed in its proper setting.' In the eighth game both the fortunes and the play of the French champion reach their lowest ebb; he can do nothing right, and as early as the 15th move (over which he takes three-quarters of an hour) his game is hopeless. By this time (Delannoy informs us) the Cercle des Echecs is in a state of utter despair; George Walker across the Channel proudly proclaims that England has at last found a player worthy to succeed McDonnell; retired Waterloo veterans at the Brighton Chess Club express 'energetic satisfaction' at the new English triumph; and supporters of both sides look upon the match as over. But St. Amant sits down for the ninth game; and it is here, faced at the end of eight hours with the loss of his Queen or a clear piece, that he hits on the desperate resource which leads to the first English setback of the match. Staunton, who calls his opponent's 32nd move 'a splendid coup, as ingenious as unexpected,' is left with only one winning continuation. In the heat of battle he misses it; immediately after, robbed of certain victory, he throws away a clear Rook and resigns. Staunton at the conclusion (Doazan tells us) 'congratulates his opponent with a majestic smile.' 'You have broken the ice,' graciously observes Captain Wilson to St. Amant. 'The match,' continues M. Doazan (not altogether impartially) 'only really begins now, and is fought with the utmost energy to its conclusion.'

The tenth game after running to 61 moves is won by Staunton; in the eleventh he loses a pawn at the outset, but fights back with a vigour 'which draws repeated expressions of admiration from the surrounding spectators.' On the point of achieving the victory, however, he turns it into defeat by that celebrated endgame blunder which he deplores at such length both in the 'Handbook' and in the 'Companion.' But for his lapses in games 9 and 11 he would have actually won the match without losing a single game. The twelfth game, a great struggle of many vicissitudes, deservedly goes to Staunton after eighty-nine moves and nine hours' play. 'In spite of all our countryman's victories,' wrote a keen follower of the match to George Walker, 'I never quite gave St. Amant up until to-day, when I played over the twelfth game; but I am now satisfied, once and for all, that Mr Staunton is the better player.'

Undaunted, however, even by the loss of this last gruelling battle, St. Amant returns next day to the arena and suddenly begins to 'hand it out' himself. He wins the famous thirteenth game 'in glorious style, dashing into the heart of the English citadel and scattering outworks and inner defences like chaff.' Notwithstanding the state of the score, the French Press fairly lets itself go. According to one expert, 'the first half-dozen games never count in a match. It is only now that St. Amant is beginning to play, and we have no fear of the result'; according to another, 'St. Amant has now penetrated all his opponent's chess secrets and will henceforward demolish him!' 'Such,' Walker is rude enough to observe, 'was the stuff gravely set forth by these learned scribes.' The fourteenth game, one of the few really dull ones of the match, ends in a draw; the fifteenth, steadily and admirably conducted throughout by Staunton, perhaps shows him, more than any other game in the series, as the forerunner of modern position play. Victorious after 56 moves and seven hours' play, the English champion has now arrived within one point of final conquest. At this juncture, however, he loses the services and companionship of Captain Wilson, who, to his own intense disappointment, is forced by ill-health to leave Paris and return home, 'delighted at having recorded 10 out of 11 games won for old England, and deploring the illness which deprived him of participation in the crowning triumph of the eleventh British checkmate.'

The sixteenth game begins. Staunton with the move sets out on his last lap with every confidence, but lo! at the critical moment he overestimates his position, and after some forced exchanges is left on his 37th move with a pawn to the bad. Even then, he makes a fine effort to finish off the match, and comes within an ace of doing it; but St. Amant stands fast, weathers the storm, and wins cleverly on the 58th move. Two bitterly contested drawn games now follow: the seventeenth in 54 moves and eight hours, the eighteenth in 57 moves and seven hours. In the former, Staunton ends up with King and pawn against his opponent's lone King, which 'gets in front' just in time; in the latter the Englishman is again a pawn up at the finish – but this time there are Bishops of opposite colours.

The match is not over yet, and 'a loud acclamation' from the spectators greets the Frenchman when he scores the nineteenth game after 79 moves and nine-and-a-half-hours' play. This game, rather than the more spectacular thirteenth, is perhaps St. Amant's best effort of the match, and shows, as Wayte says, 'that he was really a great player.' But the strain is clearly telling on Staunton, who next day conducts the twentieth game in a manner quite unworthy of him, losing in 30 moves 'the worst-played partie of the match.'

'Five times has the Englishman returned to the charge in vain' – his intrepid adversary has held up chess history for eleven days. A great crowd assembles for the twenty-first game. 'Many Paris celebrities' are present – both players and spectators seem to feel instinctively that the climax is at hand. Only 29 moves are made each side in the first eight hours. A decision then seems so far off that the 'no adjournment' rule is waived for the first time in the match, and the players are allowed an hour's break. On the resumption Staunton makes his supreme effort. 'Le Joueur Anglais,' handsomely observes *Le Palamède*, 'semble retrouver cette énergie des premières parties du Match qui, depuis quelque temps, l'avait abandonné.' By the 54th move it is evident that the final game has come at last, but it is now past midnight, and a second adjournment is agreed upon. Next morning, the two champions face each other for the last time,

and on December 20th, 1843, after 66 moves and fourteen hours' play, the Englishman achieves his eleventh and final victory. At its close the score stands:

Staunton	11
St. Amant	6
Drawn	4

In summing up the match, George Walker says: 'Had St. Amant played as well at first as he did at the last, we are persuaded that he would have been equally defeated, though he might have put up a better fight, winning perhaps one or two more games. Mr Staunton has shown himself the better player at every point. Nothing could be better than St. Amant's notes to these games in *Le Palamède*. He personally bears up against his defeat with the same manly spirit which sustained him in his heroic struggle to the last. No cavilling, no querulous complaint escapes him. We earnestly hope that a new match will be made up to take place in the coming year.'

'Unhappily,' writes Mr H.J.R.Murray, 'the Fates ruled otherwise.' We cannot here deal fully with Staunton's ill-fated second visit to Paris in October 1844, with the attack of pneumonia which laid him at death's door four days before the return match had been fixed to begin, and with his narrow recovery and subsequent return to England utterly unfit for play, and indeed, as Mr Murray truly observes, 'really unfitted for all serious match-play from that time forward.' For he brought back with him that permanent weakness of the heart which as the years went on was to show itself more and more painfully in the unevenness both of his play and of his temper. He still had his victories to come in 1846 against Horwitz and Harrwitz; but when the crash came in 1851 he was already the shadow of his former strength, and in 1853 we find him excusing himself, owing to 'my old enemy, palpitation,' from playing a friendly game he had arranged one evening with Von der Lasa, whom more than any of his other contemporaries he liked and respected. 'I dare not play to-day,' he writes pathetically. 'The excitement would be too much for me. . . . My trouble is, I believe, brought on in part by irritation at how sadly I have fallen off in my play.'

That he again excused himself five years later, this time from playing a match against the greatest player of the century, then at the zenith of his youth and fame, was no tragedy for chess. The contest would have been a fiasco. But it would have been happier, both for the young champion and the old, had the latter never said he would play at all.

Master Prim *by James Whitfield Ellison*

The extract from this book covers the game between Julian Prim and Eugene Berlin in the last round of an imaginary US *championship. I say imaginary but no reader of the book or this extract will have the slightest difficulty in identifying the originals of Prim and Berlin in real life. While I don't regard the book as a literary masterpiece the author does, I think, convey something of the cruelty of chess – the bitterness of defeat for the ageing champion by a younger and greater talent with an ambition at least as obsessive and unrelenting as his own. Chess rivalry does not have to be as impregnated with hostility as here; it depends on the players. But something of this feeling does exist in most needle encounters; you need a lot of aggression to be a great master – and, if you have it, to be overthrown, especially by a younger rival, is hard to accept.*

Julian had won his must game and now he had seven and a half points to Berlin's eight, and victory against Berlin would bring him the United States Championship. During the night the weather broke, and on Sunday fierce, blue clouds, mapped dramatically on the face of the sky, opened intermittently in torrents on the city, and by two-thirty in the afternoon the day was very dark.

The last round, like the two before it, was closed to the public; Eugene Berlin had insisted in his agreement with the Foundation that he play his final three rounds in private if the tournament had not been decided. Almost a thousand spectators gathered in the ballroom downstairs and followed the games on a demonstration board where five grandmasters analysed the play.

The room on the fifth floor of the hotel was airless; the tables constructed on wide circular iron stands were set against the wall beneath candy-striped draperies, and the grey carpet was spotted with cigarette burns. When Julian noticed that his table wobbled, play was held up for ten minutes while a small scarred card table was brought up from the hotel's basement. Julian then asked that a container of iced tea with two teaspoons of sugar be brought to him every half-hour.

As he stood waiting for the pieces to be set up on the card table, Alan Pollenz approached him and said, 'I see that Sturdivant contrived to blow his game with you. . .' Berlin, who was resting on a couch against the other wall, opened his eyes and smiled, nodding in agreement.

Julian did not answer. His motionless and expressionless gaze was fixed on the table, and he seemed in a state of stupefaction. But then, as he sat down in his seat, he leaned across the table and said to Berlin softly, 'I saw you smile. I saw you smile at what Pollenz said. . .' Suddenly his face, every muscle in it, was quivering with nervous excitement; his eyes, which had seemed dull before, almost bemused, gleamed now with full, vivid fire, and in an even softer voice he said, 'Well, Master – here we are. We are supposed to shake hands. It's the way things are done. Have you forgotten?'

They shook hands across the table and their eyes locked until Berlin, with an embarrassed clearing of his throat, looked away. While the Tournament Director set their clocks, Julian leaned back in his chair, his thumbs hooked in his trouser pockets, and stared at Eugene Berlin, trying to catch him in the web of his own intensity. But Berlin busied himself lighting a cigarette, then wiped his glasses carefully on a clean white handkerchief.

He did not look at Julian once in the next four hours.

Some of the players still walked around the room as they waited for play to begin. When they stopped in front of Julian's table they looked at him with an expression that combined dislike and a kind of frightened reverence; they all paused there, waiting, as though he might look up and acknowledge them, acknowledge something in them they were not sure they possessed – but he never noticed them, and they walked on.

Now a new depth of quietness filled the room. The nervous, sporadic ripples of sound – the whispered conferences, clicking cameras, coughing, shuffling of feet – abruptly came to an end. The Tournament Director walked up to each table, smiled briefly, and started White's clock. Two and a half hours for forty moves. Two and a half hours for Julian Prim to try and invent a winning design of moves from the possible billions upon billions of variations that a forty-move game can take. Two and a half hours in which he could use his brilliant imagination and his fine perception for spatial relations to become chess champion of the United States.

A photographer hovered in the back of the room waiting for Julian's poised hand to fall. A fly buzzed near Eugene Berlin's nose; he swiped at it impatiently with the fingers of his left hand. The fly floated slowly toward the ceiling. Julian breathed in deeply and let the air seep out in one sustained exhalation – then down came his hand.

1.   P–Q4

And a white flash filled the room. As Berlin stared at the move in evident amazement, pursing his cherry lips, Julian, after depressing the button on his clock which automatically started Berlin's, rose from the table. With a jabbing finger he pushed the cameraman towards the door. 'Out, out,' he said. 'You know enough to obey the rules. You speak English.'

'Now you just hold on –'

'*You* hold on,' Julian said, pushing the white-faced cameraman out the door with the help of the Tournament Director. 'You ruin my concentration.'

Jason Cook looked up from his table, grinned, and said, 'That will be the day.'

Julian slumped down in his chair and closed his eyes. Berlin, stroking his heavy cheeks, still stared at Julian's opening move. Not once as a professional, not once, perhaps, since the childhood game he had played with Jacob Solovey, had Julian opened with the Queen's pawn. Five minutes passed and Berlin still stared at the board. By that time the other players had paused by the table (for to them, this was the stage where the drama was) and all of them walked away talking about Julian's opening, discussing what his plan might be. Six minutes, seven minutes. Finally, Julian shrugged, got up from the table and went into the bathroom for a drink of water. When he returned Eugene Berlin had responded.

1.   ...   P–Q4

As Julian stared at the chessmen his eyes assumed the green, glazed-over quality of profound concentration. His glance flicked quickly across the chessboard, his right hand touched his forehead lightly in the movement of a small cross, and then shot out.

2.   Kt–KB3

Eugene Berlin, frowning at the board, rubbed the tips of his fingers together slowly and then moved.

2.   ...   Kt–KB3

Sighing, he removed his glasses and wiped them again. He did not look away from the board. He used the handkerchief he held in his hand to blow his nose; mucus rattled in his throat. He rolled the handkerchief into a ball and jammed it into his jacket pocket and started massaging his neck with his fingertips. He was never still.

Julian was very still. When he moved a piece, his arm did not seem attached to the rest of him.

3.   P–B4   P–K3
4.   Kt–B3   QKt–Q2
5.   P–K3   B–Q3

Julian squinted his eyes until they were almost shut, ran his tongue slowly across his lips, and then moved.

6.   Kt–QKt5

Paul Marcus, sitting beside me, whispered into my ear, 'Berlin's last move was poor. Just a plain blunder. He should have played B–K2, in my opinion. I don't know about that Knight move of Julian's either.'

Neither, apparently, did Berlin, who took ten minutes to decide on what seemed to be an obvious move in his position. After studying his pocket set more carefully, Paul Marcus said, 'I think Julian should have played pawn to Bishop five. That would have forced the Black Bishop back, and then he could have advanced the Queen Knight's pawn to four. As it is, he's lost time. It could really hurt him.'

'I expected a very careful opening from both of them,' I said. 'Not this. Maybe they're both nervous.'

Paul Marcus scratched his head and looked sceptical. 'Julian can't have studied the Queen openings enough. Chess has specialties like anything else. You specialise in openings.'

'Maybe he's depending on the element of surprise.'

'When everything rides on one game?' Paul Marcus said. He shook his head. 'I don't know. He's a very quixotic boy in some ways – playing to Berlin's strength.'

'He likes to gamble,' I said.

'The point in chess is to minimize the risk,' Paul Marcus said. 'I just don't understand him.'

'Well,' I said, 'if he beats Berlin at his own game, then it's a more impressive win. Maybe that's what he's thinking.'

'A win is a win,' Paul Marcus said. 'But it would be like him to think that.'

Eugene Berlin made his move.

6.	...	B–K2
7.	Q–B2	P–B3
8.	Kt–B3	0–0
9.	B–Q3	PxP
10.	BxP	P–B4

Paul Marcus put an exclamation point after Berlin's last move, and Julian's game, for the first time, slowed down. Twice he started to move, but each time he drew his hand back. Finally, he took the pawn.

| 11. | PxP | BxP |
| 12. | 0–0 | P–QKt3 |

After his twelfth move, Berlin had used thirty-five minutes on his clock and Julian fifteen. Paul Marcus and I went out into the hall so that we could talk more easily.

'I think Berlin will keep the championship,' he said. 'He has an excellent game now. It's too bad, too, because he isn't nearly as interesting a player. Julian will probably try to force things from now on, complicate them. That Knight move of his was a real lapse – the kind he doesn't often make. And Berlin is great at making you eat your mistakes. . . .'

Paul Marcus was right. Julian played

| 13. | P–K4 |

still trying to force the pace. I could only guess, along with Marcus, that Julian was overextending himself in the hope of regaining the initiative.

Berlin took an interminable amount of time before making a reply.

13.	...	B–N2
14.	B–KKt5	Q–B1
15.	Q–K2	B–Kt5

Peter Sturdivant looked at the game and then said to Paul Marcus, 'The fireworks have really started. How about an exclamation point for Berlin's Bishop move?'

'Definitely.'

'I like Berlin's game,' Peter Sturdivant said. 'But I never count Prim out. If Berlin drifts just a little Prim will come fighting back.'

| 16. | B–Q3 | BxKt |
| 17. | KR–B1 | |

Berlin looked pale now, and there were dark rings of exhaustion beneath his eyes. After long reflection (more than twenty minutes), he picked up his Knight with his pudgy hand and captured the pawn at K4.

| 17. | ... | KtxP |

Julian looked at the move, and then, for a full twenty seconds, at Berlin.

| 18. | BxKt | |

I thought I could see a slight smile start up on Julian's face; he continued to stare at Berlin but the Champion deliberated, rigid and silent, his head bowed to within inches of the chessmen.

Paul Marcus said, 'I'm beginning to wonder *who's* winning.'

'I think Julian thinks he is.'

'I'm sure he does,' Paul Marcus said. 'He always does. That's part of his secret. He wants to win so much he wills the victory.'

'But everyone wants to win,' I objected.

'No, I don't agree. A chess player – a master, at least – works hard to win. He prepares. But no one knows until he plays any given game just how deeply he wants to win that one. Something can go limp inside of you. The creative energy can falter. I have never seen this happen to Julian Prim yet. Not once.'

'You make it sound mystical.'

'Well, of course it is.'

Berlin glanced at his clock and then exchanged Bishops.

18.	...	BxB
19.	QxB	Kt–B4
20.	Q–K2	B–R4
21.	QR–Kt1	Q–R3

Almost immediately Julian responded with

22.   R–B4

which created a glissando of sound – a blend of surprise and excitement – throughout the room. A daub of colour burned now on Julian's cheeks. He stared at Berlin for a moment and then got up and walked quickly around the room, pausing at each table to examine the various positions, and when he came back he had to push his way through a number of the players, who, when they were free to leave their own games, gathered around to follow the course of play.

Berlin lighted a cigarette and bowed down over the table, his head bent low. He coughed, pulled back to wipe his mouth with the palm of his hand, then leaned over the pieces again. His forehead gleamed with sweat. Julian, sprawled out in his chair, stared at the ceiling. Slowly, Berlin's hand moved out, hovered an instant above the chessmen, then descended on the Knight.

22.   ...   Kt–R5

Julian sat up straight and rested his elbows on the edge of the table, his head cupped in his hands. After a moment he slumped and rubbed his eyes and then leaned his cheek against his bent left wrist. He looked over at me – or rather, right through me – and then turned his gaze on the board. For fifteen minutes he was perfectly still. A glass shattered on the tiles in the bathroom. A maid came in with a broom and cleaned it up. All through this, Julian stared at the board, not moving. His eyes rested immovably on the board, his lids drooped, and toward the end of the fifteen minutes his mouth opened slightly, which gave him a vaguely bemused look.

Then his hand shot out.

23.   B–B6

Mark Friedman walked away from the table, shaking his head and smiling.

'Well,' Paul Marcus said, 'that is a move. Worth two exclamation points at least. Berlin may be in trouble now. He can't take the Bishop with his pawn. If he does, Julian checks with the Rook and wins his Queen. And the Rook pawn can't move, because Julian can sacrifice his Queen and mate in three.' Paul Marcus smiled. 'This move illustrates the difference between my game and Prim's. I see the move once he makes it, but I can't think it up.'

'Berlin is a great defender,' I said.

'Yes. He may have an answer.'

Now Berlin had only half an hour left on his clock.

23.   ...   KR–B1

Julian played without hesitation.

24.   Q–K5

Berlin looked at his time clock as his hand hovered over his Rook.

24.   ...   R–B4

Julian instantly played

25.   Q–Kt3

and Richard Sturdivant, standing beside us, said, 'Berlin's Knight is gone. Look at that line-up on his Queen side – five pieces! No symmetry. He must feel like vomiting!' He laughed and Julian looked up at him sharply. Sturdivant, grinning boyishly, shook his head in apology, and then whispered to Paul Marcus, 'We all thought he would fold. He was very nervous last week. All hung up. But you have to admire his guts and the kind of game he plays. Queen pawn opening!'

Berlin's next move was forced.

25.		...	P–Kt3
26.	R x Kt		Q–Q6
27.	R–KB1		Q–B4
28.	Q–B4		

Julian pushed the button on his clock and Berlin's clock started running. He glanced at it – there were fifteen minutes remaining. He removed his glasses and put them on again. A vein throbbed in his temple. He pushed his lower lip out, drew it in, pushed it out again. He lighted a cigarette, put it in an ashtray, and immediately lighted another one. He jutted his chin out of his collar repeatedly, then pushed his lower lip out again. And the minutes ran out.

Julian stared across the table at him, and I thought I saw a softening in his eyes – perhaps an element of pity.

Berlin opened his mouth to speak, and then moved his Queen instead.

28.   ...   Q–B7

After Julian's prompt reply

29.   Q–R6

Berlin cleared his throat a number of times, then slowly rose to his feet.

'I resign,' he said. 'Congratulations.'

'Thanks,' Julian said.

They stood a moment looking at each other, then they shook hands briefly, and Berlin turned and walked out of the room.

The Royal Game *by Stefan Zweig*

Here we have another fictional struggle, between the World Champion Mirko Czentovic and the mysterious Dr B. The players are examples of two types with a strong appeal to writers caught by the fascination of chess. Czentovic is the freak – the chess equivalent of the calculating prodigy; uneducated, uninterested in any other intellectual field and apparently devoid of general intelligence, lacking indeed in any emotions except pride in his skill and determination to exploit it, he has a marvellous gift for chess. Dr B. is very different; imprisoned in solitary confinement by the Gestapo (The Royal Game was published in 1944), his only book was one of 150 championship games, which he stole from a pocket of one of his inquisitors' coats. With no other outlet, he soaked himself in chess to preserve his sanity; from playing endlessly through these games he went to playing invented games mentally. Originally saved by chess, he became obsessed by it and finally had a breakdown after which he was released. On board ship he is drawn into a game with Czentovic; the question is, 'could this highly intelligent man forced by circumstance to give his whole time to chess beat the prodigy?'

We must not be deceived by the excellence of the writing into believing wholly in Czentovic, Dr. B. or the result. This is far better written than Master Prim *– but it is much less true to life. Czentovic is a real, though rare, type of chess master in his lack of other intellectual interests; I don't believe however in his stupidity – I would expect any chess master, however limited his interests, to have a high I.Q. And Dr B.; I would like to think that Dr B.s exist, but they don't. Solitary study cannot supply the practical technique, width of experience and ability to resist pressure that only comes from meeting live opponents.*

Nevertheless the extract from this story, through the excellence of its writing, gives an insight into the psychology of chess and chessplayers which makes it well worth reading. The story is translated from the German by B.W.Huebsch.

We assembled in the smoking-room the next day promptly at the appointed hour, three o'clock. Our circle had increased by yet two more lovers of the royal game, two ship's officers who had obtained special leave from duty to watch the tourney. Czentovic, too, not as on the preceding days, was on time. After the usual choice of colours there began the memorable game of this *homo obscurissimus* against the celebrated master.

I regret that it was played for thoroughly incompetent observers like us, and that its course is as completely lost to the annals of the art of chess as are Beethoven's improvisations to music. True, we tried to piece it together from our collective memory on the following afternoons, but in vain; very likely, in the passion of the moment, we had allowed our interest to centre on the players rather than on the game. For the intellectual contrast between the contestants became physically plastic according to their manner as the play proceeded. Czentovic, the creature of routine, remained the entire time as immobile as a block, his eyes unalterably fixed on the board; thinking seemed to cost him almost physical effort that called for extreme concentration on the part of every organ. Dr B., on the other hand, was completely slack and unconstrained. Like the true dilettante, in the best sense of the word, to whom only the play in play—the *diletto*—gives joy, he relaxed fully, explained moves to us in easy conversation during the early intervals, lighted a cigarette carelessly, and glanced at the board for a minute only when it came his turn to play. Each time it seemed as if he had expected just the move that his antagonist made.

The perfunctory moves came off quite rapidly. It was not until the seventh or eighth that something like a definite plan seemed to develop. Czentovic prolonged his periods of reflection; by that we sensed that the actual battle for the lead was setting in. But, to be quite frank, the gradual development of the situation represented to us lay observers, as usually in tournament games, something of a disappointment. The more the pieces wove themselves into a singular design the more impenetrable became the real lie of the land. We could not discern what one or the other rival purposed or which of the two had the advantage. We noticed merely that certain pieces insinuated themselves forward like levers to undermine the enemy front, but since every move of these superior players was part of a combination that comprised a plan for several moves ahead, we were unable to detect the strategy of their back-and-forth.

An oppressive fatigue took possession of us, largely because of Czentovic's interminable cogitation between moves, which

eventually produced visible irritation in our friend too. I observed uneasily how, the longer the game stretched out, he became increasingly restless, moving about in his chair, nervously lighting a succession of cigarettes, occasionally seizing a pencil to make a note. He would order mineral water and gulp it down, glass after glass; it was plain that his mind was working a hundred times faster than Czentovic's. Every time the latter, after endless reflection, decided to push a piece forward with his heavy hand, our friend would smile like one who encounters something long expected and make an immediate riposte. In his nimble mind he must have calculated every possibility that lay open to his opponent; the longer Czentovic took to make a decision the more his impatience grew, and during the waiting his lips narrowed into an angry and almost inimical line. Czentovic, however, did not allow himself to be hurried. He deliberated, stiff and silent, and increased the length of the pauses the more the field became denuded of figures. By the forty-second move, after one and a half hours, we sat limply by, almost indifferent to what was going on in the arena. One of the ship's officers had already departed, another was reading a book and would look up only when a piece had been moved. Then suddenly, at a move of Czentovic's, the unexpected happened. As soon as Dr B. perceived that Czentovic took hold of the Bishop to move it, he crouched like a cat about to spring. His whole body trembled and Czentovic had no sooner executed his intention than he pushed his Queen forward and said loudly and triumphantly, 'There! That's done with!', fell back in his chair, his arms crossed over his breast, and looked challengingly at Czentovic. As he spoke his pupils gleamed with a hot light.

Impulsively we bent over the board to figure out the significance of the move so ostentatiously announced. At first blush no direct threat was observable. Our friend's statement, then, had reference to some development that we short-thoughted amateurs could not prefigure. Czentovic was the only one among us who had not stirred at the provocative call; he remained as still as if the insulting 'done with' had glanced off him unheard. Nothing happened. Everybody held his breath and at once the ticking of the clock that stood on the table to measure the moves became audible. Three minutes passed, seven minutes, eight minutes – Czentovic was motionless, but I thought I noticed an inner tension that became manifest in the greater distension of his thick nostrils.

This silent waiting seemed to be as unbearable to our friend as to us. He shoved his chair back, rose abruptly and began to traverse the smoking-room, first slowly, then quicker and quicker. Those present looked at him wonderingly, but none with greater uneasiness than I, for I perceived that in spite of his vehemence this pacing never deviated from a uniform span; it was as if, in this awful space, he would each time come plump against an invisible cupboard that obliged him to reverse his steps. Shuddering, I recognized that it was an unconscious reproduction of the pacing in his erstwhile cell; during those months of incarceration it must have been exactly thus that he rushed to and fro, like a caged animal; his hands must have been clenched and his shoulders hunched exactly like this; it must have been like this that he pelted forward and back a thousand times there, the red lights of madness in his paralysed though feverish stare. Yet his mental control seemed still fully intact, for from time to time he turned impatiently towards the table to see if Czentovic had made up his mind. But time stretched to nine, then ten minutes.

What occurred then, at last, was something that none could have predicted. Czentovic slowly raised his heavy hand, which, until then, had rested inert on the table. Tautly we all watched for the upshot. Czentovic, however, moved no piece, but instead, with the back of his hand pushed, with one slow determined sweep, all the figures from the board. It took us a moment to comprehend: he gave up the game. He had capitulated in order that we might not witness his being mated. The impossible had come to pass: the champion of the world, victor at innumerable tournaments, had struck his colours before an unknown man, who hadn't touched a chessboard for twenty or twenty-five years. Our friend, the anonymous, the *ignotus*, had overcome the greatest chess master on earth in open battle.

Automatically, in the excitement, one after another rose to his feet; each was animated by the feeling that he must give vent to the joyous shock by saying or doing something. Only one remained stolidly at rest: Czentovic. After a measured interval he lifted his head and directed a stony look at our friend.

'Another game?' he asked.

'Naturally,' answered Dr B. with an enthusiasm that was disturbing to me, and he seated himself, even before I could remind him of his own stipulation to play only once, and began to set up the figures in feverish haste. He pushed them about in such heat that a pawn twice slid from his trembling fingers to the floor; the pained discomfort that his unnatural excitement had already produced in me grew to something like fear. For this previously calm and quiet person had become visibly exalted; the twitching of his mouth was more frequent and in every limb he shook as with fever.

'Don't,' I said softly to him. 'No more now; you've had enough for to-day. It's too much of a strain for you.'

'Strain! Ha!' and he laughed loudly and spitefully. 'I could have played seventeen games during that slow ride. The only strain is for me to keep awake. – Well, aren't you ever going to begin?'

These last words had been addressed in an impetuous, almost rude tone to Czentovic. The latter glanced at him quietly and evenly, but there was something of a clenched fist in that adamantine, stubborn glance. On the instant a new element had entered: a dangerous tension, a passionate hate. No longer were they two players in a sporting way; they were two enemies sworn to destroy each other. Czentovic hesitated long before making the first move, and I had a definite sensation that he was delaying on purpose. No question but that this seasoned tactician had long since discovered that just such dilatoriness wearied and irritated his antagonist. He used no less than four minutes for the normal, the simplest of openings, moving the King's pawn two spaces. Instantly our friend advanced his King's pawn, but again Czentovic was responsible for an eternal, intolerable pause; it was like waiting with beating heart for the thunder-clap after a streak of fiery lightning, and waiting – with no thunder forthcoming. Czentovic never stirred. He meditated quietly, slowly, and as I felt, increasingly, maliciously slowly – which gave me plenty of time to observe Dr B. He had just about consumed his third glass of water; it came to my mind that he had spoken of his feverish thirst in his cell. Every symptom of abnormal excitement was plainly present: I saw his forehead grow moist and the scar on his hand become redder and more sharply outlined. Still, however, he held himself in rein. It was not until the fourth move, when Czentovic again pondered exasperatingly, that he forgot himself and exploded with, 'Aren't you ever going to move?'

Czentovic looked up coldly. 'As I remember it, we agreed on a ten-minute limit. It is a principle with me not to make it less.'

Dr B. bit his lips. I noticed under the table the growing restlessness with which he lifted and lowered the sole of his shoe, and I could not control the nervousness that overcame me because of the oppressive prescience of some insane thing that was boiling in him. As a matter of fact, there was a second encounter at the eighth move. Dr B., whose self-control diminished with the increasing periods of waiting, could no longer conceal his tension; he was restless in his seat and unconsciously began to drum on the table with his fingers. Again Czentovic raised his peasant head.

'May I ask you not to drum. It disturbs me. I can't play with that going on.'

'Ha, ha,' answered Dr B. with a short laugh, 'one can see that.'

Czentovic flushed. 'What do you mean by that?' he asked, sharply and evilly.

Dr B. gave another curt and spiteful laugh. 'Nothing except that it's plain that you're nervous.'

Czentovic lowered his head and said nothing. Seven minutes elapsed before he made his move, and that was the funereal tempo at which the game dragged on. Czentovic became correspondingly stonier; in the end he utilized the maximum time before determining on a move, and from interval to interval the conduct of our friend became stranger and stranger. It appeared as if he no longer had any interest in the game but was occupied with something quite different. He abandoned his excited pacing and remained seated motionlessly. Staring into the void with a vacant and almost insane look, he uninterruptedly muttered unintelligible words; either he was absorbed in endless combinations or – and this was my inner suspicion – he was working out quite other games, for each time that Czentovic got to the point of making a move he had to be recalled from his absent state. Then it took a minute or two to orient himself. My conviction grew that he had really forgotten all about Czentovic and the rest of us in this cold aspect of his insanity which might at any instant discharge itself violently. Surely enough, at the nineteenth move the crisis came. No sooner had Czentovic executed his play than Dr B., giving no more than a cursory look at the board, suddenly pushed his bishop three spaces forward and shouted so loudly that we all started:

'Check! Check, the King!'

Every eye was on the board in anticipation of an extraordinary move. Then, after a minute, there was an unexpected development. Very slowly Czentovic tilted his head and looked – which he had never done before – from one face to another. Something seemed to afford him a rich enjoyment, for little by little his lips gave expression to a satisfied and scornful smile. Only after he had savoured to the full the triumph which was still unintelligible to us did he address us, saying with mock deference:

'Sorry – but I see no check. Perhaps one of you gentlemen can see my King in check?'

We looked at the board and then uneasily over at Dr B. Czentovic's King was fully covered against the Bishop by a pawn – a child could see that – thus the King could not possibly be in check. We turned one to the other. Might not our friend in his agitation have pushed a piece over the line, a square too far one way or the other? His attention arrested by our silence, Dr B. now stared at the board and began, stutteringly:

'But the King ought to be on f7 – that's wrong, all wrong – Your move was wrong! All the pieces are misplaced – the pawn should be on g5 and not on g4. Why, that's quite a different game – that's –'

He halted abruptly. I had seized his arm roughly, or rather I had pinched it so hard that even in his feverish bewilderment he could not but feel my grip. He turned and looked at me like a somnambulist.

'What – what do you want?'

I only said 'Remember!' at the same time lightly drawing my finger over the scar on his hand. Automatically he followed my gesture, his eyes fixed glassily on the blood-red streak. Suddenly he began to tremble and his body shook.

'For God's sake,' he whispered with pale lips. 'Have I said or done something silly? Is it possible that I'm again . . .?'

'No,' I said, in a low voice, 'but you have to stop the game at once. It's high time. Recollect what the doctor said.'

With a single movement Dr B. was on his feet. 'I have to apologise for my stupid mistake,' he said in his old, polite voice, inclining himself to Czentovic. 'What I said was plain nonsense, of course. It goes without saying that the game is yours.' Then to us: 'My apologies to you gentlemen, also. But I warned you beforehand not to expect too much from me. Forgive the disgrace – it is the last time that I yield to the temptation of chess.'

He bowed and left in the same modest and mysterious manner in which he had first appeared before us. I alone knew why this man would never again touch a chessboard, while the others, a bit confused, stood around with that vague feeling of having narrowly escaped something uncomfortable and dangerous. 'Damned fool,' MacIver grumbled in his disappointment.

Last of all, Czentovic rose from his chair, half glancing at the unfinished game.

'Too bad,' he said generously. 'The attack wasn't at all badly conceived. The man certainly has lots of talent for an amateur.'

A Quiet Game of Chess *by Maurice Richardson*

From 'The Exploits of Engelbrecht abstracted from The Chronicles of The Surrealist Sportsman's Club' by Maurice Richardson, with illustrations by James Boswell.

This story I leave to readers in the hope that they will enjoy it as much as I do; it teaches one nothing, I fear, about anything or anybody.

It was the Boxing-day after the last Christmas before the End of the World, and, together with a sizable handful of my fellow-members, I was lounging away the remaining shreds of the tattered epoch in the Trance-Room of the Surrealist Sporting Club.

We were engaged in the traditional Boxing-day pastime of shooting down our Hangovers. Chippy de Zoete, with a shrewd left and right from his trusty old elephant gun, had just put paid to a frightful fanged Apparition who had been pursuing him hotly ever since breakfast. Nodder Fothergill was taking aim at a great grey Cloud of Unknowing that hovered over the sofa on which he lay outstretched. Wally Warlock was blazing away at the Spots in front of his eyes. Engelbrecht, the dwarf surrealist boxer, had just brought the chandelier crashing to the floor and blown off several of the Oldest Member's members in a plucky but characteristically rash attempt to dispel by rocket-fire a hideous black Shape answering to the name of the Dark Night of the Soul which was harassing his trusty but congenitally melancholic old manager, Lizard Bayliss.

At that moment the Id, who had been shouting away to himself in the Silence Room, blew in and challenged all and sundry to a quiet game of chess.

I don't know whether you've ever played surrealist chess. It's a bit different from the ordinary kind. Not only does it include additional pieces such as the Tank, the Fighter Plane, and the Atomic Bomb which were introduced into the game by King Abdulla of Transjordania to bring it into line with modern power politics, but it is played with human Kings, Queens, Bishops, Knights, and Pawns, with genuine old machiolated castles for Rooks, all on a board of positively cosmic dimensions. So much so that the doors of the Surrealist Chess Stadium have proved before now to be the portals to several other worlds besides the next.

It was with some trepidation, therefore, that I accepted Engelbrecht's invitation to join the H.Q. staff of the scratch unit which he undertook to put on to the board against the task-force of Grand Masters fielded by the Id. And, as so often happens in Surrealist Sport, there was a powerful whiff of dirty work in the ether. I noticed that nearly all the Old Hands – clutchers, most of them, if you ask me – had enlisted on the side of the big battalions, and Chippy de Zoete, always a tough and slippery customer, had been commissioned Pawn-Master.

Indeed, when our side assembled in the funereal dressing room – we had drawn Black, of course – we were reduced to

'Lull between moves'
A leaf from the sketch book of
Official Surrealist War Artist Sir John Tenniel
Now on view in the Surrealist War Museum

Engelbrecht, Lizard Bayliss and myself, little Charlie Wapentake (as defective as he is devoted) and as much of the Oldest Member and his members as could be collected from the Club carpet.

'You haven't been betting, have you, kiddo?' Lizard Bayliss asked nervously as he adjusted his crêpe chess-helmet.

Engelbrecht nodded vigorously. 'You bet I have,' he said. 'Everything we possess. Everything I could think of. Plus all the Time we got left plus what we won from Grandfather Clock. Why not?' He hiccoughed and was immediately enveloped in a dense cloud of black smoke.

Plainly the fighting dwarf was still under the direct influence. He had not even begun to approach the Hangover stage.

Presently the professional umpire, Dreamy Dan, who umpires all surrealist sporting contests, wandered in to say it was time we were getting out on to the board as the pieces had arrived. We hurried out to look them over.

It was obvious that the Id had not been letting the grass grow under his feet. The Black pieces were the most moth-eaten collection of disintegrating old hams you ever set eyes on outside the waiting room of a theatrical agency. As for the pawns they were nothing but a gang of dead-end kids and I wasn't a bit surprised to find they were out on ticket of leave from an approved school.

White, on the other hand, was as well disciplined a set as any turned out by old man Staunton himself. They lined up in formation and marched off, chanting in unison the daring slogan: 'One, two, three, four! Pawn to Queen's Bishop Four.'

Then the umpire's helicopter became airborne and not long after the boom of the Sunset Gun announced the start of play.

The Oldest Member took a pinch of gunpowder from his snuffbox and passed the flame of his lighter under his nostrils. He appeared to benefit from the resulting explosion. It enabled him to take in the situation at a glance. 'The first thing to do,' he said, 'is to submit those pawns to a severe loyalty test.'

'Better save your strength,' said Lizard. 'Every piece we got's been got at, if you ask me. Might just as well line up the whole lot on the fifth column, bump 'em off and call it a day.'

'You let me get at 'em,' said Engelbrecht, lurching forward. 'Listen to me, you spivs,' he roared. 'I don't care how often you've broken your old mothers' hearts or cheated the hangman. You're chessmen now, see. Black chessmen. And when I give the word I want you to get cracking into the middle of that board and knock hell outa them White bastards. Now ...'

His voice was drowned in a ragged cheer. The Black King started to recite Henry V, and three pawns, fired by the general élan, dashed forward in a charge.

'Get back to your squares, you bloody little stoats,' yelled Charlie Wapentake.

We held an emergency conference. Night was falling. Only one thing was clear, which was that our Captain did not know the first thing about the Game. Lizard Bayliss, living in the world of fisticuffs where the higher cerebral sports are but little esteemed, had never graduated beyond the draughts-board, and could only mutter 'Huff him, chumbs, huff the bleeders to death!' Charlie Wapentake was still concussed as the result of having been fool's-mated so often at his prep school. My own chess-lore is rudimentary. It seemed we should have to rely on the Oldest Member's Memory.

From the White end of the board a rocket soared up into the night and burst releasing a cluster of incandescent stars which arranged themselves in the symbols PK4. The Id had moved.

Engelbrecht reeled up to our King's Pawn and aimed a savage kick at the child. 'Two squares forward! March!' he roared. Around midnight the KP got through on his Walkie Talkie Apparatus to say that K4 was untenable. I jumped into a staff car and shot off to investigate.

I must say the route to PK4 was a pretty gruelling one. The car sunk under me in a bog near the frontier of K3 and K4 and I had to do the last part on foot. I found the pawn skulking about under a Upas tree. 'I don't like it 'ere, sir,' he whined. 'There's things, nasty things.' 'What of it,' I roared, 'there's nasty things everywhere. The Universe is stiff with 'em. You'll either do your duty and hold this square or be court-martialled and shot on the spot.' Just then there was a moaning gibbering noise and something in a white sheet flitted by. I took a pot-shot at it and heard a frightful but all too familiar curse. It was Chippy de Zoete, trying some of his favourite psychological warfare tactics.

Shortly after I arrived back at H.Q. another rocket signal went up. The Id had castled on the King's side.

'Castled has he?' said Engelbrecht. 'Well we'll castle too. How do we do it?'

How indeed? For no sooner did we start to move our King's Rook than the entire structure collapsed in a shower of brick-dust and plaster, jackdaws' nests, and bats. We heard a thin voice somewhere in the middle of it all say: 'I'm very old and very tired.' And that was how a very gallant edifice passed over to the other side.

We called for volunteers to rig a temporary structure on KB1, put Lizard Bayliss inside it to make it stand up, and just managed to get the job done before the time signal went for us to move. But we had reckoned without the Id. When the King took up his position on KKt1 there was a violent explosion. While we had been busy reconstructing enemy paratroops had mined the square. An attempt to take advantage of the confusion and kidnap the Queen was discovered in time by QP and QBP who heard the old girl holler and gave the alarm.

The preliminary phase of court intrigue was now over. The middle game, and with it all the horrors of mediaeval warfare, had begun in earnest. Soon the board was one vast panorama of carnage. The screams of hapless pawns being dragged away to captivity with all its nameless horrors, the wheezy death rattle of Knights, the whining supplications of crafty Bishops, the sadistic frenzy of Queens, resounded on all sides. It was too much for poor little Charlie Wapentake. He developed Chess-shock. 'I can't stand it,' he said, burying his face in his hands. 'I can't stand it I tell you. It's too horrible.'

'And what about me shut up in this here bloody tower,' said the hollow cardboard voice of Lizard Bayliss. Sternly we ordered him back to his square...

At dawn on the seventh day I returned to H.Q. weary and travel-stained after a long-distance recce up in the mountains at QR6 where one of our pawns, a boy scout type, had been making some progress. Engelbrecht was snoring on his camp bed. The Oldest Member was at the control panel. 'Let me put you in the picture,' he said. 'We've had a pretty severe pranging but I think we can say that our position is still defensible. We've got rid of the worst of our fifth column by process of exchange which is whizzo so far as it goes and we've held our own in pieces. But we're badly behind in tempo, and I'm afraid we shall feel it as soon as the secret weapons come into play. The purple's up already.'

Next moment Dreamy Dan's voice sounded on the loud speaker: 'Tank to Tank's twelfth, Check. And Flame Thrower to Flame Thrower's sixth, Double Check.'

'I expected as much,' the O.M. went on. 'Well, we must evacuate our King to safety. I've booked him a room at the Palace.'

The next twenty-four hours were hellish. We were attacked on all sides by newly invented pieces including bacteriological warfare units in flagrant defiance of the rules of all forms of chess. All appeals to Dreamy Dan were met with his invariable formula – accompanied by a schizophrenic chuckle – of: 'Can't say I noticed anything special. You must be seeing things.'

Our own shock-pieces proved, as we had feared, markedly inferior to the enemy. The Tank moved straight into a trap. The Fighter Plane was held immobilized by a Ray apparatus on Rocket Bomb's ninth . . .

The concrete bunker which was our H.Q. was given over to black despair, so black you could scarcely see your hand in front of your face. Our Atomic Bomb had been taken *en passant* before it had had a chance to go off. The White pieces were milling all round the Palace Hotel where our trusty old Monarch was sitting shivering in the Winter Garden humming *God Save the King* to keep his spirits up. 'It's Mate in two whatever we do,' said the Oldest Member. I had never seen Engelbrecht so downcast.

There was a scratch at the door and Lizard Bayliss poked his head round.

'What are you doing, Lizard?' I said. 'I thought you'd been taken years ago.'

'So I was,' said Lizard, 'but I escaped. Had a hell of a job to get across the board. I got a message for you. It's from the little bleeder of a pawn, you know the boy scout type what was so keen. You should see where he's got to. Way out behind their lines 'e is. 'E couldn't let you know before because Chippy de Zoete smashed his Walkie Talkie App way back on QR3. 'Ere, read this. It's hot.' He handed over a crumpled note.

Engelbrecht read out: 'Have infiltrated to QR 666th disguised as brushwood stop Enemy's Atom Bomb en prise stop Chance of Mate in two stop Move me quick. Sgd. QRP.'

The Oldest Member positively leapt to the controls. 'QRP takes Atom Bomb and Atom Bombs, Check!' he announced. 'It's Mate in two whatever they do.'

We heard over the intercom a shaky voice saying: 'White resigns!' But it was too late. The dizzy height of promotion from Queen's Rook's Pawn to Atom Bomb had gone to our little boy scout's head. 'I'm not accepting any resignations,' he squeaked, 'I detonate.'

Next moment there was a blinding flash and the Universe turned into a nebula.

'This,' said the Oldest Member, 'is where I came in.'

The End

Bibliography

The following are some of the books which have helped me in writing this one. In their different ways, I have enjoyed all of them, and would like to acknowledge my indebtedness. I have grouped them by the areas where they have most helped me, but a number have been of value in more than one place. If you want to get any of them, by far the best thing to do is to write to one of the specialist chess magazines. In England, write to *Chess*, Sutton Coldfield, or to *British Chess Magazine*, 9 Market St, St Leonards-on-Sea, Sussex. In America, write to *Chess Life Review*, 479 Broadway, Newburgh, New York 12550, USA. For books on problems write to *The Problemist*, Hon. Sec. G.W.Chandler, 46 Worcester Rd, Sutton, Surrey. If you are interested in endgame studies, then there is an endgame magazine called *E.G.*, Editor A.J.Roycroft, 17 New Way Rd, London NW9.

The books listed here are, of course, only a tiny fraction of the total number of chess books. Not all of these books are in print; should you want one which is out of print, you may be able to get a second-hand copy through one of the chess magazines. One of the advantages of writing to a specialist magazine is that it immediately opens up a much wider choice.

Quotations
Coles, R.N.   *Chess Player's Weekend Book* (Pitman)
Knight, Norman   *Chess Pieces* (Chess)
Reinfeld, Fred   *Treasury of Chess Lore* (Dover)

Prologue
Skopje 1972: The Chess Olympiad (Chess)

The Nature of Chess
Alexander, C.H.O'D.   *Fischer v. Spassky, Reykjavik 1972* (Penguin)
Capablanca, J.R.   *My Chess Career* (Bell)
Sunnucks, Anne   *The Encyclopedia of Chess*, Professor Euwe's article 'Computers and Chess' (Hale)

Fourteen Centuries of Chess
Murray, H.J.R.   *History of Chess* (OUP)
　　　　　　　　　Shorter History of Chess (OUP)
Richards, D.J.   *Soviet Chess* (OUP)

The Dialectic of Chess
Alekhine, A.A.   *My Best Games of Chess* (Bell)
Botvinnik, M.M.   *One Hundred Selected Games* (Dover)
Euwe, M.   *Development of Chess Style* (Bell)
Kotov, A. and Yudovich, M.   *Soviet School of Chess* (Dover)
Nimzovich, A.   *My System* (Bell)
Réti, R.   *Modern Ideas in Chess* (Bell)

Chess for Blood
Korn, W.   *Modern Chess Openings* (Pitman)
Larsen, B.   *Larsen's Selected Games of Chess* (Bell)
Levenfish, G. and Smyslov, V.   *Rook Endings* (Batsford)

Chess for Fun
Berliner, H. and Messere, K.   *World Correspondence Chess Championship* (British Chess Magazine)

Variants
Anderson, G.F.   *Are There Any?* (Stroud News and Journal)
Bell, R.C.   *Board and Table Games* (OUP)
Dickens, A.S.M.   *A Guide to Fairy Chess* (Stroud News and Journal)
Japan Shogi Federation   *Shogi* (Nihon Shogi Remmei, Tokyo)

Problems and Studies
Harley, B.   *Mate in Two Moves* (Bell)
Havel, M.   *Bohemian Garnets* (Chess Amateur, Stroud)
Lipton, Matthews and Rice   *Chess Problems: Introduction to an Art* (Faber)
Roycroft, A.J.   *Test Tube Chess* (Faber)
Sutherland, M.A. and Lommer, H.M.   *1234 Modern End-game Studies* (Printing Craft Ltd)
Weenink, H.   *The Chess Problem* (Chess Amateur, Stroud)
White, A.C.   *Sam Loyd and his Chess Problems* (Dover)

Go
Haruyama and Nagahara   *Basic Techniques of GO* (Ishi Press GO Series)
Kawabata, Yasumari   *The Master of GO* (Tuttle)
Smith, Arthur   *The Game of GO* (Tuttle)

Literature
Ellison, J. W.   *Master Prim* (Macdonald *in Great Britain*, and Little, Brown, *in the USA*)
Zweig, Stefan   *The Royal Game* (Cassell & Co.)
Richardson, Maurice   *The Exploits of Engelbrecht* (Phoenix House)

Index

Page references in bold indicate an illustration, those in italic a diagram

Thanks are due to the following for permission to reproduce illustrations and extracts from published works:

Staunton versus Saint-Amant, G.H.Diggle, and British Chess Magazine © G.H.Diggle, 1943
Master Prim, Macdonald and Co. (Publishers) Ltd. (in Great Britain) and Little, Brown and Co. (in U.S.A.) © James Whitfield Ellison, 1968
The Royal Game, Estate of Stefan Zweig, and Cassell and Co. Ltd. © Stefan Zweig, 1944
The Exploits of Engelbrecht, Maurice Richardson, and J.M.Dent and Sons Ltd. © Maurice Richardson, 1950

Sources of illustrations
Endpapers: Escher Foundation, Haags Gemeentemuseum, The Hague
Frontispiece, 37: British Museum
17,51,69: The Bettman Archive Inc
18,19,38,65,66: Novosti Press Agency (A.P.N.)
21: *The Saturday Magazine*, 3rd July and 28th August, 1841
28–9: USIS:IU: Photos
35: The Tate Gallery, London
43,132: Illustrated London News
53,55,60,83,84–5,109: Radio Times Hulton Picture Library
73: Penguin Books
76: R.D.Keene and D.N.Levy *Siegen Chess Olympiad*, Chess Ltd, 1970
86: Ger Dijkstra
95: *The Saturday Magazine*, 3rd August 1844
113: J.Boyer, *Nouveaux jeux d'échecs non orthodoxes*, Paris 1951
129: F.Lanier Graham, *Chess Sets*, Studio Vista, London, 1968
134: Royal Opera House, Covent Garden
134: AB Svensk Filmindustri, Stockholm
135: Bradford and Bingley Building Society
136: Galeria Schwarz, Milan
136: Philadelphia Museum of Art
140: G.H.Diggle/*British Chess Magazine*
148: *Przekrój*, Kraków, 1947
152: Estate of James Boswell

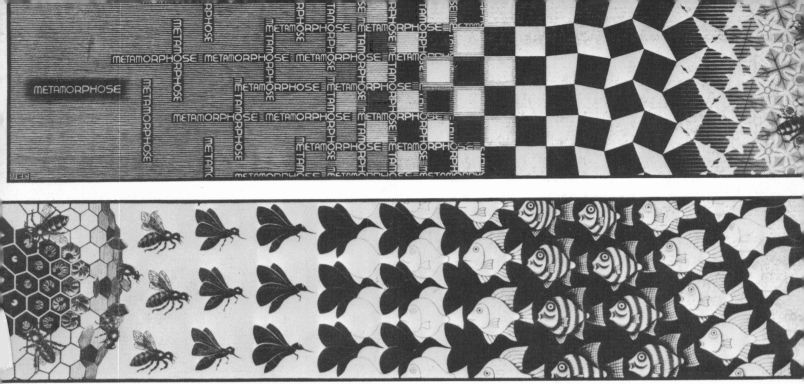